CROSBIE'S DICTIONARY OF Puns

CROSBIE'S DICTIONARY OF Puns

by John S. Crosbie
Illustrated by Janet Sutherland

Speeding thru your book
I think I've lost my grip

Harmony Books
New York

To the memory of the late Bennett Cerf,
a great humorist and a kindly man.
His prowess in punning was only exceeded
by his joy in sharing.

Book and Cover Design by Janet Sutherland

Publisher: Bruce Harris
Editor: Pamela Riddle
Production: Gene Conner, Murray Schwartz
Typography: B.P.E. Graphics, Spring Valley, New York

H·A·R·M·O·N·Y B·O·O·K·S
a division of Crown Publishers, Inc.
One Park Avenue, New York, New York 10016

Published simultaneously in Canada
by General Publishing Company Limited.
Printed in the United States of America.

Library of Congress Cataloging in Publication Data
Library of Congress Cataloging in Publication Data
Main entry under title:
Crosbie's Dictionary of puns.
1. Puns and punning.   I. Crosbie, John S., 1920—
PN6231.P8D5 1977   423'.1   77-10181
ISBN 0-517-53124-0
ISBN 0-517-53125-9 pbk.

Third printing

contents

introduction

THE PUN—
IS IT HERE TO SLAY?

The pun has been said to be the lowest form of humus—earthy wit that everyone digs. It compresses into the shortest possible length the basic elements of comedy. It appeals to the intellect (sick?) and allows the recipient to feel superior to someone who might not catch the ball-up.

H.W. Fowler, in his "Dictionary of Modern English Usage," says, "The assumption that puns are *per se* contemptible—betrayed by the habit of describing every pun not as a *pun,* but as a *bad pun* or a *feeble pun*—is a sign at once of sheepish docility and a desire to seem superior. Puns are good, bad and indifferent, and only those who lack the wit to make them are unaware of the fact."

It has been observed that many people have in common an awkward reaction to hearing a pun. They try to reward the perpetrator by overresponding (usually with loud groans). This can be gratifying to the author's ego as long as the pun was intentional. Otherwise, it can cause some confusion.

One recalls the story of Eleanor Roosevelt at a state dinner, discussing democracy with an Oriental ambassador. "And when did you last have an election?" she asked. "Before blekfast," he replied with some embarrassment.

The history of puns is a long one. Punning was very much in vogue, for example, during the 16th, 17th and 18th centuries in England. In *The Spectator,* Addison in sketching the history of puns from the time of Aristotle (*Appendix A*), said that a pun "is a conceit arising from the use of two words that agree in sound but not in sense."

In "The Life of Samuel Johnson," Boswell quotes his mentor as saying, "I think no innocent species of wit or pleasantry should be suppressed and that a good pun may be admitted among the smaller excellencies of lively conversation."

Dr. Johnson himself is credited with several puns. Shakespeare's plays abound with them. In the Bard's time, the pun was a literary device not always intended to be humorous. Lady Macbeth says of murdered Duncan, "If he do bleed, I'll gild the faces of the grooms withal; for it must seem their guilt."

An industrious Britisher, Dr. F.A. Bather, F.R.S., delivered a paper on Shakespeare (*Appendix B*) at the Wimbledon Public Library in 1923 in which he expressed reverence for the man who had such a command over language that he could perpetrate ten hundred and sixty-two puns. (We, in turn, must revere Dr. Bather; he not only counted the puns, he cataloged and classified them by types!)

Nor were puns a pervasive element in Elizabethan literature alone. Through such writers as Addison, and Swift (disguised as "Tom Pun-sibi"*), we can look back to puns in the Pentateuch, in the great dramas of the Greeks, in Cicero and Virgil. German, French and Italian texts exist on the subject. In Japanese poetry, noted the enthusiastic Dr. Bather, "word play and similar artifices are among the most admired ornaments." The Romans even had a word for pun-making: *paronomasia*.

From this, I give you a new word with which to conjure: *paronomania*. I suspect that it is a growingly common affliction. In the early stages, you are the life of the party. In the later stages, you don't get invited.

To protect you from becoming a victim, I recommend that you take this dictionary in small doses. The consequences of reading it through in one sitting are greatly to be feared. You might become so infected as to progress overnight to that ultimate and horrible stage where you begin to compile a dictionary of your own!

Should this happen, there is no known cure. However, out of my own suffering, let me offer a word of advice: Don't tell anybody. Like leprosy, dictionary-making is a form of affliction that has little social acceptability. People simply don't know how to handle it. It is better to suffer in silence than to see friends, confronted with the news, turn pale and withdraw, leaving you alone with your cocktail, the focus of inattention.

Oh, one other word: Beware of including puns that are based on events so long gone that the average reader won't know what you are talking about. It is for this reason that many of Shakespeare's puns are not to be found here—at least in the form he used. In like manner, I have tended to shun puns on people's names where those names, perhaps once famous, have passed or may soon pass from general awareness. It is, admittedly, an area of judgment; I have struck Bach but stayed off the Bachrach and have not dallied with Salvador. Just as I have avoided puns that are the product of innocent mispronunciations, so, except where the basic word or phrase is in fairly

---

*"The Art of Punning; or, The Flower of Languages; In Seventy-Nine Rules; For the Farther Improvement of Conversation and Help of Memory," Dublin, 1719.

common use in English,* I have excluded puns involving other languages, even though the temptation is great to add to this repast when the soupçon or to acknowledge the brilliance of young students of Latin under the guidance of easygoing headmasters *(facile princeps)*. The handling of multiple puns has been a problem. It has not been easy to catalog those gems whose meanings can be taken several ways.** In future editions, I will try harder with this rara avis.

The things about which people make puns are constantly changing, for humor changes with the times. In fact, a case can be made for humor reflecting mores. Within my lifetime, I believe I have discerned a diminishing tendency among English-speaking people to tell what are commonly called dirty stories. (This is not to say that only English tastes in humor are changing, but rather that I cannot speak of languages that I cannot speak.)

What this change suggests is that—since we are now in a period when the natural is no longer made to seem unnatural, when we can speak freely of the human body and its functions without being deemed vulgar—intercourse and alimentation are no longer funny *per se*. Situations involving them can still produce humor, for both are functions involving privacy, and the sudden disruption of privacy or the intrusion of the unexpected can still produce laughter.

Yet unless one is listening to a person who is emotionally immature or in need of the catharsis that vocalizing unattainable acts can provide, one rarely encounters those stories which were once the conventional stock-in-trade of the travelling salesman and the tours de farce of vaudeville.

There is a happiness in laughter we have not known since the childhood of the race.

In this book, you will find some vestiges of the old approach to humor. Even so humble a compendium would not be complete without them. If the variants on "arse" offend you, bear with them—and with Shakespeare. Like the codpiece, they have been hanging around a long time—for though this may be the Age of Aquarius, much of our humor is still hairy. As Charles Lamb wrote in an essay on puns *(Appendix C)*, "A pun is not bound by the laws which limit nicer wit."

I offer here not only examples of pure puns—homonyms and words which so interchange the forty phonemes of the English language as to make them seem similar to other words—but also seek to explain some common words or phrases which are used (or can be used) to cause confusion. Where possible, I have tried to avoid what I term "nudgers"—puns so strained that recognition of them requires that the hearer be nudged either physically, as with the elbow in the ribs, or orally by repetition until, by one means or the other, a reaction is produced.

---

*e.g. coup de grâce: a dessert made with creme de mènthe ice cream and marihuana.

**e.g. She was only a fisherman's daughter, but when she saw my rod she reeled.

While we have ventured into the topsy-turvy of language so far as to include a few spoonerisms in which initial sounds or other sounds of words are transposed,* most spoonerisms are not deliberate and are therefore, while often a source of delight, beyond the intent of this book except where a pun results. ("Let me sew you to your sheet," said the usher.)

Nor have I succumbed, I hope, to mere malapropisms except where a pun, though unintentional, has been involved as when a woman on a New York elevator was overheard saying, "I always read Time magazine because of the way it capsizes the week's news," or when Jane Ace said of her husband, Goodman, "He always gets up at the crank of dawn."

In a like manner, I have tried (not always with success) to avoid humorous definitions such as "Gigolo—A hired hand." This has sometimes been difficult. I did succumb for instance, to "Rapscallion—A man who hates onions," and "Hors de combat—Camp followers."

I found that a good test was to ask, "Can the word or phrase be used in a sentence which seems to make sense when taken as it stands?" ("The camp followers were all hors de combat.") Admittedly, I have had to be lenient. ("The chef is kitchen up.") When in doubt, I listened to Addison, who said that if a piece of wit translated into another language vanishes in the experiment, you may conclude it to have been a pun.

While a finite number of puns exists, an infinite variety of presentations seems possible. It is one of my regrets that it has not proven feasible to credit all sources. Should a reader encounter a pun expressed in a form that he believes he originated, I hope his pride of authorship won't be dimmed.

There are few people, I'm sure, who will realize the sacrifices that have been made to bring this paronomasiac dictionary in to the world. Not that I wish for sympathy, for the decision to create the book was entirely my own, and each man must bear his own guilt. As far as I can discover, it is the first book of its type that has ever been written. Perhaps this fast-changing world will make it unnecessary ever to write in this vein again. Perhaps, in fact, I have already sufficiently written in vein.

—John S. Crosbie

---

*In the manner of the Reverend W.A. Spooner of Oxford, who was heard to ask in church, "Is this pie occupewed?"

Allegro is a chorus line.

aaaaaaa

A
The Scottish student couldn't have mastered the 3 Rs e'en though he worked for A.

aardvark
Heavy labor: "It's aardvark, but it pays well."

abalone
Reference to average TV commercial.

abash
Party.

abb
Gaelic word for marking (hence English "dab"). Specifically, the colored marking of the wool on Irish sheep to distinguish herds—a dying practice. In all of Ireland there is only one abb stainer.

abbé
Geographical term.

abbess
Henry VIII found walking difficult, you see,
Because he had an abbess on his knee.

abbreviate
The kind of cheese we had yesterday.

abdominal
Refers to legendary mountain creature, The Abdominal Snowman, so called because he walks erect, with abdomen exposed.

aberration
A homosexual club soon becomes a mutual-aberration society.

abnegate
The entrance to Dogpatch.

abominable
Term applied to a bomb swallowed by a male bovine.

abomination
He couldn't get married in her church because he belonged to a different abomination.

abortion
Dislike of Russian soup.

absinthe
French aphrodisiac. Hence the saying, "Absinthe makes the heart grow fonder."

absurd
Mab and Ab joined the army at the same time. Mab never rose above private, but Ab soon became a sergeant. The reason was absurd.

abundance
Like a tea dance. A hot-cross fox trot.

Acadian
Resident of Nova Scotia, so called because of that area's cay shape.

Acapulco
Singing without musical accompaniment.

accelerator
Wine connoisseur.

acclaim
In Massachusetts, when a politician wants to get reelected, he frequently invites his constituents to acclaim bake.

accost
A basic fault in the novel "Murders in the Rue Morgue" is that the author failed to determine how much a trained gorilla would accost.

accouter
Fumigator.

accumulate
Convenient way of asking, "Why are you so tardy?"

acerbity
A small knight.

acetate
The chemist was asked by his company to work on acetates but he refused, knowing that he who acetates is lost.

ache
Broadway is the street of ham and aches.

achoo
Sneezing is often much achoo about nothing.

acid
If you suffer from acid indigestion, chew a Tums and you can bet your acid will go away.

acidic
Sentence often found in children's readers.

acidulate
Southern U.S. expression repeating an accusation of tardiness.

acolyte
Advice to priests: If you want to keep your acolyte, trim his wick.

acoustic
What you use to shoot pool.

acquire
Chorus.

acre
1. Small dog of mixed parentage.
2. A doctor's mistakes go six feet under; a dentist's cover an acre.

acrimony
1. Another name for marriage, sometimes called holy.
2. What a divorcee often gets.

acronym
Name for resident of Akron, Ohio.

across
A motorist, going 80 mph, tried to beat a speeding train to an intersection. He got across, all right—a beautiful marble one.

acrostic
Angry insect.

Adam
Why had Eve no fear of the measles?
Because she'd Adam.

adamant
1. The first insect.
2. It was a nuisance to adamant Eve.

adder
1. I thought she was a boa until I adder.
2. When the flood had abated, Noah sent the animals off the Ark, enjoining each couple to "go forth and multiply". As he was clearing up afterwards,

he came upon two snakes. "I thought I told you to go forth and multiply!" he exclaimed. "We're sorry, but we can't," one of them replied. "You see sir, we're adders."

3. The Year of the Snake in the land of Confucius was filled with adder confusion.

addict
An opium den is the Oriental version of an addict rendezvous.

ad infinitum
The man who thought he was through having children sometimes finds that to his budget he must now ad infinitum.

adieu
Since he couldn't fare well, he left without further adieu.

admonition
Song from the Salvation Army: "Craze the Lord and Parse the Admonition."

Adolph
"Knock, knock!"
"Who's there?"
"Adolph."
"Adolph who?"
"Adolph ball hit me in de mowf. Dat's why I dawk dis way."

adore
Why is a lovely young lady like a hinge?
She is something to adore, especially if she is a swinger.

adultery
Adolescence is the stage between puberty and adultery.

adumbrate
The facile artist can outline things quickly: the less apt proceed at adumbrate.

advance
Said the banker to the girl with a groan,
"I know how slim are my chances,
"But I'd like to get you a loan
"And then make a few advances."

adversity
Madison Avenue.

advice
Dry martinis.

Aeneid
For Virgil Aeneid a translator.

Aesophagus
Author of Aesop's Fables.

affaire de coeur
1. Love-in.
2. Pigeon bazaar.

affiliate
Remnants of small steak.

afflict
A bad movie.

à fond
Source of money.

agate
1. After weeks without a girl friend, the young printer finally reported, "I'm all set! Agate a new type; Ruby. She's very font of me!"
2. As girls who love diamonds know, adore is not adore when it's agate.

agenda
If you're going to have a meeting of the sexes, you really need agenda.

aggrandizement
He has just ordered a new, custom-built piano. Could it be aggrandizement?

Agnus Dei
The day when Agnus took it on the lam.

agoraphobia
Morbid dread of bullfights.

ah
When it comes to ingenuity, our Japanese friends frequently have the situation ah-so'd up.

ahead
Just as he was about to trip the guillotine, a friend presented the executioner with a new recipe book ("Chops and Steaks"). "Thanks," said the preoccupied official, "Would you mind putting it in the basket? I like to keep ahead with my reading."

aide
Said a modest young miss to de Sade,
"I'm simply too shy and afraid
"To take part in your pranks,
"But to show you my thanks
"I'd just love to become your first aide."

aim
"Will you tell me," asked an old gentleman of a lady, "what Mrs. Jones's maiden name was?"
"Why her maiden aim was to get married, of course!" exclaimed the lady.

ain't
Sister of one of your parents.

aisle
1. What does the bride think when she walks into the church? "Aisle, Altar, Hymn."
2. Robert Burns was given to drink. In fact, he would drink any given amount. This sometimes inhibited his church attendance because he could not find the road to the aisles.

alabaster
Money left to illegitimate child.

à la mode
An alert San Antonio restauranteur has this suggestion printed atop the dessert list on his menus: "Remember the a la mode!"

Alas
Abbreviation for Alaska. (Suggested by Texas).

alder
Open-air wedding ceremonies are fine, especially if held in front of an alder.

ale
1. *Here's to a stout end*
   To bitter days.
   Ale's well that ends well.
2. So what the ale!

alibi
Escape route, as in "the alibi which he got away."

alike
"You southerners are all alike!"
"Alike to think so."

alimentary
"Tell me, Holmes, what is the purpose of laxatives?"
"Alimentary, my dear Watson."

allay
Popular female.

allegro
Chorus line.

alles
A couple in Germany had a dozen daughters. All of them were given names beginning with "B" except the last. Her name was Alice. "Did you run out of names beginning with 'B'?" the mother was asked. "Ach, no," the mother sighed, "but when the nurse told Poppa it was again another girl, he cried, 'Das ist alles!' "

alliance
Soporific, commonly provided in liquid form (Alliance Cordiale).

alligator
1. A youngster found a salamander in his back yard and put it into a tank with his pet alligator. The alligator promptly swallowed the salamander. The youngster rushed wailing to his mother. "Something awful's happened! Sally's in our alli!"
2. This is not the same youngster who returned from a trip to New York City and reported that he had visited the Empire State Building and had ridden to the top in an alligator.

alliterate
To take the census.

allude
Pornographic picture.

allusion
Unusual sunglasses can create an optical allusion.

almond
Nuts are becoming so expensive these days they cost you an almond leg.

aloha
A Pullman berth.

alone
The president of a big bank fell off a seagoing yacht. While his friends frantically sought a life preserver, a sailor shouted, "Hey—can you float alone?"
"Of course I can," gasped the floundering banker, "but this is a hell of a time to talk business!"

aloof
Top of a Chinese house.

aloud
Sign on a boys' club: "No Girls Aloud."

Alp
From Zurich, bankrupt Debbie·
Sent her pa a little note:
"Every little bit Alps"
Was all the sly minx wrote.

altar
A bachelor is an unaltared male.

alter
The pride of a seamstress is her alter ego.

altercation
The pupils were given a holiday while the school was closed for altercations.

alternative
A person born during his parents' wedding ceremony.

Amazon
"You can pay for the eggs but the Amazon me."

ambassador
Ardent fisherman.

ambassadress
Fishing place.

ambivalence
Following the Watergate incident in Washington, there were so many lawyers trying to get involved in the settlement of conflicting evidence that they became known as "ambivalence chasers."

amende honorable
Proper repair (of clothing).

amends
A room at the back of the bar.

ammonia
"The shoes look beautiful, but have you tried ammonia?"

amnesty
The way that I react on nasty days.

amorous
Cry of conflict. Two little boys caught beating up a bigger boy shouted, "It's amorous!"

amour
Arab lover, e.g. Othello.

amourette
Consequence of Arab cannibalism.

amour propre
Dock piling.

amp
One of the reasons nylon underwear has never been popular with men is because it sometimes gets loaded with static electricity—and who wants amps in his pants?

amphibian
"So you think amphibian, do you?"

ampoule
Cosmetic surgery gave her an ampoule bosom.

amuck
The frenzy had were deep in amuck.

anapest
Beset by an urge to divest
Himself of all rules and the rest

Of writing's strict forms in the past,
The poet became at the last
Unable to scan anapest.

anastomosis
What God gave in order to transport those heavy tablets down Mount Sinai.

Andalusian
A Spanish drum is a snare Andalusian.

anecdote
Of all the ages of man, the most telling is the anecdotage.

anemone
A man wanted to buy his wife some anemones, her favorite flower. Unfortunately, all the florist had left were a few stems of the feathery ferns he used for decoration. The husband presented these rather shamefacedly to his wife. "Never mind, darling," she said, "with fronds like these, who needs anemones?"

anesthetic
If glue-sniffing can damage the brain, can inhaling chloroform produce anesthetic?

anode
A shocking piece of poetry created by a positive Pole.

ant
1. There are two kinds; insects and lady uncles. Sometimes they live in holes, and sometimes they live with their married sisters.
2. If you think Fanny Hill was colorful, you should have seen her Ant Hill!

anteater
Aunt Emmet's foe,
She'd have you know,
Was destined to defeat her.
He'd probe her hill
Then at his will
He'd pick her up—anteater.

antediluvian
One who was opposed to creating the Paris Museum.

antelope
Type of family scandal.

anthem
In the interests of peace, all national songs should be sung quietly; a soft anthem turneth away wrath.

antic
Hugh Hefner, publisher of Playboy, is famous as an antic collector.

antidote
1. A funny story.
2. A condition related (usually by marriage) to the Oedipus complex.

antifreeze
"How can I make antifreeze?"
"Hide her woolen pajamas."

antipasto
Weight-watchers.

Antwerp
Small bird. Colloquially, a little person.

ape
"Where," demanded an old gnu, "do you fool monkeys pick up all those wild rumors you keep circulating?"
"Why, we get them," explained one monkish monk, "over the apevine."

aplomb
Politically, a payoff or lucrative assignment, as in "The Honorable Mr. Spleen has aplomb."

apocryphal
Hippety-hop to the corner shop for apocryphal of candy.

apologist
Short summary of the first moon shot.

apostle
A package from the Bronx.

apparent
Member of the lost generation.

applaud
One who leaves the stage too slowly.

apse
The reason the old church in our village has irregular recesses in its walls is that the builder lost the plans. In consequence, the edifice suffers from an apse of memory.

aqueduct
Water fowl.

arbor
Every industrial city needs a port. Detroit, for example, has Ann Arbor.

arc
Because he was a man, Noah had a bigger arc than Joan.

arcade
A beverage invented by Noah.

arch
A school essay informs us that King Solomon reigned for 40 days and 40 nights while Noah was building that arch.

archaic
The wife of a distinguished classical scholar planned a special birthday cake for him. It was carefully decorated with quotations from Greek poets. Unfortunately, it tasted terrible—proving once more that we can't have archaic and eat it, too.

archdeacon
Coy ecclesiastic.

archipelago
A long run in music.

ardor
Sign over fireplace in fraternity house: "If at first you don't succeed, try a little ardor."

area
If you wish, your hat can be quite flat
Or be all puffed up like a rumpled bed.
You have your choice of this or that,
So long as it covers the area head.

argon
State immediately north of California.

Argus
"Juno, what happened to Argus's eyes?"
"We think the peacock's been tailing him. Argus is as good as yours!"

aria
The aria,
An extended song,
Too oft goes on and on too long,
Until the singer has explored
All aspects and the listener, bored,
Has had his fill of her and it
And hopes that soon they both will quit
The aria.

ark
Injunction to listen, as in "Ark, I think it's raining!"

arm
A Turkish visitor to the Guggenheim Museum asked an attendant what the lumpy protuberances were sticking out of a pillar of brass. "That statue is called 'Woman,' sir, and those are her arms." The Turk wandered off muttering, "Arms, for the love of Allah! Arms, for the love of Allah!"

Armageddon
1. As St. John said after his dream, "Armageddon out of here!"
2. Title for a western movie with a Biblical background: "Armageddon For the Last Roundup."

armor
I fancied myself as a knight errant—but some other guy had his armor round her.

aroma
Vagabond.

arose
It is interesting to trace the sources of famous songs. For instance, it was after the opening of a new hydroelectric development in Virginia that "Mightly Lake" arose.

arrears
"My brother and I both hate to wash behind arrears."

arrival
American highways have evolved into arrival of the fittest.

arse
Ancient misspelling of "horse." Hence, "Lady Godiva rode through town on her _____."

arsenic
Horsebite.

arson
Horseplay. Example: "Stop arson around."

artesian
Said a cat as he playfully threw
His wife down a well in Peru,
"Relax, dearest Dora:
"Please don't be angora;
"I was only artesian you."

Arthur, King
His real name was Ralph. However, he abandoned that the day he first met Lady Guinevere and she asked, "Arthur any more at home like you?"

artichoke
Dorothy Stickney, invited to dinner with a President of the United States, was so nervous she quavered to him, "What an imposing building the White House is! Who was the artichoke who designed it?"

artillery
The blood vessels are the veins, arteries and artilleries.

asbestos
Comparative, as in "I like her asbestos."

ascend
> The bottom.

ascent
> Unpleasant odor.

ash
> How to catch an elephant: Dig a big hole and fill it with ashes, then surround it with a ring of peas. When the elephant comes along to take a pea, you kick him in the ash-hole.

asp
> When Antony saw how Cleopatra handled snakes, he tried to make an asp of himself.

aspen
> 1. It is an old belief that the aspen's leaves quiver in shame because it was the tree of which Christ's cross was made. Actually, it is because, at His birth, the only place big enough for all the visitors He had was the aspen.
> 2. Stop aspen why that tree's so poplar alder time.

aspersion
> Donkey from Iran.

asphyxiation
> Fanny fetish.

aspic
> Edward Lear: "His house stood on a Cliff, it did.
> In aspic it was cool."

ass
> 1. Old song we haven't heard for a donkey's age: "The Green, Green Ass of Home."
> 2. Communism is the opiate of the asses.

assail
> *In less than a week, if she did not ground,*
> *I'd assail this hooker the wide world round!*

assassinate
> It was his last meal, but you should have seen how the assassinate!

assault
> Perhaps it was because no one peppered him with questions—sort of an assault-free diet.

assay
> A bearded prospector marched into an assayer's office back in the California gold rush days and planted two whopping nuggets on the counter. The clerk registered amazement. "Well," rasped the prospector angrily, "don't just stand there. Assay something!"

asset
1. In ancient days, wealth was expressed in many forms. A man might be judged by his sheep herds, dog packs or even assets.
2. The rumba is an asset to music.

asterisk
Little Mary on the ice
Went with her friends to frisk.
Wasn't Mary being nice,
Her pretty *?

astute
Vulgar sound.

ate
Social Note: Mrs. L.B.R. Hunter held a small dinner party on Thursday evening last. Places were set. Four ate.

Atlas
When Zeus banished him to Africa to uphold the heavens, his faithful girl friend went with him, sighing, "Atlas, we are alone!"

atoll
Hardly. As in "That's not a Bikini atoll."

atom
A scientific item says there is a war on between the electron and the atom. Up, Electrons, and Atom!

atonal
Atonal music is so called because someday somebody is going to have to atonal the sins involved.

atrophy
Reward for political service, etc.

attar
When he told me Rose's perfume was delightful, I had to take his word because I couldn't get attar.

auction
If you're seeking bargains, you've got to go where the auction is.

audit
Bookkeeping term, as in "It's audit hasn't balanced this time."

au fait
Negro term for white man.

aught
A. Wag says: "A printer who set $10,000 to read $1,000 might have prevented his mistake with a little fourth aught."

aunt
Philadelphians are proud of William Penn, yet few know that he had a couple of aunts named Natalie and Ellie who were themselves famous, especially in the art of whipping up a mince pie or an apple strudel. When Quakertown bakers formed a combine and tripled the price of their pastries overnight, Aunt Natalie and Aunt Ellie decided to teach the greedy merchants a lesson. They put their delectable concoctions on the market at bare cost—and then proceeded to reduce the price by two cents a day. In no time, the good citizens of Quakertown were discussing only one topic: the pie rates of Penn's aunts.

aural
Aural sex should be heard but not obscene.

author
Asked to use "author" as a subject of a sentence, a brave child wrote, "Grammar is just an author subject to me."

auto
They don't make cars like they auto.

autobiography
A history of motor cars.

auto-da-fé
Car owned by foolish person.

autoerotic
A drive-in movie.

autoerotism
Love of cars.

autoharp
Backseat driver.

avail
He was an old and not very handsome widower.
"You are the sixth girl to whom I have proposed without avail," he sighed. "Well," said the girl kindly, "when making your seventh proposal, maybe you'll have better luck if you wear one."

avant-garde
French chastity belt.

avaunt
Actress Greta Garbo's famous line: "Avaunt to be alone!"

avenue
"I avenue baby sister."

aversion
A white lie is aversion of the truth.

Avon
From Shakespearian song
"Are You Avon Any Fun?"

away
"You are good-looking, in a way."
"What way?"
"Away off!"

aweigh
A group from the U.S. Navy was rehearsing a special rendition of "Anchors Aweigh." For the climax, each man was supposed to pop up and sing one word of the song. The commander who was listening grumbled, "It's still pretty ragged! Did you see that man who stood up to sing 'Anchors'?" "You think he's bad?" commented his aide. "You should have seen the one that got 'Aweigh'!"

awful
The commonest kind of fertilizer is awful.

awkward
Bird sanctuary.

awl
The tools of acupuncture are believed by some to be cure awls.

awry
Once you've developed a taste for corn liquor, you'll never go awry.

aye
Sailors in the Russian navy are prone to pink aye.

ax
What you use if you can't sign your name.

*An Italian fog is a **bigamist**.*

B

1. *A play on B*
   Is easy to C.
2. Drunk in apartment-house lobby: "2B or not 2B?"

Baal

To the Phoenician mariners, he was the deity who governed shipwrecks. Even to this day, sailors on sinking ships may be heard to cry "Baal! Baal!"

Babylon

Infant buying ground in southern California.

bacchanal

A Venetian alley.

bacchic

Sound produced by overindulgence.

Bach

1. He loved the organ player, especially when she was on her Bach.
2. The famous TV star Cleo the basset was sometimes required to play the piano. Even though a gentle dog, it was still true that her Bach was worse than her bite.
3. Whenever Bach worked away from home he developed a prodigious appetite. So every time he went on a trip he packed a valise with sandwiches, apples, cheese and cookies. This became known as a "Bach's lunch."

bachelor

Lover of females in batches.

backward
Hospital section for sacroiliac cases.

badger
The minx was hard if things went well
But softened soon if ill befell.
Her eyes were wont in tears to melt
Whene'er she heard how badger felt.

badinage
Jack Benny's insistence on always being 39 proved that he was good in comedy but badinage.

bag
The baby kangaroo was asked why it wouldn't jump into the adult kangaroo's pouch.
"I can't," the baby explained. "It's not my bag."

bagel
A bird with a loud voice.

Baghdad
Father of the aging bride.

bail
When her lover was charged with her rape, she couldn't stand the court scene and finally cried out, "Bail Hans! I loved beside the Shalimar!"

bailiff
One who will post your bailiff you can afford it.

bairn
Scottish and North-English form of barn, as in, "Breeding is just one bairn thing after another."

bait
1. It is a cat skill in the Catskills to eat cheese and then wait beside a mousehole with baited breath.
2. You can't bait it.

baking
"This job of bringing home the bacon is no joke," sighed one married man. "No," growled another. "And on top of that, I always have to stop at the bakery and bring home the bakin', too."

bald
1. In news photos, Eisenhower and Khrushchev stood out in bald contrast.
2. Samson loved Delilah—until she bald him out.

ball
1. Women's Liberation Movement motto: Don't Ball Us, We'll Ball You.
2. Or, to quote Xaviera Hollander, "The bigger they come, the harder they ball."

3. "Do you like masked balls?"
"No, I prefer to know with whom I am sleeping."

ballyhoo
The English owl has a cry all its own.

balm
Contraceptive jelly: an antipersonnel balm.

bambino
Expression of reprimand used by a mother deer.

bamboo
Italian baby.

banana
U.S. colloquialism, as when the detective on TV asks his secretary, "Banana messages for me?"

bandage
An American epoch, circa 1940.

bandeau
French: Bath water.

bandicoot
A flea with rickets.

Bangladesh
Eastern diplomats are not always diplomatic; if they can't get attention by thumping the drum, they will often Bangladesh.

banshee
Stag party.

barbiturate
Two lions strolled into a roadside tavern in search of refreshment. "Get a load of that babe at the end of the bar!" one whispered to the other. "Man, you must be really hard up!" his friend replied. "No, sir, she looks good enough to eat," said the first lion. He thereupon got up and went down the bar and ate her. The next day, when he met his friend, he complained of stomach pains.
"I told you!" said his friend. "It's that barbiturate."

bard
1. One hot day in spring, Shakespeare decided to desist from writing sonnets to his Anne and take her for a swim at a nearby beach. They had to don their swimsuits from the previous season, of course, and it suddenly occurred to Shakespeare that moths had very possibly been feeding on the back of his trunks. "Wouldst thou investigate, my love and life?" he asked his companion. She made a thorough if discreet examination and then reported cheerfully, "No holes, Bard."
2. Disgruntled by his failure to make a living, an unsuccessful poet forsook bard times for good.

3. Once upon a time, a group of poets were marooned in manacles on an island which, they soon discovered, had only one other resident, a beautiful woman. In their efforts to reach to her, they began to thrash one another, thereby illustrating that bards of a fetter flog to get her.

bare
1. A Buddhist nudist is one who practices yoga bare.
2. As a boy, Al Jolson was so poor that he had a bare Mitzvah.
3. A pair of stripteasers named Betsy and Beth were grinding it out before an audience of all-male art lovers when Betsy noticed that Beth's G-string was slipping. Betsy whispered urgently, "Oh, Beth, where is thy string?" Beth looked down and shrugged. "They'll think it's part of the act," she whispered back, "if you'll just bare with me!"

bargain
Profits from sale of alcoholic beverages.

bark
1. You can always tell a dogwood tree by its bark.
2. As the little dog said when he fell overboard, "My bark is on the sea."
3. *A dog that*
   Barks a lot
   Is not
   A friend to man.
   So, if you can,
   Get a cat,
   And leave the sot
   In a barking lot.

baroque
One of the grotesque aspects of 17th- and 18th-century art is that if you buy too much of it, you end up baroque.

barouche
A Russian pub.

barque
A wealthy yacht owner decided to give his crew a Christmas party in port. He went ashore to round up evergreens, food, musicians and gifts. When he returned, he found all the greens being installed—but on the wrong ship. "Ahoy!" he shouted, running down the dock. "You're treeing-up the wrong barque."

barracuda
Despite her big teeth, she's a barracuda girl.

bartender
One termite to another in a saloon:
"You've been here before. Where is the bartender?"

barter
Smetana showed up by mistake one night at a theater across the street from

the one in which his opera *The Bartered Bride* was playing. He didn't know which side his bride was bartered on.

basic
Upset by ground swell.

bask
On your first trip to the beach you may get more sun than you've basked for.

Basque
When some Spaniards tried to flee to France over a single open bridge, they found they had put all their Basques in one exit.

bass
The Compleat Angler is all about the way of a lad with a bass.

bat
The mad scientist in the old castle had a strange secret—but he kept it under his bat.

batter
The Old Lady who Lived in the Shoe had little trouble keeping her numerous progeny in line. She knew which side her brood should be battered on.

bauble
As Margie told the wealthy old man after her first visit to his apartment, "I hated the champagne—but I just loved the baubles!"

bawdy
A young woman widely famous for her lust for life became known as the bawdy beautiful.

bawl
1. Making love in the onion patch is one sure way of having a bawl.
2. Bagpipes were the original Scotch high bawl.

bay
A chemist has discovered a drug that will keep dogs from howling at night. Now, not every dog will have his bay.

bazaar
A church fair is a bazaar experience.

beach
A female.

beachcomber
A hairdresser.

bead
The pearl puncher pocketed plenty of punched pearls—and then decided to bead it.

beam
The yachtsman bought his girl friend a small bikini and watched her beam with delight.

bean
The brawniest and most imposing delegate at a recent U.N. assembly was a seven-foot, two-inch giant from a newly formed African state. "You are a magnificent specimen of mankind!" gushed a lady reporter. "What do you eat to keep in such superb condition?" "Beans" was his laconic reply. "Beans!" echoed the unbelieving reporter. "Do you mean soy beans? Navy beans? String beans?" "I do not," growled the delegate. "I mean HUMAN beans."

bear
1. "Do you hunt bear?"
   "Not in cold weather!"
2. None but the brave deserves the bear.

beard
Shakespeare was so busy writing plays that he never had time to shave. That is why he is called the Beard of Avon.

beat
"This can't be beat!" said the farmer as he pulled up a carrot.

beatnik
Santa Claus on the day after Christmas.

beauty
A student returned to his boardinghouse from a party at Big Sur sporting a black eye and a badly swollen lip. "Run into a door?" he was asked. "No," replied the adventurer ruefully. "I was struck by the beauty of the place."

beaver
As winter approaches, the eagerness of these Canadian animals to build dams is at a beaver pitch.

beck
Jewish opposite of "frond."

beckon
Beck plus conjunction, as in "beckon frond."

bed
1. O.E. spelling of "bad." Hence, houses of ill repute offer "bed and bored" and thus, in turn, one speaks of going from bed to wurst.
2. Bed Riddance—book by Ogden Nash.

bedder
Comparative, as in "Tis bedder to have love than lust."

bedeck
A Cape Breton term believed to have originated in shipbuilding.

bedlam
Rushing to bed.

bedouin
1. A harem-scarem heiress invaded a Turkish seraglio and demanded a bedouin and bath.
2. An Arab will always win in a race with a Jew because no matter how good a runner the Jew may be, the Arab is bedouin.

bedraggle
Argument in bed.

bee
Al Jolson's famous song of sex: "Climb Up on My Bee, Sonny Boy."

beef
"Home on the Range" was originally written in beef-flat.

bequest
Hunting for honey is like a legacy.

beer
1. I'm very thirsty, so beer with me.
2. Goldie Lox and The Three Beers.
3. Guinness's Stout is known as a beer of the realm.
4. Or so they would make it a beer.
5. To beer not to be.

Beethoven
Famous European distiller whose products gained world recognition through Sir Winston Churchill's famous gesture of raising his index and second fingers in the form of a V (the Latin symbol for five), indicating his readiness for another opening of a Beethoven fifth.

beetroot
Lettuce forget those leeks of gossip and beetroot to each other.

beg
A community chest is an organization that puts all its begs in one ask-it.

begorra
This word, says *The Oxford Dictionary,* is an Irish corruption. That probably explains why there is a Dublin bar for homosexuals called Sodom and Begorra.

beguile
When she was small
No one would fall.
But with her teens
Stretching her jeans,
The boys avow
That she's a beguile now.

beguine
As his biographer said to George Gershwin,
"Let us beguine at the beginning."

belfry
A.T. & T. under socialism.

belle
The sunburn season is ushered in by the peeling of the belles.

bellicose
1. "Don't hit me in the bellicose it hurts."
2. A neat shave by a Chinese barber.

bellow
"The fire is going out!" he bellowed.

belly
James Howe III of the Lewis-Howe Company ("Tums for the Tummy")
recalls that when his grandmother first heard the name and slogan proposed
she humpfed, "Why not say Bells for the Belly?" Might have been a good
name at that, for, as every user knows, Tums works belly well.

bend
Yoga is the be-all and bend-all.

benedick
One who is addicted to "bennies," of which the best known vendor was
Benedict Arnold.

benefactor
One who makes "bennies."

benefit
An overdose of drugs.

benign
What you can't wait to be when you're eight.

Beowulf
Mother of Uncle Remus (and another Roman boy whose name I don't
remember).

beret
Loud, baying sound.

Berne
The amateur skier would be well advised to do a slow Berne.

berry
To inter, as in the folk song "Berry Me Not on the Loan (Prayer E)."

besot
Rural invitation: "Come in and besot a spell."

Bessemer
Mexican for "kisser," hence "Bessemer Moocho": one who steals kisses.

best
The curler got stoned when he played it too close to the best.

better
For years, the travelling salesman had lavished his attention on the statuesque show girls of Las Vegas. He finally tried dating a short one, but she wouldn't let him leave the gambling tables, which proved she was only a little better.

bey
Once upon a time an Arab sheik fell off the merry-go-round of a country carnival and was promptly gobbled up by the second of three hungry sheep grazing nearby. The owner of the carnival, angry at losing a customer, seized the offending animal and exclaimed, "Middle lamb, you've had a dizzy bey!"

bibelot
Child's apron.

bidding
Pleasant-faced people are generally the most welcome, but the auctioneer is always pleased to see a man whose appearance is for bidding.

bidet
D-Day minus two.

bier
A drunk staggered into a funeral parlor and demanded a Scotch and soda. When the undertaker explained where he was, the drunk pulled himself together and announced with dignity, "Well, sir, in that case, you may give me a bier."

big
The proper term for an important desert sheik is "a dune biggie."

bigamist
An Italian fog.

bigamy
Brigham Young was explaining to a French journalist his reasons for having so many wives. "But," interrupted the journalist, "M'sieu, that is rather a wonderful thing you have done; to have married so many!" "Yes," conceded Young, "it *is* bigamy!"

bight
An old seadog's barque is worse than his bight.

bigotry
An Italian redwood.

bilious
Feeling you get when you open your mail on the first of the month.

billet
1. Hill dweller. Hence American redundancy (Cajun).
2. "Hill billet," meaning illicit distiller (moonshiner).

billet doux
Money owed moonshiner.

billing
Alimony: the billing without the cooing.

bind
A girdle: bind over matter.

biracial
How Jacob begat.

bird
Badminton players are for the birds.

biscuit
She was a very confused bride. She found she had put all her eggs in one biscuit.

bisexing
Geometry is the science of bisexing angels.

bisexual
Southern U.S. prostitute's greeting.

bishopric
Organ of the church.

bit
Many horses feel a bit down in the mouth.

bitch
A bitch in time saves nine.

bite
The first pun ever made is credited, logically enough, to Adam. Eve teased him, "What's wrong with eating this little old apple?" and Adam answered, "I'll bite." The next day, they both had to give up Eden.

bitter
A wife is sometimes defined as the bitter half.

bivalve
Oysters breathe bivalve.

blade
An enterprising American manufacturer has just put on the market a new brand of razor blades designed for homosexuals (some of whom are quite thin-skinned). He calls them "Gay Blades."

blancmange
A disease of the scalp (exclusive to blondes).

bleach
When the blonde he married faded into brunette, he sued for bleach of promise.

bleachers
He was so crazy about blondes that every time he went to a football game he headed for the bleachers.

blight
1. Genocide is one way of maintaining blight supremacy.
2. "It's not your dog's mange that bothers me; his bark is worse than his blight."

blinks
Japanese armored-car service.

blizzard
Part of a hen's insides.

bloat
Fat person. Hence the exercise song "Row, Row, Row, You Bloat!"

blond
1. In the Waldorf Astoria, there is only one man to look after all the Venetian blonds.
2. *Said a happy old hooker named Bond,*
   "I've a wile of which clients are fond;
   "When I've hairsprayed some gold
   "Where my labia fold,
   "I'm a gilt-edged negotiable blond."

bloomer
Blunder, hence "Bloomer Girl"; early 1900's designation for girl who pants after a man and then complains, "I bloomer chances."

blouse
Nautical version of "blows," as in "Thar she blouse!" (First noted in Moby Dick's novel *Four Years Before She Asked.*)

blow
1. If you go into a bakery that has just had an explosion, you are likely to find that the cause is a Napoleon blown apart.
2. When he came to a tacit passage, the novice horn player blew it.
3. An observing man claims to have discovered the color of the wind. He says he went out and found it blew. If this is so, then *Gone With The Wind* is a blew movie.

bluff
She threatened to throw herself off a 300-foot cliff, but it turned out to be a lot of bluff.

blunderbuss
1. Vehicle used for random travel.
2. Errant osculation.
3. Baby carriage.

boa
Shortly after the pregnant snake swallowed the rubber ball, she gave birth to a bouncing baby boa.

boar
1. Many of the world's great masterpieces have been inspired by love. When the Russian composer's lady was willing to forego her customary diet of fine foods to share his humble meal of wild boar, he was inspired to immortalize her gesture of love in the now-famous opera *Boar Is Good Enough.*
2. The word "pig" is often used in a derogatory sense about a person who is really just a boar.
3. *The sow*
   Somehow
   Boar
   More.

body
Popular song among ghosts: "I Ain't Got No Body."

boisterous
"Mary and I like playing with girls; what are you boisterous?"

bold
When the U.S. elected Stonewall Jackson, it got a bolder president.

boll
After the boll weevil all go home.

bolt
1. She ordered red wool from the store—but it came as a bolt from the blue.
2. "So you're a locksmith!" rumbled the judge. "What has that to do with being in that gambling house when it was raided?"
   "Well, Your Honor, you see—I was making a bolt for the door."

bombard
A bad poet.

Bonaparte
Famous men have a different skeletal structure from other people. This is proven by the fact that Napoleon was a Bonaparte.

bone
Blessed event in southern U.S.

bonkers
U.S. colloquialism: A city in New York, hence a reference to all Americans who are in that state.

bonspiel
A drinking bout. From French *bon* (good) and Dutch *spiel* (spill or spilling).

bonus
"Christmas," sneered the bitter employee, "is the time when the boss throws us dogs a bonus."

boot
Approximately, as in, "Isn't it a boot time for another wee drop?"

booty
When some local Nova Scotians went to Oak Island and found the legendary treasure of Captain Kidd, they were afraid the owners of the island would have them arrested. So the leader of the group hid the loot in his grandfather's apiary. He then passed a note to the rest of his conspirators: "Booty is in the beehives of the older."

bordello
Laconic greeting.

bored
A girl who is just waiting for someone to give her a fur coat is apt to get bored.

boring
George Jessel, a toastmaster at so many banquets who was reported by Bennett Cerf to be thinking of calling his autobiography "Dais without End," advises: "If you haven't struck oil in your first three minutes, stop boring!"

Bosphorus
A Turk clerk, feeling the effects of too much Kirsch, moaned to his noontime companion, "We can't go back to the office now. Who'll tell the Bosphorus?"

botany
Australian wool lately?

botch
Term of contempt for a German.

bottle
When it came to drinking, comedian W.C. Fields was a veteran who suffered from bottle fatigue.

boulder
The psychiatrist told the man who said his girl friend treated him like every other pebble on the beach that he would have to be a little boulder.

bounce
There's nothing like the Christmas season to put a little bounce in your checks.

bound
The zoo's kangaroo lacks zip: He is frequently discovered out of bounds.

bourbon
1. A pink elephant is a beast of bourbon.
2. There is now a cocktail called Bourbon Renewal.
   Two of them make the whole neighborhood look different.

bovine
There once was a tolerant cow who stood for absolutely anything her favorite bull tried to get away with. She reasoned, "To err is human, to forgive, bovine."

bow
The pretty violinist never married—but she always had her bow.

boy
1. They had to let the plumpest ballerina go, because they couldn't find anyone to boy her up.
2. A bachelor is a thing of beauty and a boy forever.

brag
A press agent is a person who has hitched his braggin' to a star.

braid
In the days when young ladies prided themselves upon the length of their hair, it was reported that one youth was actually saved from drowning when his companion cast her braid upon the waters.

braise
Look upon the rainbow, and braise Him who made it.

brandish
Cereal bowl.

brass
This house, where once a lawyer dwelt,
is now a smith's. Alas!
How rapidly the iron age
Succeeds the age of brass!

braziers
Night watchmen don't look liberated—and they've been burning their braziers for years.

breadth
On the menu in a restaurant that specializes in low-calorie foods: "Our dishes will take your breadth away!"

break
Some girls break dates by going out with them.

bream
The song of the fisherman's nightmare: "To Dream the Impossible Bream."

breast
A Los Angeles radio announcer once tried to urge his audience to "get the best in bread," but he didn't make it.

breath
1. The doctor was examining a pretty young girl who had a chest cold. "Now, then," he said, raising his stethoscope, "big breaths!" "Yeth, thir," she replied proudly, "and I'm only sixteen!"
2. Friend of mine had a drinking companion who was a big rabbit. Wanted to be a writer, my friend. But he couldn't concentrate because the rabbit kept breathing down his neck. Missed fame by a hare's breath.

breathless
As every literary critic knows,
Poems without punctuation
Are often breathless prose.

bred
It is a little-known fact that while the animals went onto the Ark two by two, by the end of the trip some had multiplied. Thus Noah became the first man to have bred his cast upon the waters.

breech
1. An older husband deliberately threw his out-of-style trousers into the furnace, then told his young wife, "Now you can't accuse me of being a stick-in-the-mud! I have just burned my breeches behind me!"
2. "Hot pants" are breeches of promise.

breeze
In Chicago, every prospect breezes.

brew
1. A hangover is when the brew of the night meets the cold of the day.
2. A couple of vats at a brewery in Milwaukee were struck by lightning. Not only were they undamaged, but experiments showed that the beer in them was actually improved in quality. The brewmaster smacked his lips over the unexpectedly fine flavor and wrote the head of the company, "We believe that this is the first case on record of a storm actually brewing."

bridge
1. The hunter in Ceylon got so excited when he shot his first leopard that his teeth fell out. Ever since, he has been searching for his bridge on the River Kwai.
2. A flood is a river too big for its bridges.

bridle
When he tried to smuggle his horse into the hotel, they gave him the bridle suite.

brief
One of the guards at the Tower of London is so in love with his job that his colleagues call him "the brief eater."

bright
Genius is the brights' disease.

bristle
The British navy used to insist on short haircuts. They liked their crews to be shipshape and bristle fashion.

broad
There's a rich old lad on Wall Street who still has an eye for the girls. He's generally acknowledged one of New York's natural athletes: He makes every broad jump.

broadtail
The Hollywood wife was offered the gift of a broadtail coat by an admirer. "Oh, anything but that!" she cried. "You've no idea what it's like being married to a comedian!"

brocade
Welfare.

brogan
Irish, from "brogue" (accent or accident), as resulting from shillelagh blow: "Faith, my head is brogan!"

brontosaurus
Anthology of works by 19th-century English sister authors.

brood
1. The modern method of teaching very young children to swim by simply tossing them in proves the value of the Biblical injunction, "Cast thy brood upon the waters."

2. Tea is not something to brood over.

brook
When the visitor to the village was finally persuaded to visit the brook, he was dismayed to see it emanating from a pipe. He protested that it was really a sewer. But his host replied, "Oh, you can't tell a brook by its cover!"

brothel
One of Toledo's best-known houses of ill repute was invaded by a band of unromantic robbers. All the cash and valuables on the premises were taken. The moral of this sad tale is that too many crooks spoil the brothel.

brouhaha
French: the joy of cooking.

bruin
When Johnny tried to ride the bear
He found he'd made a grievous error,
As, borne toward his certain ruin,
He cried, "Get help! There's trouble bruin!"

bruise
What you hear played when it's Mardi Gras on the Ginza.

brutish
Marc Antony: *"For Brutus is an honorable man....*
O judgment! thou art fled to brutish beasts..."

buccaneer
First Pirate: "How much did those earrings cost?"
Second Pirate: "Two dollars."
First Pirate: "Not bad for a buccaneer!"

buck
He oft would whale Jack with the cat
And say, "My buck, doe you like that?"

bucket
Uncle Oscar had a close call the other day: He fell into his well and almost kicked the bucket.

Buddha
Many an Oriental, brought up to believe in Buddha, has come to North America and developed a fondness for margarine.

budge
Pity the poor man who has a big load of debt and doesn't know how to budge it.

budgie
Mother's Whistler.

buff
The striptease artist got arrested in mid-act; her buff was called.

buffalo
Greeting between two nudists.

buffet
A gay shoeshine boy.

bug
An exterminator in Idaho announced that he invented a new spray, one application of which will remain effective for a full season. "Of course," he warned, "I've still got a few bugs to iron out."

bugaboo
Primitive means of getting rid of insects by sneaking up behind them and frightening them to death.

bugger
When Whistler was told that his enemy, Oscar Wilde, was writing a new work in Reading Gaol, he commented, "It must be known as 'The Bugger's Opera.'"

buggy
Q. What's the best way to drive a baby buggy?
A. Tickle its feet.

bulldozer
A man who sleeps through political speeches.

bullet
A missile of lead
Can play hell with your head,
Causing drafts and much mental ado.
The cure, so I'm told,
Is to be quick and bold
And brazenly bullet right through.

bulletin
"Pa got in a fight and now he has a bulletin his leg."

bum
1. A "bum steer" is a lazy longhorn.
2. The teacher was putting her young class through a bit of abstract training. "Now, Willie," she asked, turning to a freckled youth in the end row, "if a policeman found a watch on a tramp, what would you naturally infer about the watch?" "That it was on the bum!" came the prompt answer.

bumpkin
An unpleasant Mafia assignment.

bungle
1. An unexpected baby is a bungle of joy.
2. After the Watergate affair, many politicians in the U.S. found themselves living by the law of the bungle.

buoy
A boat is called a she because: There's always a great deal of bustle about her; there's usually a gang of men around her; she shows her topsides and hides her bottom; and, when coming into port, she always heads for the buoys.

bouyant
"You aren't as gallant as when you were a boy," pouted the wife. "No," admitted the husband, "and you aren't as buoyant as when you were a gal!"

burden
"Dad went hunting, but he didn't get a burden he came home mad."

bureau
When he got the writing desk home from the auction and opened it, a dozen people fell out. Apparently, it was a missing persons' bureau.

burp
"Well!" exclaimed the wife, "I hear that all those drinks you had at the club today didn't agree with you." "How did you hear that?" the husband demanded indignantly. "Oh," said the wife darkly, "a little burp told me."

burro
To get ahead in the early days of America's west, many a man had to beg, burro and steal.

bury
When good old Chief Shortcake died, the whole tribe mourned and the lamentations of his faithful squaw were heard for miles around. Neighboring chiefs arrived with pomp and ceremony and announced, "We come to make funeral for Chief Shortcake." "Not on your life!" announced his widow. "Squaw bury Shortcake!"

bus
A bird in the hand is worth two in the bus.

bushwhack
Female Australian soldier.

bust
A brassiere is a bust stop.

butcher
Lady in meat store, confronted by a new female clerk: "Are you a butcher what?"

butt
1. Research shows that cost-conscious Canadians take an extra couple of puffs on a cigarette before putting it out, while U.S. smokers are noticeably more prodigal. This suggests that you can always tell an American by the size of his butt.
2. A homosexual is often the butt of jokes.

butte
The trouble with a man who makes mountains out of molehills is that when he makes a mistake, it's a butte.

butter
1. She wanted to go, butter mother wouldn't let her.
2. Since he found a whey to make money he's doing much butter.

butterfly
And then there was the dairymaid who was so eager that she made the butterfly.

buttress
A woman who makes butter.

buxom
Thin girls love their men passively. Fat girls buxom.

buy
1. The hard part of being broke is watching the rest of the world go buy.
2. Lottery motto: If at first you don't succeed, buy, buy again!
3. Famous American novel about a dishonest purchasing agent: "The Catcher in the Buy."

byre
When you're selling cows, it's often a byre's market.

*The guillotine
is a French **chopping** center.*

CCCCCC

C
The new shipboard choir was doing well with its opening number until the tenors got lost on the high C's.

cacciatore
If a Liberal hawk can catch a Conservative chicken, he has chicken cacciatore.

cache
In desperation, the Czechoslovakian midget pounded on his friend's door. "The Russian police are after me!" he cried. "Can't you please cache a small Czech?"

cachet
In small-town nightclubs, you can sometimes cachet falling star.

caddie
He isn't the caddie used to be.

Cadillac
A Cadillac mean if you pull its tail.

Caesar
Did Julius Caesar with decorum in the forum?

Cain
The real reason Adam was thrown out of the Garden of Eden was because he raised Cain.

caisson
The medical officer in our unit drank so much that even when we went on a forced march, he had a caisson.

calabash
When his supporters wanted to persuade President Coolidge to run for a second term they decided to give calabash.

calk
"And where is your father?" asked the minister who had come to call at the farmhouse. "Oh," replied the little girl. "He's out in the barn calking the mare." "Dear me!" said the minister to himself. "Perhaps that Kinsey Report was right!"

call
Before birth, the fetus of the gorilla is protected by the call of the wild.

Callas
Maria Callas, temperamental former star of the New York Metropolitan Opera Company. Known to other members of the company as "Pretty Callas."

calling
"How would you classify a telephone operator? Is hers a business or a profession?" "Neither. I rather think that it's a calling!"

Calvary
New York clothier's ad: "Men! Solid Tan Calvary Twill Suits!" Just in time for Easter, if you have a religious hang-up.

Calvin, John
The father of the doctrine of particular election and redemption. It is a theologically sound presumption that the papal bull is not Calvin.

camel
My camel
burns at
both ends;
It will not last
the night;
But oh, my foes,
and oh, my friends—
It gives a lovely bite.

camphor
"I thought you were staying for dinner." "No, I just camphor tea."

can
1. Thomas à Becket built a fireplace in his outhouse and thus had a can for all seasons.
2. Perhaps the problem of the homonym is best illustrated by the story of the Englishman visiting the U.S. who was told by a fruit-grower, "We eat what we can, and what we can't, we can." On returning home, the Englishman reported this bit of whimsy as, "They eat what they can, and what they can't, they put up in tins."

Canada
"You bring the wieners, and I'll bring a Canada-best sauerkraut."

canard
They call a sensational report a canard because one canardly believe it.

candy
Valentine: candied opinion.

cane
To be able, as in, "Cane Chew Here Me Calling, Caroline?"

cannon
Cannon fodder: The author of a church decree.

canoe
"I'm going to sail across the Atlantic by myself."
"Canoe?"
"I think so. As long as it's big enough."

canon
If you're making a mess of the Mass, pass the canon to someone else.

Cantab
British low-calorie pop (not to be confused with Vox pop).

cantaloupe
"Knock, knock!"
"Who's there?"
"Cantaloupe."
"Cantaloupe who?"
"My father's watching. We cantaloupe tonight."

canticle
A little song which canticle your fancy.

caper
There once was a hot-blooded draper
Who grabbed at a shop girl to rape her.
But instead of a cherry,
He grew a bit wary
To find himself cutting a caper.

capitol
1. Polonius: *I did enact Julius Caesar. I was killed i' the capitol. Brutus killed me.*
   Hamlet: *It was a brute part of him to kill so capital a calf there.*
2. When the government taxes you to get capital so that it can go into business in competition with you and then taxes your profits to pay for its losses, that is capitol punishment.

capsize
1. When that crafty old seadog Don Martin's boat sank, the first thing he did was dash to a haberdashery to buy a new yachting cap. The hatter asked sympathetically, "Capsize?" Martin answered, "Seven and an eighth."
2. "I always read *Time* magazine because of the way it capsizes the week's news."

carafe
A political soirée sometimes becomes a carafe tea occasion.

carat
She: "You got fooled on this diamond ring."
He: "I guess not. I know my onions."
She: "Maybe—but not your carats."

carcass
The burlesque queen was rushed to the hospital because she had caught a strip-de-carcass infection.

carp
1. When a man in Japan has to choose between fishing and farming, he usually puts the carp before the horse.
2. Young fish like to play carps and robbers.

carrot
If you just want something to drive around the farm, this carrot to do.

Caruso
Famous Italian tenor who became marooned on a desert island.

cascarets
National instrument of Spain.

case
"What's that you're building?"
"I'm trying to make a case for beer."
"You don't have to. I'm convinced."

cashew
Those who work for peanuts are always shelling out. It's those with cashew can salt some away.

casket
A-tisket, a-casket,
They're coming with the basket.

cassowary
A kind of large running bird related to the ostrich. When you see one coming you should cassowary eye.

cast
1. His only qualification as a drama critic was that he had once had a leg in a cast.
2. A motion picture director wanted to do a movie about eunuchs but he couldn't get his budget approved because of the cast ration.

castor
If we want to get rid of the beaver dam fast we should castor oil on it.

cat
The origin of this word is not clear. We find early uses of it in terms such as "cat house," which suggests that the original spelling may have been "ghat,"

a Persian word meaning ashes. This etymology seems confirmed by the still-current expression, "Getting his ashes hauled." Hence "catatonic." See "catnip."

cat-a-mountain
The Animal trainer sighed. "That leopard is too quarrelsome. There's no hope of that cat-a-mountain to anything!"

catgut
Our dog got fleas but our catgut kittens.

catnip
A quick catatonic.

caucus
1. A dead animal.
2. To assault sexually: "They said they were going to caucus, but they seem to be tied up in a meeting."

caul
"Caul me early, Mother dear, for I'm to be Queen o' the May."

caulk
As the sailor cried when offered his choice in the brothel, "I could caulk the hull lot!"

cauterize
1. The Cockney doctor rushed home and cried, "I cauterize today!"
2. His nurse became very friendly when his new paycheck cauterize.

cavort
Swedish beer: Two pints make one cavort.

caw
1. A Mississippi State University entomologist has reported that the crows of that state do not respond to crow calls recorded in New York. It seems to be a problem of caws and effect.
2. While most of the flock settled on trees or power lines, one crow always headed for telephone cables. Once there, he seemed to spend all his time talking to himself. Another crow finally asked him why he did this. "Oh," said the gabby one, "I just like to make long-distance caws."

cedar
Go to Beirut and cedar Lebanon.

celibacy
A disease of the brain cells.

celibate
"Tell me, Sister, how do you feel about celibacy?"
"Good idea! What will we celibate?"

cell
1. "How did that play they put on in the jail turn out?"
   "Marvelous! It was a cell out."

2. "The vault, dear Brutus, is not in our stairs but in our cells."

cellar
Q. Why is coal the most contradictory article known to commerce?
A. Because, when purchased, it goes to the cellar.

cellulite
Pimp to client: "If you'll reduce, I can cellulite."

census
Q. What did the man say when they told him he'd just become the father of triplets?
A. "I can't believe my census."

centaur
The world's cheapest prostitute.

centimeter
Asked to use the word in a sentence, a young student said, "If you see a centimeter, step on it."

centipede
In South America, no dining-room table is without its centipede.

centurion
Leicester *Evening Mail:* "They thought she was ninety-nine but are now convinced she is a centurion."

cervix
The gynecologist's office: a cervix station.

chafing
The pretty girl on the elevator kept tugging at her dress and wiggling uncomfortably. The other passengers could see that she was a chafing dish!

chain
My doctor discouraged me from chain smoking, so I've switched to tobacco.

chair
1. British exclamation, as in, "Three hearty chairs!"
2. They really should be more chairy.

chairman
British social comment: "It's been chairman!"

chamois
"I try to keep everything polished," she sighed. "I wish I could chamois like my sister Kate."

Champlain
1. The Canadian who failed to keep the wolf from the back door while his horses were Champlain at the bit.
2. A Chinese term for effervescent wine.

chandelier
A French rooster.

change
"Now, tell me, why did you steal that purse?"
"Your Honor, I wasn't feeling well. I thought the change would do me good."

chant
1. Two cheerleaders ended up at the altar. They met by chants.
2. We chant say more about them.

chap
A woman who flirts is like a person whose skin cracks in cold weather; she is likely to end up with chaps on her hands.

chapter
1. "I hear that the police raided your fraternity."
   "Yes, I'm afraid that's a closed chapter now."
2. An inveterate punster is not a chapter give in.

char
It is bad form to sit with your legs over the arm of your char.

charge
"That pretty new widow down the street wants me to come to her party tonight and pretend to be her houseboy."
"Are you going to charge her?"
"No, I think I'll just wait until all the guests are gone and sneak up on her quietly!"

charisma
The proper holiday wish for a politician: "Merry Charisma!"

chary
1. He wanted to use her love seat, but she was chary.
2. Seduction was what she suspected he was after, for he was known as a chary picker.

chassis
Sean O'Casey, in *Juno and the Paycock:* "The whole world is in a state of chassis."

chatter
Bridge is the triumph of mind over chatter.

Chaucer
The young student of literature was dawdling over a second cup of coffee one Sunday morning while reading *The Canterbury Tales.* His father demanded, "What have you got there?" "Oh," answered the boy, "just my cup and Chaucer."

chauffeur
He advertised for a limousine but had nothing to chauffeur it.

chauvinism
Bellicose patriotism. From Chauvin, veteran of Napoleonic wars. Hence "Who are you chauvin?"

check
"Do you accept checks at this restaurant?"
"Certainly, sir, as long as they behave themselves!"

checked
"Have your eyes ever been checked?"
"No. They've always been blue."

checkers
Chinese checkers: Oriental grocery clerks.

checkoff
Masochism: A Russian concept (from Chekov, the Russian playwright).

cheep
An aviary is a cheep place.

cheese
"Oh, what a friend we have in cheeses," sang Tom Swift, Kraftily.

cheetah
A kind of leopard in India trained to hunt deer. Unfortunately, you can't trust it.

cherry
1. One should be cherry of virgins.
2. We know one man who gave up Cherry Heering because he was tired of listening to them.

chew
1. We think a backyard barbecue is a very tasty thing—don't chew?
2. As many a postman knows, some dogs are pretty chewsy.

Chianti
His wife likes wine. Why Chianti?

chic
1. The social set in Mecca is known as the chic of Araby.
2. Modern fashion designs are often presented with tongue in chic.

chief
The chief of the cannibals asked his captive what his occupation was. "I am an editor." "Congratulations!" exclaimed the cannibal. "Tomorrow you will be editor in chief."

Chile
A group of Cuban delegates to a convention were expelled on arrival at Santiago, after getting a Chile reception.

chimpanzee
A gay monkey.

chintz
When you go into the drapery business, you have to take your chintzes.

chivalry
What you feel when you are cold.

choir
After years of practice, she finally came to a choir a good voice.

choker
Mrs. reported to Mr.: "It says here that a man on the next block throttled his mother-in-law yesterday." "Hmmm," mused Mr., "sounds to me like he was a practical choker."

choler
A zebra is a horse of a different choler.

chop
When comedian Ed Wynn was playing the role of a waiter years ago in *Manhattan Mary,* a customer demanded lamb chops au gratin. Departing from the script, Wynn shouted to the kitchen, "Cheese it, the chops!"

chopping
The guillotine is a French chopping center.

chowder
The chef chowder how to make the soup.

chub
If someone tends to carp, don't let him chub you around.

chump
Reporter to star: "Is it true that your new bride has been married five times and that you have been married just twice?" Star; "Yes, she's three chumps ahead of me."

churn
When Mrs. Worts gave her neighbor a nice new butter churn, the neighbor gave her one, too, explaining that it was only fair, since one good churn deserves another.

cider
Happiness is in cider all of us.

cigarette
Cigarette life if you don't weaken.

cinnamon
Scottish colloquialism, as in: Old McIntosh is a bit of a stick. When it comes to being canny, I've never cinnamon like him."

cipher
Even though you have a code, I still cipher you.

civil
There is no such thing as a civil engineer.

claim
"That's my gold mine!" he claimed.

clamor
"Another dozen shells for me!" he clamored.

clap
VD is nothing to clap about.

clash
The late poet J. Ogden Nash
Always made of his English a hash.
When asked where it led
He flippantly said,
"It gives it a great touch of clash."

clause
1. To protect the credulous, the government has inserted into its fair-trade legislation a Santa clause.
2. Women lawyers are quick to show clause.

climax
Noun: a mountain tool.
Verb: result of using the noun.

cling
Wrestling is the sport of clings.

clip
A New York City garment manufacturer increased production 53 percent by introducing clip-sew music.

clock
For years he stayed at home and collected clocks. Then, one day when he was sixty-nine, he finally admitted his real problem was that he was a clock sucker.

clod
In the airport at Lima, someone inscribed below the name of a local Andes-hopping air service "Chariots of the Clods?"

cloister
1. *Wrangling in the quad*
   May seem very odd,
   But many do
   Get in a cloister stew.
2. *Don't let the priest disrobia*
   Or you'll get cloisterphobia.

close
1. Like Lady Godiva on her ride, the year is approaching its close.
2. When the British bachelor went looking for accommodation, his search had a close finish.

clothe
Sign by gate to nudist colony:
"Come in. We Are Never Clothed."

clothes
1. He raced her to the bedroom; it was a clothes thing.
2. Perhaps she suffered from clothestrophobia.

clown
One day Prince Jacques and his sister, Jill, went for a walk with the court jester. Unfortunately, Jacques fell down and broke his clown—and Jill came tumbling after.

clue
To be a good writer of detective stories, you have to operate a clue factory.

coal
It is hard to keep warm if you have a bad coal.

coarse
1. Defecation is the natural coarse.
2. Coarse it is!

coat
A checkroom is a place where the sheep are separated from the coats.

cobra
Brassiere for Siamese twins.

cochineal
If you are dying for fish you will see red if you cochineal.

cock
1. Brighton has a 24-hour brothel. It offers round-the-cock service.
2. *There was an old abbess quite shocked*
   To find nuns where the candles were locked.
   Said the abbess, "You nuns
   "Should behave more like guns,
   "And never go off 'til you're cocked."
3. The Toronto *Sun*: "Police yesterday swooped down on a secret cockfighting center in southern Illinois, arresting 19 men and three women and seizing 23 cocks."

cockatoo
"Why do whorehouses have parrots in their parlors?"
"I guess they figure they can always use a cockatoo!"

cocksure
Condom advertisement: Don't be half safe—be cocksure!

cocktails
"Do you enjoy cocktails?"
"I certainly do! Heard any good ones lately?"

cod

1. "Cod" and "codpiece" are archaic words largely out of use since Elizabethan times (when, apparently, people thought there was something fishy about the whole business). Last known reference in the theatre occurs in the opera *Porky and Buss* when the baritone hero, suddenly deprived of vital equipment, sings the soprano aria "My Cod! What a Mourning!"
2. The opera was written during the cod war.
3. Which was followed by the cod peace.

code

Bass-voiced actor Lorne Green was trying to place a call with a long-distance operator. When he gave the number, the operator asked, "Have you a code?" "No," Lorne rumbled, "I talk this way all the time!"

codify

Archaic—from "cod" and "codpiece." Defiance of the cod; first indications of the suffragette movement to come.

coed

A U.S. high school paper informed its readers that their football coach was up and around again, "after being laid up for a week with a bad coed."

coffin

1. An undertaker was sliding a coffin into the hearse on a cold winter's day when it slipped out of his hands, landed on the icy pavement, skidded down a hill, sailed through the town drugstore entrance and slid past the prescription counter. The undertaker came puffing along and implored the druggist, "For heaven's sake, give me something to stop this coffin!"
2. *It isn't the cough*
   That carries you off.
   It's the coffin
   They carry you off in.

Cohen

There once was a little girl named Carmen Cohen. Her mother called her Carmen but her father, for reasons only he could explain, always hailed her by her last name, Cohen. As a result, by the time the unfortunate little girl had reached puberty, she didn't know whether she was Carmen or Cohen.

coin

The queen may not be a pal.
But it's funny; on money,
She's my coined of gal.

coincide

What to do when it starts to rain.

Coke

"I'd like two bottles of pop," said Tom Swift, Cokesingly.

collar

When my mother was learning to drive she accidently backed into our

Chinese laundryman, Hum Wing. He went down with flying collars.

cologne
A man who was chipping at stone
Said, "I really am terribly prone—
"If I don't go quite slow—
"I get strong B.O.
"And that's why I wore cologne."

colon
He thought his life was coming to a full stop. But thanks to his surgeon, it only came to a semi-colon.

colt
Feed a colt and starve a beaver.

column
Samson understood advertising. He took two columns and brought down the house.

comb
1. Q. What did Paul Revere say when he passed a London barbershop?
   A. "The British are combing."
2. Song heard by a hive? "Bee it ever so humble, there's no place like comb."

come
1. Good girls don't come cheap.
2. *There was a young plumber of Leigh*
   Who was plumbing a girl by the sea.
   Said she, "Stop your plumbing,
   "There's somebody coming!"
   Said the plumber, still plumbing, "It's me."

comical
A compound is a comical combination of two or more elements.

comma
What a medium falls into.

commander
A commander is under an admiral—but who does an admiral commander?

commonplace
"Take that pencil out of your mouth, Tommy, and commonplace it on my desk."

compassion
A sex orgy is filled with compassion.

compére
A speaker who needs no introduction is beyond compére.

complement
At Wright-Patterson Air Force base near Dayton, Ohio, a newly assigned colonel walked into his office and asked the cute young stenographer, "What

is the normal complement of this office?" "Why, Colonel," exclaimed the girl, "I reckon the most normal is 'Howdy, honeypot, you're sure lookin' luscious this mornin'!'"

compromise
The Atlanta Journal: Men compromise only 1.5 percent of the South's nursing students.

concord
When United States Senator Edward Muskie was campaigning for party leadership in New Hampshire, he exclaimed happily to a reporter, "We have just concord the statehouse!"

concrete
Mr. Roe, who had just supervised the pouring of a fine new walk outside his home, was outraged when he caught his three children pressing their hands into the still-wet concrete. He walloped the three of them until they howled for mercy. "You brute!" chided his wife. "Don't you love your children at all?" "Yes," replied Mr. Roe, "in the abstract—but not in the concrete!"

concubine
The state flower of Colorado.

concupiscence
To have an awareness (Latin: *sence*) of how to overcome (Latin: *con*) with love (Latin: *cupi, cupid*).

concur
A yes man is one who stoops to concur.

condom
The Boston *Herald American* quoted an irate woman who was giving testimony at a legislative hearing on the reform of rape laws as saying, "If you're going to let these people out on the streets, you're going to be condoming what they do!"

condominium
A prophylactic for midgets.

conduct
Life has its ironies, as witness the time a jail guard handcuffed to a prisoner, was shot at. His life was saved because the conduct.

cone
A couple with a mutual craving for something sweet drove to an ice cream shop. Having bought ice-cream cones, they returned to the car to be comfortable. As they settled back to enjoy them, two birds landed on the car hood and began to chirp and flutter and peck at the windshield. The husband finally figured out what they wanted. He opened his window and put his cone on the hood, whereupon the birds settled down to eat it. "You're wonderful, George!" complimented his wife. "How did you ever think of it?" "Nothing at all," he said. "It was just a case of stilling two birds with one's cone."

Confucius

An Egyptian led his party into Cairo's largest mosque and announced: "Here the sons of our great leader Nasser and his friends learned to worship God and his prophet Mohammed." A Maoist from Shanghai interrupted from the edge of the crowd, "That's not the way my Chinese ancestors tell it." The guide looked pained and remarked, "There seems to be a little Confucian around here."

congeal

A harassed husband in Hoboken hit his wife with a bowl of Jell-o. She emerged messy but unscathed—and then had him arrested for carrying a congealed weapon.

congestion

"T.b. or not t.b., that is the congestion."

connoisseur

A sewage inspector. (Term believed to have originated in Connecticut.)

consecrated

"May I have some consecrated lye?"
"You mean concentrated lye."
"It does nutmeg much difference. That's what I camphor. What does it sulphur?"
"For 35 scents. I never cinnamon with so much wit!"
"Oh, ammonia novice. Thank you. That's a condiment."

conservative

A kind of greenhouse for looking at the moon.

consommé

"How is your soup?"
"'Tis a consommé devoutly to be wish'd."

consonant

A large body of land surrounded by water.

container

"When I told the old bag to wrap it up, that we could go on the package tour, she couldn't container self."

contrite

"William writes beautiful poetry but I contrite a thing."

contusion

A skier often jumps to contusions.

convenience

Chivalry is a man giving up his seat to a lady in a public convenience.

convention

Necessity is the mother of convention.

conversation

1. The process of turning steam back into water.
2. Natural conversation is about preserving the birds and the bees.

convex
They are kept in a prism.

conviction
Even a convict has the courage of his convictions.

coo
"We've taken over the government!" the general cooed.

cook
Once, when the Reverend Spooner was visiting a friend at his new country cottage, the Reverend complimented the host on his "nosey little cook."

cooler
Judge: "I'll fine you just ten dollars, this time. But if it happens again tomorrow, I'll throw you into jail."
First Offender: "I get it, Your Honor. Fine today, cooler tomorrow."

coop
The rural reverend decided to try raising chickens on the side. Each morning, he would go out to see if the eggs he bought had hatched. Finally, one morning, there they all were: dozens of little fluffy chicks! "Ah," he murmured thankfully, "my coop runneth over."

cop
Detective Charlie Chan was once assigned to discover who was stealing cargoes of tea being imported from the Orient. He thus became America's first China tea cop.

cope
Where there's life...

copse
If you think there's someone hiding in the underbrush, you should cull the copse.

copper
The Archbishop of York: "My ignorance of science is such that if anyone mentioned copper nitrate, I should think he was talking about policemen's overtime."

coppice
No two pictures of forests are the same, although there may be a similarity in the coppice.

coq d'or
Entrance to the men's room.

core
1. When Adam ate the fruit and fell from grace, it was a case of cores and defect.
2. Perhaps this was because the apple was hard core.

corn
An Iowa farmer is a cornographer.

cornea
Her jokes are like her eyes; blue as the sea, only cornea.

coroner
1. Cornet player.
2. What death is just around.

corps
1. Dead male. (Dead female: corpse.)
2. *She was never a stingy lady*
When an officer asked for more,
But she held a thing against privates
And was rotten to the corps.

corsair
A bawdy song, as in, "O Shed a Private Tear for Captain Morgan, Boys; He's Gone and Lost His Barbary Doll!"

corset
Supporters of the Women's Liberation movement are rumored to be discarding not only their bras but corsets without foundation.

cortege
When taking a girl to a dance, you should always buy her a cortege.

cosmos
The cosmos may be universally liked as a flower, but a space-age traveller the cosmos not.

cost
Love's Labours Cost.

cough
The reason the Smith Brothers (Trade and Mark) never shaved was because they were too busy swelling their coughers.

counterirritant
A woman who shops all day and doesn't buy anything.

country
Hamlet: *Lady, shall I lie in your lap?*
Ophelia: *No, my lord.*
Hamlet: *I mean, my head upon your lap?*
Ophelia: *Ay, my lord.*
Hamlet: *Did you think I meant country matters?*

coupe
A trusty at a state prison farm roused the warden from his bed, shouting, "There's a convict outside attaching an airplane propeller to your old jalopy! I think he's preparing to fly the coupe!"

course
1. Teacher: "And you, Willie, can you tell the nationality of Napoleon?"
Willie: "Course I can."

Teacher: "That's right."

2. Mary Ellen eloped in her sophomore year at college. Like many a student, she thought she would sophomore if she didn't put the heart before the course.

cover

Lancashire Evening Post: "The man was wearing a mustard covered V-necked pullover or cardigan, and using a large white car."

covert

Spy novels are so exciting that you want to read them from covert to covert!

cow

1. *Cow, shall I love thee?*
   Let me count the ways...
2. He was like a bull in a china shop until she cowed him.

Coward, Noel

Famous playwright whose name became a household word—as applied to a husband afraid to come home from the office Christmas party.

cowslip

If you fall in a pasture, it may be a cowslip.

crab

Once there was a girl
Who kept fishing for a pearl,
But her chances were drab for it—
Until she made a crab for it.

crack

The bore who constantly repeats the same joke has a one-crack mind.

crane

The trustees of the Madrid Zoo read that there were only 30 whooping cranes left in the U.S. and decided that they must have one before the breed became extinct. A bird was soon dispatched via air freight. Alas, when the fool bird arrived at the Madrid airport, he flatly refused to debark. The moral of this story is that cranes in Spain stick mainly to the plane.

crank

Jane Ace once said of her husband, "He always gets up at the crank of dawn."

crash

1. Humpty Dumpty must have made a crash move.
2. He should have called an ambulance and asked for crash-and-carry service.

crass

The ass
Is decidedly middlecrass—
Conventional, obtuse.

Reason, abuse,
Are equally no use.
It is a platitude
That only a halter
Can alter
The middlecrass assitude.

creator
If you climb to the top of an active volcano you can see the creator smoking.

craze
None knew thee but to love thee,
Nor named thee but to craze.

crèche
"Well!" exclaimed Mary, "If you expect me to have the Baby in *that* thing, I'll have to go on a crèche diet!"

creep
The problem with short skirts is the upcreep.

cremate
One of the advantages of nuclear warfare is that all men are cremated equal.

crew
Sailing is a crewed business.

crewel
On the morning after Richard Nixon was elected President of the United States, his daughter Julie presented him with a Presidential Seal that she had stitched and framed. Mr. Nixon later described it as, "the kindest thing that I had happen, even though it's crewel."

crick
Q. What is a crick?
A. The noise made by a Japanese camera.

criminal
"Mamma's broke all the time because Papa's got to have rich criminal his food."

critic
A husband is the critic on the hearth.

croak
1. *Raising frogs for profit*
   Is really a bit of a joke.
   How can you make any money
   When so many of them croak?
2. The wise old bird finally came to the day when all the others admitted that he was croaking.

Croat
Near the conclusion of World War II, a jeepload of Tito's soldiers was

speeding along a winding road in the Yugoslavian mountains. Rounding a curve at high speed, the jeep plowed into an oxcart filled with natives. After the crash, they had a hard time separating the jeep from the Croats.

cross
The Crusaders were cross people.

crossroad
A cloverleaf is a crossroad puzzle.

crotchety
Wearing tight pants.

crow
As the mother bird said to her offspring, "If you've got to crow, you've got to crow!"

crowbar
Raven alcoholics are caused by a crowbar.

crowd
To a pickpocket, every crowd has a silver lining.

crude
Interest is a crude income.

cruiser
When the panhandler on the dock tried to slip aboard the tour ship, the officer at the gangplank stopped him politely. "I'm sorry," he said firmly, "but beggers can't be cruisers."

cruller
1. A small boy delighted in meeting Patrolman O'Reilly on the same corner each morning. The boy would buy a doughnut and feed it to O'Reilly's grateful horse. One morning, however, the horse would have none of the doughnut. "What's wrong with Brownie today?" asked the puzzled urchin. To which O'Reilly replied, "Oh, this isn't Brownie. This is a horse of a different cruller."

2. *Dear Pet Vet:*
   I want to give my pet goldfish a bedtime snack. What would you recommend:
   Dear Chub Chum:
   Why not feed them night crullers?

crumb
Archimedes said: "Give me a full crumb and I will move the world."

crunch
When the zoo keeper discovered that his boa constrictor had escaped, he hung a sign on the cage: "Out to Crunch."

crusader
Every navel surgeon is a crusader.

Crusoe
Why was Robinson Crusoe's man Friday like a rooster? Because he scratched for himself and Crusoe.

crust
Man does not live by bread alone—but many get by on crust.

cub
A ruminant is an animal that chews its cub.

cuckoo
"We have a new cuckoo makes nice tarts."

cudgel
"I have just found a new club that is very cudgel."

cuff
"Last month my tailor told me I could have no more cuffs on my pants. Now he says I can have no more pants on the cuff."

cul-de-sac
French term: "Throw out that bag."

cull
As they say in casting offices, "Don't cull us, we'll cull you."

cuneiform
When the Persian war correspondent was captured, he was stripped of his cuneiform.

cunning
He was not only a great swordsman, but also a cunning linguist.

cur
Why is a tin can tied to a dog's tail like death?
Because it's something bound to a cur.

curb
New York City has a new cocktail called The Stock Market Special: Three of them gets you a seat on the curb.

curd
Only a jerk would milk his firm of expenses when none have been in curd.

curl
Labia majora: the curly gates.

current
1. "Where do jellyfish get their jelly?"
   "From ocean currents?"
2. The current practice at boarding kennels is so much per dog per day.

curry
If you have decided to prepare Indian food for your guests, you must have the curries of your convictions.

curse
Lay off The Pill and let Nature take its curse.

curtail
He went to the costume party as a dog, and found himself curtailed.

curtain
1. When the great Barrymore, badly intoxicated, appeared upon the stage, it was curtains for him.
2. Even though, as an actor, he had that curtain something.

cuspidor
In the days when this receptacle was in its glory, a bartender in Chicago wagered a British customer that the saloon had four doors: "The front door, the back door, the cuspidor and me, Isidore." The visitor took the joke home with him, giving the punchline as, "The front door, the back door, the proprietor and the spittoon."

cut
1. My cut runneth over.
2. Recipe for a slow-growing lawn: Plant the seed deep and soak with beer. The grass will come up half cut.
3. A lovelorn butcher in Maine stabbed himself with an icicle last winter and died of his own cold cuts.

cycle
1. A long-haired youth in California was hauled into court for the fourth time for the same offense: riding off on somebody's motor scooter. The judge remarked, "Young man, you are obviously a cycle-path."
2. It was true; he had been going around in a vicious cycle.

cyclone
"Do you like cycling with a group?"
"No, doing things in groups gets the wind up for me. I prefer to cyclone."

cygnet
If a swan sings its swan song, does a young swan sing its cygneture tune?

cymbal
Banging together brass plates in an orchestra is not as cymbal as it looks.

*Cleopatra was the queen of **denial**.*

D
The second note of the natural major scale. Hence the observation that many modern singers are D-ranged.

dab
It strikes me that a dab hand probably has something fishy about him.

dace
Now that the rivers in Europe are getting cleaner, happy dace are here again.

daguerreotype
Sherlock Holmes was always photographed in street attire. He was a cloak and daguerreotype.

dais
When the platform collapsed in the middle of his lecture, the professor picked himself up and sighed, "Some dais are like that!"

daisy
"Ma's always glad when school starts because Andy's such a nuisance on the daisies at home."

dam
Bassano, Alberta's entrance sign: "Best in the West by a Dam Site."

dame
Floods can be avoided by using large dames.

damp
Sex is just one damp thing after another.

dance
A stupid or ignorant person.

Darjeeling
"Would you like some tea, father?"
"Yes, my Darjeeling daughter."

date
1. You can tell that a palm tree is old if it's dated.
2. Did you hear about the Arabs who were sitting under a palm tree eating their dates?

dawn
The frustrated husband awoke with a hard dawn.

daze
And then there was the traveller on a liquid diet who went around the world in a tea daze.

deacon
A signal fire placed in a prominent position to warn people.

dead
1. The Undertakers Association of the World (UAW) decided to promote their product. What they came up with was a dead giveaway.
2. Title of novel by Sir Alan Patrick: "Holy Deadlock."

debate
What lures de fish.

debenture
Niagara Falls Gazette: "New Technique Implants Set of Debentures Direct to Patient's Jawbone."

debt
An income-tax review can become a sudden debt payoff.

deceit
"Ma makes me wear pants with patches on deceit."

deceiving
All banks have two windows. One is marked "Paying," the other "Deceiving."

decoy
Sign in a window featuring a line of brassieres: "This is the Real Decoy."

decree
A divorcee is a woman who gets richer by decrees.

deer

A CAT-ASS-trophy

"DEER girl," chortled OWL man BULLitt, "my father's sister in TURKEY—you know, my FEZAUNT—finally mailed me that hundred BUCKS she owed me."

"WALLABY a song-of-a-gun!" laughed Mrs. Bullitt. "OCELOT of DOE. How's for GIBBON some to KITTY?" "I let my secretary BURRO it," admitted Mr. Bullitt, SHEEP-ishly.

"That peROCside CHEETAH! EWE did this on PORPOISE!" WHALEd his outraged wife. (In tense moments she lapsed into a French patois she had picked up in LIONS.) "I MOOSE keel her one day," she snarled. "No wonder ze loafers WEASEL at her on ze street corners! Her dress, eet is always so low ZE BRA shows!"

"OSTRICH to the facts," suggested Bullitt wearily. "WEASEL get by. POSSUM of those GNU spareribs you've cooked. I declare, that recipe ought to be triple-starred in the next BULL-etin of Miss Duncan HYENA's." Completely mollified, Mrs. Bullitt beamed. "I could eat a PLATTER, PUSS, myself! But BEAR in mind that Duncan is not a miss. He's a MON, GOOSE!"

CUR-tain

-AnonyMOUSE

defeat

Every time the prince found a girl he thought might be Cinderella, he went down to defeat.

defect

To get a young lady pregnant and then to leave town is to be guilty of cause and defect.

defence

Repairing the Great Wall of China: a good example of defence-mending.

defer

The draftee ran through fire and got deferred.

de Gaulle

As a tribute to their great leader of the past, the French plan to take over the Rock of Gibraltar and rename it "de Gaulle Stone."

delegate

There's a sandwich shop across the street from the U.N. called "The Delegate-essen."

delight

1. To darken the boudoir is to lower delight.
2. The firefly that got caught in the threshing machine was delighted.

denial

Cleopatra was the queen of denial.

denier
If you're going to rob a bank, wear a stocking mask. Denier won't be recognized.

Denise
Once upon a time, after a trawler fisherman had gone to sea, his wife gave birth to twins. Aware that her husband seldom agreed with her decisions yet needing names for the children, she turned to his brother for help. Upon his return, the fisherman, having admired his new son and daughter, asked his wife what she had named them.
She confessed that she had let his brother make the choice. "He called the girl Denise," she explained.
"Well, that's pretty good," admitted the father.
"And what did he call our son?"
"Oh," his wife replied, "he's Denephew!"

dent
Garage advertisement: "May we have the next dents, please?"

depart
1. Gauguin tired of superficial painting styles and moved to depart.
2. He is easy to understand on the surface, but I can't plumb the depart.
3. That's depart that baffles me.

depend
These days, it's getting so that a diving-board is the only thing on which you can depend.

dependant
"Why is a once-successful man like you working in a jewelery store like this?" "Because all I have left is dependants."

deplore
The whale
Bewail.
When gone from sight,
Then we will write:
No more;
Deplore.

deploy
Spreading out your troops isn't always a good idea, but sometimes deploy works.

depravity
Arriving home for the holidays from reform school, a teenage delinquent called out, "Look, Mom, no depravities!"

deprecated
Canadian Army notice (Northern Italy, 1944):
LATRINES: All troops will ensure that faces are covered with soil after each person has deprecated."

depress
They called him "Sad Sack" because his pants were so depressed.

desert
The sand which is here.

Des Moines
"What did you do last summer?"
"I worked in Des Moines."
"Coal or iron?"

dessert
And then there was the Swedish chef who refused to make pastry. He didn't want to waste his Swedeness on the dessert area.

detention
The truant officer's rationale: Necessity is the mother of detention.

detergent
Leicester Mercury: "This is a particularly serious offense which we have to deal with severely, as a detergent to anyone in the same mind."

devotee
A bridge player's social event.

dew
When rain falls, it gets up again in dew time.

diatribe
What the North American Indians used to do before going into battle.

dice
How were Adam and Eve kept from gambling?
Their pair o'dice was taken away from them.

dick
"Ahab a Moby Dick."
"That's better than Ishmael one!"

dido
1. The same; usually represented by dido marks.
2. From Dido, Queen of Carnage, who had marks like these on Aeneas.

die
1. The sheep died in the wool.
2. "We have no room for all this," said the city editor, glancing despairingly at a two-column obituary.
   "It must be cut down to proper diemention."
3. An American tourist in London, forgetting that traffic there bore to the left instead of the right, looked the wrong way and was run down. He regained consciousness in an emergency ward and moaned, "Did I come here to die?" "Oh, no, sir," the Cockney nurse assured him. "You came yesterdie."

dig
A gossip columnist makes many a martial grave with little digs.

dilate
"I'm at your cervix," said the gynecologist.
"Dilated to meet you," replied his patient.

dill
Attempts to save money by doing it yourself don't always work out. Even if you want to preserve your own pickles, you will find that dill waters run steep.

dilute
It is a sin to water good scotch. Compelled to do so to meet the proof standards of his market, the conscientious distiller was heard to say to his vats: "We who are about to sigh dilute you."

dim
There was a young lassy from Limerick
Whose eyes were all shiny and shimmerick.
When asked why her stare
Seemed to float on the air
She said, "I moist up when it's dimmerick."

dime
The two coin collectors got together for old dimes' sake.

din
The Towel of Babel was a din of iniquity.

dink
A daisy chain is no stronger than its weakest dink.

dinosaur
Restaurant term relative to complaints about bad food or service. As in, "What made that dinosaur?"

disbar
As distinguished from another.

discharge
The spouse of a pretty young thing
Came home from the wars in the spring.
  He was lame but he came
  With his dame like a flame—
A discharge is a wonderful thing.

disgusting
As the weatherman said, "Disgusting is going to come to blows."

dish
Knock, knock!
Who's there?
Dishes.

Dishes who?
Dishes me. Who ish you?

dismal
Method of counting invented by Arabs.

distaste
A Brooklyn bard has been credited with saying of cunnilingus: "Distaste is da best taste in da world."

distress
To read dramatically, you should put more distress in one place than another.

divan
"Mah deah," exclaimed the southern belle to her overweight friend, "you-all look simply divan!"

divider
No expert he on freeway speeds,
Sober or with cider.
In the graveyard now his headstone reads,
"He crossed the Great Divider."

dizzy
The Reverend Spooner, calling on the dean of Christ Church: "Is the bean dizzy?"

doe
A-hunting we will go!
A-hunting we will go!
That's the way to get a buck—
Or at least a little doe!

dog
1. *The dog comes*
   on little fat feet.
   It sits looking
   over the harbor and city
   with silent hunches,
   and then moves on.
2. It may seem cruel, but when an Eskimo runs out of firewood, he simply throws another dog on the fire.
3. One symptom of puppy love is when the boy dogs the girl's footsteps.

doge
La Mancha's best friend is its doge.

doggerel
A particularly untalented poet persisted in submitting his material to a tough editor of a national magazine. The editor finally wrote him, "For heaven's sake, curb your doggerel!"

dogma
A puppy's mommy.

dogmatize
"You really can't train a terrier," he dogmatized.

domain
The world of dishonest bookkeepers is one of ledger domain.

doormat
The sex urges of a henpecked husband may lie doormat for years.

double
When Columbus sailed across the Atlantic and back without taking a bath, the Queen of Spain called him a dirty double crosser.

dough
The upper crust is a lot of crumbs held together by dough.

dour
1. The taxi driver thought that the passenger said he wanted to be taken to a dour house, and dropped him at a funeral parlor.
2. The organist there was playing "O God, Dour Help in Ages Past."

dowager
One who bets on the New York Stock Exchange averages.

dowel
When the cabinetmaker tried to open her drawers, he finally threw in the dowel.

dower
A beach boy charges by the day. A playboy charges by the dower.

down
1. As the eider duck remarked, "If you want to line a nest, you really must get down to it."
2. *Singapore Straits Times:* "Six girls struggled from sick beds on Thursday and downed their swimsuits for a last-minute rehearsal for the final ceremony."
3. "Linda Lovelace for President" concluded with "...the first woman president to go down in history."

drain
Gutter language puts a drain on society.

dram
Not all cows are contented. The other day one muttered to her farmer, "Go ahead and milk me. See if I give a dram!"

drape
The famous stripper Gypsy Rose Lee woke up fully dressed one morning and cried, "Good heavens, I've been draped!"

draper
It would have been curtains for him if she had found out who her draper was.

draw
The bank sent our statement this morning.
The sheet was a sight of great awe.
Its figures and mine might have balanced.
But my wife was too quick on the draw!

drawer
The dictum "He who would make a pun would pick a pocket," was attributed first to Ben Jonson, then to Oliver Wendell Holmes. Its real source seems to have been the critic John Dennis (1657-1734). When he and the composer Henry Purcell were together in a tavern, Purcell rang the bell for the drawer (waiter) but no one answered it. Tapping their table, Purcell asked Dennis, "Why is this table like the tavern?" He then supplied his own answer, "Because there is no drawer in it." Dennis replied, "Any man who would make such an execrable pun would not scruple to pick my pocket."

drawing room
Dental parlor.

Dresden
Formerly a type of lace, now used in reference to all female clothing, as in, "My God, look what she's dresden!"

dressing
"Want to do something naughty, Jimmy?"
"What, Billy?"
"Let's go into the kitchen and watch the salad dressing!"

dribbling
What happens to teachers who retire? They lose their principals. And to principals who retire? They lose their faculties. And to professional basketball players who retire? They just go on dribbling.

drill
Going to the dentist can be a drilling experience.

drip
A drizzle is a drip that's going steady.

drogue
An air force shoot-out, usually held outside a drogue store.

drool
You can always tell an Alabama baby because it has a southern drool.

drug
A man in Canada was charged with pulling a woman along the street by her hair. The magistrate asked the policeman, "Was she drugged?" "Yes, sir," he replied. "A full two blocks!"

druid
> There is a mysterious circle of stones near Killarney—but no one knows who druid.

dry
> 1. Sign on liquor store door next to hospital: "Dry, Doc?"
> 2. I hate to see a grown man dry.
> 3. "Why am I standing on these newspapers? My feet are wet. These are the Times that dry men's soles."

Dublin
> The most popular quiz program in Ireland is reported to be called "Dublin or Nothing."

duck
> 1. On a visit to San Francisco, Bing Crosby was trying to describe to a waiter in a Grant Street chop-suey emporium a succulent dish he had been served in Hong Kong. "I'm sure it was some kind of duck," recalled Bing, "but at the same time it tasted like fish."
> "Ah, yes," beamed the waiter. "Hadduck!"
> 2. The nicest thing about a pool are the ducks in it.

ducky
> Wife of a duke.

due
> 1. The credit manager's song: "Beyond the Due Horizon."
> 2. The minister of a small church was his own bookkeeper. He kept his bills in a drawer marked, "Due Unto Others."

duel
> As any lover of shish kebab knows, a sword can be used for duel purposes.

duenna
> A woman employed by Spanish parents to make sure that no one can duenna thing to their daughter.

duet
> Pity the man who couldn't find anyone to sing with! He went out and bought a duet yourself kit.

duke
> Madame: "Now remember, girls, when handling royalty, the important thing is to keep up your dukes!"

dun
> 1. For years, Mary Spender couldn't balance her budget. Then she wrote a book and became so rich that she had no more problems. Her book? Oh, she called it "The Man Who Came to Dun Her."
> 2. At its conclusion, the hero exclaims, "It is a far far better thing I'm due than I have ever dunned!"

dunce

A series of rhythmic concerted movements and steps timed to music, so named after the inventor, Mavis Dunce, whose name became a customary salutation before joining in the activity, i.e.: "Mavis Dunce with you?"

dung

1. Agricultural word from North American dialect, as in, "White man speaks with forked dung."
2. Also occurs in a staff song used in fertilizer plants: "When the Work's All Dung This Fall."

dusk

Little bits of stuff that fly about in the air.

dybbuk

A publisher who specializes in novels about zombies, goblins and demons has just established the Dybbuk-of-the-Month Club.

dye

1. She was a suicide blonde; she dyed by her own hand.
2. Would hue and dye have helped her?

"I've got to jump,"
the pilot **explained**.

E

The editors of *Look* magazine heard that their competitor, *Life* magazine, had employed a distinguished statesman to write a series of revealing articles on backstage Washington. Unfortunately, they did not know the man's name. Even at *Life*, he was referred to only as "Mr. E." Anxious to scoop the *Life* team, *Look* assigned one of its senior editors to track down the statesman. He succeeded in doing this by the simple device of following one *Life* editor assigned to the articles until he saw him one day in a bar talking to a famous politician. Sure that he had his man, the *Look* editor waited until the editor from *Life* had gone to the men's room, then dashed up to the alarmed politician and exclaimed, "Ah, sweet 'Mr. E' of *Life,* at last I've found you!"

each
Minor irritation.

eagle
American symbol of democracy: "All men are created eagle."

ear
1. You ear some awful corn these days.
2. "Your wife never stops talking. How on earth can you stand it?" marveled a henpecked husband's best friend. "I know," sighed the husband, "I've given that woman the best ears of my life."

earl
When his lordship's crew mutinied during a storm, the first thing they did was to pour the earl on the troubled waters.

earn
"Well," said the call girl defensively, "you live and earn."

earnest
The pun in the title of the play *The Importance of Being Earnest* was a Wilde idea.

earring
The lobe was the original earring aid.

earthquake
It's nobody's fault but it has taken us until recently to fissure out what makes the earthquake.

earwig
Hairpiece with built-in hearing aid.

easel
When the artist protested that he couldn't paint his hostess because he hadn't brought his equipment, she refused to let him easel out of it.

Easter
Good Friday Easter be a national holiday.

eat
1. Why the cannibal decided to become a missionary: "If you can't eat them, join them!"
2. There is reported to be an outdoor restaurant in Florida called "The Garden of Eatin'."

eaves
The farmer shot his stable because it had the eaves.

eavesdropper
Adam.

ebony
In Scotland, a black girl is known as ebony lass.

echelon
Wartime drinking song: "Echelon Way to Tipperary."

eclair
Small French cake filled with bird meat: *eclair du loon.*

Ed
When twins came, their father Dan Dunn
Gave "Edward" as name to each son.
When folks said, "Absurd!"
He replied, "Ain't you heard
That two Eds are better than one?"

Eden
Adam was rejected for Eden the apple.

edifice
Sign on a junkyard fence: "Edifice Wrecks."

edit
When Jacqueline Kennedy Onassis got a job with a publishing house, an admirer hoped she would soon edit to her laurels.

Edith
A young Air Force cadet managed to get himself engaged to two beautiful girls at the same time. One was named Edith, and the other Kate. Unfortunately for the cadet, the two girls met, discovered his duplicity and confronted him, crying, "We'll teach you that you can't have your Kate and Edith, too!"

eek
A sharp cry, sometimes of dismay, e.g., as heard from a professional mourner trying to eek out a living.

eel
1. "Do you have much in your creel?" the returning fisherman was asked. "Oh, yes, a good eel!"
2. There once was a fisherman in the Gulf of Mexico who caught an eel in which he found a very large diamond ring. He sold the ring and retired on his eel-gotten gains. And never again had to put his shoulder to the eel.

efface
The secret of success for the Mother Superior was that efface was her fortune.

effete
A gentleman farmer has effete of clay.

effrontery
A restaurant featuring topless waitresses.

Eiffel
For the tourist, Paris offers many attractive views. That is why its most famous tower is called an Eiffel.

Eire
Their constant conflicts must someday lead the Irish to see the Eire of their ways.

elastic
He crossed a rubber tree with a potato plant and produced Baked Elastic.

elate
Counsel to incipient old maids: Better elate than never.

election
Eleanor Roosevelt, discussing democracy with an Oriental ambassador, asked: "And when did you last have an election?" The ambassador, with some embarrassment, answered: "Before blekfast."

elementary
1. Even the most primitive of animals has an elementary canal.

2. When Dr. Watson came around to 221B Baker Street one afternoon, the housekeeper told him that Sherlock Holmes had a visitor, a schoolgirl. Watson sat down to wait but then heard muffled sounds coming from the study. Fearing that the schoolgirl might be an assassin in disguise, he broke open the door—only to find the great detective and the girl engaged in a rather shocking activity.

"By Gad, Holmes!" huffed the doctor. "Just what sort of 'schoolgirl' is this?"

"Why," said Holmes, smiling down at her happily,

"Elementary, my dear Watson."

elephant
Well-timed silence hath more elephants than speech.

elevate
"Going up! What floor, sir?"
"Elevate!"

elf
The librarian at Wimbledon has explained that the reason the library is not adding any more fairy tales is that it has run out of elf space.

elite
In Tangier there is an American-style restaurant known as "Elitery."

elk
The moose is a member of the deer family and its elk.

elliptical
The feel of a kiss.

elm
Noah's bark set sail with his wife at the elm.

elocution
In the U.S., many people are killed by it.

elope
When the cowboy and cowgirl decided to run off and get married, they went eloping down the road.

embarrassed
Emmy's condition after losing her pants.

ember
Much has been written about dispassionate women. Perhaps the best known novel on the subject is "Forever Ember."

emery
The song of the love-struck manicurist: "Thanks for the Emery."

emissary
Person sent on a special mission and frequently given special treatment at borders. Hence the passport officer's query, "Is this trip emissary?"

emotion
Climate is caused by the emotion of the earth.

empress
Royalty is pretty empressive.

emu
Being afraid of felines, the Australian bird cassowary eye when he hears emu.

enamor
You can get some girls' attention with flowers. For others, you have to use enamor.

enclose
Some fences deal in jewelery, others enclose.

encroach
One of the plagues of printers used to be type lice. Today, what with increasing mechanization, they are also having trouble with the encroach.

encyclical
Daisy, Daisy,
Give me your answer, do!
I'm half crazy
Over Pope Paul's point of view.
It may lead to world starvation,
But constant procreation
Is what we're for
It says in your
Encyclical made for two.

end
Hermaphroditism is an end in itself.

endive
Olympic swimmers in training favor the endive.

endow
"I am most impressed by your university. Could it use some financial assistance?"
"Endow!"

endure
"Perhaps it would endure need."

enema
A lady in a hospital, recovering from a minor operation, was awakened from a nap by a knock on the door. "Who goes there?" she inquired warily. "Friend or enema?"

engineer
Casey could always tell if something was wrong with his locomotive because he had a good engineer.

engrave
The stonemason who misspells a word on a tombstone is engrave trouble.

enlarge
A photo salesman makes more money by enlarge.

enormous
Enormous is bigger than an isthmus.

eon
A reflex muscular reaction of the jaw indicating the passage of time.

epicure
One who edits epics.

epidemic
Medical term: Needle used for injections.

epistle
What an apostle is always firing off.

epitaph
Short sarcastic comment.

epoch
Commemorative tablets and statues leave many a European town epoch-marked.

era
1. A fad is something that goes in one era and out the other.
2. The Churchill Era was his mistake.

ere
A popular theory of Earth's creation is that it was hot ere.

erg
When you want your team to make a power play you erg them on.

Erin
1. A pretty colleen awoke on the morning of New York's annual St. Patrick's Day Parade and sighed, "I dreamed I marched up Fifth Avenue in my Erin-go-bragh."
2. To have really done so, of course, would have been an Erin judgment.

erotic
She was confused by the bank's erotic behavior.

errant
A roving reporter frequently goes on a fool's errant.

erratic
A famous potter used to keep all his broken efforts on the third floor of his house. He referred to that floor as the erratic.

erroneous
"My husband is a great lover; he knows all the erroneous zones."

error
Every day is the dawn of a new error.

escalator
A man recently arrived in New York from Rome approached the floorwalker in a big department store and asked, "You tella me, please, where is rest room?"
The floorwalker pointed to the left and answered politely, "Escalator, sir."
"Escalator!" echoed the Italian indignantly. "Hell, mister, I gotta go now!"

escapement
When the Russian watchmaker finally managed to slip out of the country no one knew what his escapement.

escargot
At Ford Motor Company's testing grounds, all prototype autos are identified by letters. Last year, models A through R were failures, but you should have seen the escargot!

eschew
There's a new kind of chewing gum for people who simply loathe the brands now on the market. It's called eschewing gum.

eskimo
Sam and Mo, two enterprising young men from New York, got the job of leading a tour of ladies through Alaska. Unfortunately, their knowledge of the area was far slighter than they had alleged. Consequently, when one of the ladies demanded, "Where are the igloos you promised?" all Sam could do was point at his partner and reply, "Eskimo."

espousal
Bride auction.

Essex
Make of car popular in the thirties. An instance was reported then of an owner standing beside his after a collision and moaning, "My Essex! Oh, my Essex!" His wife, climbing out with difficulty, commented, "Hell, Sam, so does mine!"

esteem
The psychiatrist's office: esteem valve.

estrange
The Ku Klux Klan meets as estrangers in the night.

etch
Engraving gives one the satisfaction of scratching the etch.

eternal
The degree of Doctor of Philosophy is granted to those who are qualified to practice eternal medicine.

ether
"Doctor, will I be given a general or a local anesthetic?"
"You can have ether."

ethyl
"Do you put ethyl in your car?"
"No, I usually take her to a motel."

et tu
Calpurnia, Caesar's wife, came up with a new recipe for pizza pies. "Did you like them?" asked Brutus. "Et tu, Brute," answered Caesar, loyally. Said Brutus: "Gesundheit!"

eucalyptus
In California, these fast-growing gum trees were once sold to a railway as ties, but they proved to be unsatisfactory and the railway's owners cried "Eucalyptus!"

Euclid
The geometry professor was trying to explain his devotion to his work: "It's like this: I love my wife but, oh, Euclid!"

eugenic
"How do you feel about eugenics?"
"Oh, I think people with small ones are just as sexy."

eunuch
Being castrated is a eunuch experience.

euphemism
Euphemism and I'm for youse'm.

eureka
When Archimedes had his bright idea in the bathtub, he jumped out and ran down the street just as he was, yelling "Eureka!" The cop at the corner asked "Eureka what?" "Eureka garlic!" said Archimedes, beginning to feel a little foolish.

European
Those European floor-level urinals can be a problem for North American males. If you run into trouble, the best thing to do is to turn to the man beside you and say politely, "Pardonnez-moi, m'sieu, but European on my foot."

evanescent
"Well! Evanescent my old pal, Oscar!"

evidence
Divorce lawyer, meeting his newest and prettiest client at a party: "May I evidence with you?"

evil
Beware of Satan or evil have his way.

ewe
As one ram said to another, "After ewe!"

ewer
Baseball's Philadelphia Phillies once had a wide-mouthed pitcher who was always yelling at the umpire, "Ewer cracked!"

excess
Saving money is one area where nothing succeeds like excess.

exchequer
A retired supermarket employee.

exclaim
"I've lost my gold mine!" he exclaimed.

excrete
Former native of Greece.

excretory
Former Greek politician.

exorcise
The only way a medicine man can keep fit is to exorcise.

expectorate
As the tough cowgirl said, "You've got to chew tobacco, if you expectorate with me."

explain
"I've got to jump," the pilot explained.

extradition
"Eat all you want, there's extradition the pantry."

eye
1. Scientists claim to be able to tell the age of a deer by its eyes—which makes it an interesting eye-deer.
2. Asked to explain her success, the dress designer confessed, "I was just lucky at the start. The hook and eye hung around together."

eyeball
A nearsighted lady turned up for dinner very much disturbed. "I can't see," she explained. "I couldn't put in my contact lenses because my poodle bit me in the eye this afternoon."
"What did he do that for?" asked the hostess.
"Heaven knows," replied the guest. "Probably he felt like having an eyeball before dinner."

eyeful
In these waning days of burlesque, one sees some amazing names on the marquees. Among the strippers so advertised one might find Miss Eyeful Tower, Miss September Maugham and Miss Berthe Daye Sute. At one time, there was in Hollywood (and may still be) a school for striptease artists

which also supplied noms de plumes under which the artists could bust forth. As the stature of the art has declined, so has the gentility of the names. Some printable examples, however, include Ima Bigwon, Irma La Douche, Lotta Bounce, Gay Deceiver and Rachel Prejudice.

eyrie

Climbing a mountain gives most of us an eyrie feeling.

*The Three Musketeers were pretty **fency** fellows.*

F

1. There was once a fighter pilot who was so modest that he was known as "The F Ace."
2. One day, his colonel said, "I would like to make you F.O." The diffident young man replied, "Fine sir, I'll leave right now."
3. F only he had!

fable

The lurid illustration on the cover of a paperback novel is often a fable of contents.

fade

To a believer in apartheid, miscegenation leads to a fade worse than death.

fag

"I'd blow smoking tomorrow, if it weren't such a fag."

faint

The cowardly fencer faints.

faith

They came together in a waltz. The girl gazed up at him and whispered, "You're the kind of man I feel I can trust." "Really?" replied the boy. "We must have met someplace before! Your faith seems familiar."

fake

An imitator of Erskine Caldwell's writing style was once termed by a critic "God's little faker."

fall

There was a young fellow named Hall
Who fell in the spring in the fall.

'Twould have been a sad thing
Had he died in the spring,
But he didn't—he died in the fall.

fallow
"My fallow Americans..."

falsify
"When I put a book on my head it falsify move."

falter
In the spring a young bull's fancy
Lightly turns toward the herd.
Later on, his search is chancy
Stepping 'round the big faltered.

famine
Process of tilling soil in Massachusetts.

fanatic
"We like to dress up in the old things we get out of fanatic."

fanny
At the Miss America Contest, Miss Florida undulated by in her little orange bathing suit. Young Whitney Whitney Whitney Whitney IV felt his heart beating faster and declared to his friend, "This has to be love at first sight!" "Don't be silly," counseled his friend. "It's just a passing fanny."

farce
The traveling vaudeville show of old was often a tour de farce.

fare
K-Ration is war fare.

fart
Unpleasant onomatopoetic word to indicate an explosion. References are recurrent in the anals of literature of which grafitti are fart and parcel.

farther
While out walking, a young lady heard for the first time of her mother's intention to marry again. She was obliged to sit right down and cry. She could not go a step farther.

fastidious
You could tell that she was likely to be fastidious; her father was fast and her mother was hideous.

fate
On the punster's tombstone one should inscribe:
   R.I.P.
   Fate Accompli.

faucet
Compared to men, women have more faucets of emotion.

fault
After a major earthquake in northern California, a group of concerned citizens set up the San Andreas Fund, proving that Californians can be generous to a fault.

Faust
1. "Do you sing Faust?"
   "Certainly. Of course, I can also sing slow."
2. Faust in war, Faust in peace, and Faust in the hearts of his countrymen.

faux pas
Most of a dog's mistakes are caused by its *faux pas*.

fawn
Playing with deer is fawn.

feat
Motto: "Better footwork; bigger feat."

feces
"Where have you been?" she asked.
"Out walking the dog," he replied. "Looking for the old, familiar feces."

fecund
Punning was fecund nature to Shakespeare.

fee
A gigolo is a fee-male.

feed
1. The penalties of living a fast life most often come from exceeding the feed limit.
2. Breast-fed: a female F.B.I. agent.
3. The mess call is the battle cry of feed 'em.

feet
One has to admire those natives who walk on live coals; that's no mean feet.

feline
Sensory experience, as in, "He's feline his oats".

felon
If you feloniously fell on a felon, who's the felon—the felon you fell on, or you?

fence
The Three Musketeers were pretty fency fellows.

fender
"I was so surprised, you could have knocked me over with a fender."

ferrous
The nonferrous metals industry was holding its annual convention. A secretary, sent to find the one ferrous expert attending, solved her problem

by going to the powder room and asking, "Mirror, mirror on the wall, who's the ferrous one of all?"

fertilize
1. My new girl friend has fertilize.
2. But she also tells them.
3. Because of that, I'm not going to give her a coat or any fertilize sure of her.
4. Fertilization is a process by which aliens can become citizens.

fervor
An old maid is one who will only go so far and no fervor.

fetal
The best position for sleeping is curled up. Besides, your fetal feel better.

fete
Social events at the YMCA are known as athletes' fetes.

fetish
The way you feel on your way to a fete.

fever
Oliver Wendell Holmes, Sr., was a physician as well as an author and lecturer. He is said to have remarked of his medical career that he was grateful for small fevers.

fez
A famous Egyptian boatbuilder became known as "the fez that launched a thousand ships."

fiancée
At first, she seemed his dream come true but in the end he decided she was really just a passing fiancée.

fiddle
1. "Let's burn down Rome before that Nero gets here. I'm all for eliminating the fiddle man."
2. In France it is customary to avoid playing La Marseillaise on the violin. The French believe it is bad form to fiddle with the national anthem.
3. But it's all right to do it elsewhere, fiddle give you pleasure.

field
Baseball player's motto: "You're only as young as you field."

fife
When trumpeters marry
They oft come to blows.
Where tympanists tarry
Nobody knows.
But a flautist is fortunate all of his life:
"That was no piccolo. That was my fife!"

fig
As Adam said when Eve hung a leaf on him,
"I'm a fig boy now!"

figment
However, Eve wasn't much of a botany student; she didn't know what a figment.

figure
She said, "What's this figure talking about?"

file
The new bride asked her lawyer to get her a divorce. "My husband is too large for me," she complained. "Then," said the lawyer, "I think you should file your petition." "The heck with that!" she exclaimed. "Let him sandpaper his! What a file idea!"

fillet
There's no point in having a creel if you can't fillet.

fillip
Automotive term from the Philippines, as in, "Fillip the tank." (Spanish equivalent: "Eso si.")

finch
1. Completed. (Telephone operator's terms: "Are you finch, sir?")
2. Tarzan went out to get the evening meal, but all he could catch was a couple of small birds and two baby chimpanzees. When Jane saw what he had brought home, she sighed. "Not finch and chimps again!"

finish
I love a finished speaker,
I really, really do.
I don't mean one who's polished.
I do mean one who's through.

fink
As René Descartes wrote, "I fink, therefore I am."

Finnish
Jan Sibelius is said to have been the first to observe that nice guys Finnish last.

fireproof
The boss's relatives.

fish
Why can you never expect a fisherman to be generous? Because his business makes him sell fish.

fishy

A FISHY TALE

The prettiest she-fish in the whole aquarium was Sara Dean. Young Haddock's gills fluttered with suppressed poisson every time she and her chub Min O. slithered down the pike. Chowder kipper in comfort was his consuming obsession.

Trouble loomed, however, when the two girls worked out a sister act and opened in the Hollywood Bowl. An interested member of the audience was Rufus Goldfish, who sat in the second roe. (He was slightly hard of herring.) "Confidentially" he told a grouper friends later, "the girls' act smelt. However, one was barracuda. The other should have kept a tarpon." Young Haddock's sole shriveled at these words. That bass tard! "Only an act of cod will keep my Sara out of his clutches," he muttered shadly. Min O. tried to rally him. "Don't be blue," she counseled. "You are no common weakfish, angel. Salmon up your courage. Get in there and put that sailfish old flounder t'rout."

Had squared what passes for shoulders in a fish. "Thanks, Min," he spluttered. "By gum and bivalve, I'll get out of this pickerel yet. If that shrimp expects to mackerel have me to reckon with!"

Suiting his action to his words and casting a hook that was a real sinker, he knocked his rival off his perch and tipped the scales so effishently that poor Mr. Goldfish whaled for the carps—and a sturgeon to get the bones out of his mouth.

"I did it on porpoise!" cried the exultant Haddock, clasping Sara (who looked prettier than Marlin Dietrich) to his slippery chest.

It was all such a shark to Mr. Goldfish that he's been eel to this very day.

Finny

fissure
1. A man who sells fish.
2. God's promise to women: "I shall make you fissures of men."

fit
1. Epilepsy is the survival of the fit.
2. *Being the fort*
   Is hardly it.
   You might as well
   Have come in fit.

fizz
"Are you a doctor?" asked a young lady, stepping into a drugstore.
"Naw," replied the youth behind the white counter.
"I'm just the fizzician."

fjord
Swedish car.

flail
"It isn't often that I risk an argument with my wife because, when I do, words flail me."

flair
There is a dress shop in Beverly Hills, California, called "My Flair Lady."

flame
Last week, a fire-eater made the front pages because his flame had spread.

flare
You can see by her light touch that she has a flare for the piano.

flat
1. A brassiere manufacturer advertises, "We fix flats."
2. Pawnbrokers live on the flat of the land.
3. Tire-repair charges vary enormously; it would be better if all garages had a flat rate.

flattery
Living in an apartment house.

flaw
A Bostonian was about to be shown a new house in Naples, Florida. "Here," boasted the realtor, "is the home-owner's dream: a house without a flaw." "Without a flaw?" echoed the Bostonian. "What does one walk on?"

flea
1. To depart hurriedly.
2. Usually applied to people who are not up to scratch, but are as thick as flea soup.

flesh
1. An afternoon snack: the pause that refleshes.
2. The reason so many tycoons are fat is that they have traded the flush of youth for the flesh of victory.

flock
Not every woman likes to quilt, but they flock to make pillows.

floor
Traditional ballroom dancing is really a form of floor-play.

florist
1. The budding carpenter usually starts out as a florist.
2. Flower shop delivery boys: florist rangers.

flotation
A shipboard romance.

flour
Two-Ton Tessy was so worried about her weight she requested that her death notice read, "Please omit flours."

flu
St. Peter: "And how did you get here?"
Latest Arrival: "Flu!"

flush
A poker-loving spiritualist who needed another player for a Saturday-night session summoned the ghost of a departed friend. The ghost was delighted to sit in on the game, and on the very first hand drew five beautiful hearts. He bet all of his chips.
Unfortunately, one of the flesh-and-blood players had a pat full house and

raked in the pot—just one more time when the spirit was willing but the flush was weak.

flute
It is important to recognize the difference between an oboe and a flute. An oboe is an American transient. A flute is an Oriental homosexual.

fly
1. Q. How do you make an elephant fly?
   A. Well, first you take a gr-r-r-reat big zipper...
2. The fisherman's love song: "I Only Have Flies for You."

foal
One Kentucky horse breeder invariably has his young colts bottle-fed after they're three days old. He has learned that a foal and his mummy are soon parted.

focus
Trick photography is a lot of focus-pocus.

fodder
1. Farmers store hay in their barns so that when winter comes, they'll be fodder ahead.
2. Uncle Oscar once had a psychotic cow. Everything Oscar told her went in one ear and out the udder. Apparently she had a fodder complex.

fetal
Going to bed with some people can lead to a fetal error.

foible
While we all have our foibles, Aesop became famous for his.

foil
When the fencing team tried to wrap up the tournament, they kept getting foiled.

foist
A good buck-passer gets there foist.

fold
Breathes there a chef with sole so dead
Who never to himself hath said,
This must have been the last to land!
Whose heart hath ne'er within him burn'd
As in the grease it slowly turn'd
While all the while not smelling grand.
If such there breathe, go, mark him well;
For him no diners' raptures swell;
High though his soufflés, sweet his clams,
Moist all his cakes and tender hams,
Despite his good things, fresh off shelf,
The wretch, caught eating sole himself,
Living, shall forfeit keeping down

And, doubl'd trying, look a clown
to those who saw him steal a bite
Then, like an Arab, fold that night.

folder
Children should always show respect folder people.

folk
The English are so broadminded that on November 5 they even have a Gay Folks Day.

font
Type that was formerly lost.

football
A. A hernia (advanced).
B. A dance—usually in aid of the Fraternal Federation of Fallen Feet (4F).

footlights
"So you want to marry my daughter," said the millionaire.
"And what do you do for a living, may I ask?"
"I, sir, am an actor."
"What!" exclaimed the millionaire. "Get out before my footlights!"

fore
1. How can it be proved that a horse has six legs? He has fore legs in front and two behind.
2. *Playboy* magazine headline on a golf article: "News from the Fore Front."

forebear
"Has he ever tried to tell you about his forebears?"
"Gracious! Don't tell me he is an animal trainer!"

foreplay
My niece Janet is so innocent she thinks you can't have foreplay without three other people.

forfeit
A dog always finds forfeit better than two.

forge
The ten-year-old son of the richest, most humorless codger in town was a first-rate cheat, but the teacher hesitated to break the news to the boy's father. Finally, she compromised with this note on his report card: "Judging by his recent written exams, I'd say your son is forging his way ahead."

fork
As the Britisher warned his son, "If you keep on forking around, you'll end up forking over!"

forklift
A famous elephant was the unquestioned leader of the forest. Being a benign dictator, he decided one day to teach his subjects agriculture. He imported machinery, including a forklift that doubled as a mechanical plow. The

animals proved hard to train. One leopard insisted on using an old hoe to work the potatoes and air them. "Why are you continuing to do it the old way?" asked the elephant. The leopard answered, "It's the only way I know to aerate the soil around the spuds."
"That's as old-fashioned as hell," said the elephant. "Now watch carefully." Whereupon he climbed up on the mechanical plow and, going down the rows, showed how easily and heavenly it could be with a machine doing the work. "Now do you get the idea?" he asked. "To air is human but to forklift, divine."

formaldehyde
Mr. Hyde.

fornicate
A procurer is a fornicaterer.

fortitude
Life after forty-one.

fortunate
There's a siren in Taiwan who has just inherited five million dollars. She is one Chinese fortunate cookie!

forward
The children's nurse was asked why she had left her last post. "I didn't like the setup," she said frankly. "The child was backward and the father was forward."

four
1. Wife-swapping: sexual fourplay.
2. "Daddy can be caddy. What else is a par four?"

fowl
1. Chicken farming is a fowl occupation—and every egg a fowl ball.
2. Asked why he preferred the more mature hens in the barnyard, the rooster explained, "There's no fowl like an old fowl!"
3. A stool pigeon is a fowl of the law.

fox
The Desert Fox: an Arabian prostitute.

foyer
The manager of the Fairmont Hotel in San Francisco discovered a group playing chess in the lobby. On learning that they were not registered guests, he ordered them out. During the ensuing ruckus a lady asked the bell captain what was going on. "Oh, it's nothing, ma'am," he replied. "It's just the manager pulling his chess nuts out of the foyer."

fragrant
The pet-show judges have the right to order off any dog that commits a fragrant error.

franchise
Italian girls are pretty but they do not have the franchise.

frank
"I'll have four hot dogs," said Tom Swift frankly.

frau
It's a soft life for the German who can live by the sweat of his frau.

fray
A good seamstress is like a good poet: She knows how to turn a frays.

free
The visitor to an integrated American kindergarten was giving a speech to a class. "...And, above all," he concluded, "remember that we are all American and because we are all Americans we are all free!" A little black boy at the back of the room put up his hand. "Excuse me, sir," he lisped politely. "I am not free." "Oh?" asked the visitor, taken aback. "Why not?" "Please, sir, I'm four."

freebooter
An amateur soccer player.

freedom
The plantation owners were appalled when President Lincoln decided to freedom slaves.

frenzy
What frenzy had were nut crazy about him.

Freud
1. Sex is not for him that is a Freud.
2. Freudian slip: Garment designed to be worn under a see-through blouse.
3. A psychiatrist is a Freud egg.

friar
"Tough luck!" cracked the egg in the monastery.
"Out of the frying pan into the friar."

Friday
Robinson Crusoe originated the four-day week; he had all his work done by Friday.

frieze
The Greeks invented the deep frieze.

frog
The British rain song: A Froggy Day in London Town.

frond
"Tell me, beloved," asked Lady Chatterly. "What excuse should I use to get out to see you tonight?"
"Oh," said the gardener, "just tell your husband you're visiting a sick frond."

frontage
There was a young lady of Wantage
Of whom the Town Clerk took advantage.

Said the County Surveyor,
"Of course you must pay her;
"You've altered the line of her frontage."

frowzy
Even a linguist should never refer to a German housewife as frowzy.

frozen
The Eskimos are God's frozen people.

fruit
When U.S. Congresswoman Bella Abzug was sponsoring a bill to protect the rights of homosexuals, she told a news conference that the bill was needed "to guarantee that all individuals, regardless of differences, are entitled to share...in the fruits of our society."

fry
1. Sunbathing sometimes becomes a fry in the ointment.
2. Sign on a fish and chips shop: "We Fry Harder."

fuchsia
A Philadelphia shirtmaker offered rewards to people who could dream up new names for "dark blue," "light brown" and other stock colors. The names he received included forever amber, sick bay, hash brown, unpredictable fuchsia, statutory grape, dorian gray, gang green and hi-yo silver.

fuel
In days of oil shortage, many homeowners revert to using coal, recognizing that there's no fuel like an old fuel.

Fu-Manchu
Sax Rohmer once threatened to write a sequal to his series of novels on this villain and call it, "Many Men Smoke but Fu-Manchu."

fun
There is a place for humorists in the business world: Many a struggling company could use a good fun raiser.

fund
Giving until it hurts is said to be the fund thing to do.

fundamental
I fell off my horse yesterday, and now I have to eat fundamental.

fur
You can get fur from a skunk—if you're lucky.

fury
Lynching is trial by fury.

futility
An impotent exhibitionist is a public futility.

*Tequila is the **gulp** of Mexico.*

G
1. Abbreviation for "gravity," as in "G-force," i.e., the cavalry, who were only sent into battle when the gravity of the situation demanded it.
2. The G-string, worn by strippers, is said to have derived its name from the exclamations of the audience.

Gael
There was a Gael in Shakespeare's *Tempest*.

gal
A magician and his wife, whom he used to saw in half as the climax of his act, have retired after years on the vaudeville circuit and opened a chain of dairies. You may have seen the signs in their windows: "Milk sold here by the half gal."

Galahad
American colloquialism for "My former sweetheart."

galleon
Even before cars were invented, Spaniards were able to go for thousands of miles on a galleon.

gambit
Bitten in the leg.

gambol
Every time you cross the street it is a gambol.

game
A Princeton fellow appeared in the middle of a tennis tourney and asked casually, "Whose game?" A shy young thing looked up approvingly and murmured, "I am."

gargoyle
The reason that the British Houses of Parliament have gargoyles is that so many speakers there end up with sore throats.

gas
"Which car will get the best mileage? Your gas is as good as mine!"

gasoline
If the Arabs are getting fatter, why is their gasoline?

gastric
Political maneuver.

gastronomical
Even if you cook with oil, the costs are apt to be gastronomical.

gate
Every detective knows you can spot a fence by his gate.

gauche
Mrs. Whitney Whitney III swept out of the Plaza and was almost upended by a tipsy pedestrian. The man started to apologize, but she froze him with a stare and muttered, "How gauche!" "Just fine, lady," answered the pedestrian, adding solicitously, "how gauche it with you?"

gaucho
The signatures of uneducated cowboys in South America are known as gaucho marks.

gem
These are many kinds of gems. Perhaps the most popular are raspberry and strawberry.

genealogy
I dream of genealogy with the light brown hair.

general
"You realize," said the young army officer tactfully to the young woman he had brought into camp, "we have hired you for just one thing. But first, I'd like you to meet our General."
"To hell with that!" she responded vigorously. "Let's move from the General to the particular."

genital
Seduction is the art of genital persuasion.

Genoa
Columbus sailed with his queen's written authority; it was the Genoan article.

gentile
1. Schopenhauer hypothesized that the will of man is located in the gentiles.
2. "Father Flyn was mugged last night on the way home from our ecumenical meeting."

"I was afraid that would happen. I heard Rabbi Berger warn him: 'Do not go, gentile, into that good night'."

geranium
The old prospector for gold was mystified by new men looking for minerals that were unknown in his time. "First thing I knew," he complained to a reporter, "was when a feller showed up with a contraption he called a Goober counter and went all over the old diggings with it, saying he was looking for geraniums!"

gerrymandering
From gerry (or jerry) pot and (O.E.) *mandering,* handling. Thus, the practice of flushing out unwanted voters by pottering around with constituency limits. Erroneously attributed to Governor Gerry of Massachusetts, inventor of SKPB (The Simulated Knothole for Polling Booths) and SDB (The Self-Duplicating Ballot).
Author's Note: Both of these inventions are now obsolete in many areas, having been replaced by his later contribution, the CREVM (Conditioned Reflex Electric Voting Machine), a shocking success. As evidence of its importance, it will be recalled that the first time a voting machine was used (in Tenafly, N.J.), it elected three lemons. (The machine was later returned to Nevada.)

ghost
1. They're showing so many old films on TV these nights that you get the feeling you're watching a ghost-to-ghost network.
2. Henrik Ibsen was a Ghosts writer; many were a-ghost at his success.

ghoul
1. There's no ghoul like an old ghoul.
2. Especially one who's been raised on ghoulash.

gibbon
1. The history of the decline and fall of the Roman Empire was gibbon to bury many students.
2. Old African love song: "He Promised to Buy Me a Bunch of Blue Gibbons."

gild
Lady Macbeth: *"If he do bleed, I'll gild the faces of the grooms withal; For it must seem their guilt."*

gilt
Midas the King had a gilt complex.

gin
1. Eli Whitney invented the cotton gin, but at first it didn't sell because nobody wanted a fluffy martini.
2. Even though it was offered at bargain prices.
3. One priest to another, across the card table: "Forgive me, father, for I have ginned."

girth
Yorkshire Post: "The report said the drugs might cause girth defects if administered to pregnant women."

glacier
Man who puts glass in windows.

gladiator
What the cannibal said after he had his mother-in-law for dinner.

glance
Wife to husband staring at another woman at the party:
"May I have the next glance, please?"

gland
1. One warm spring morning, a rich old coot from Kootenay escaped from the hospital, jetted over to Tangier, and bought himself a harem. He'd gotten delusions of glandeur!
2. An orgasm is the gland finale.

glass
1. Container for beverages. Hence "glass widow" (for wife of advertising agency executive) and "glassed," as in, "Boy did I get glassed last night!"
2. Advertisement: Milk. Nature in a glass by itself.

glib
The suffragette movement has been succeeded by Women's Glib.

gloom
A day without puns is like a day without sunshine; there is gloom for improvement.

glove
The secretary of the Pilot Butte Homemakers' Club asked the members how many would be interested in a course in glove-making. They all looked a little embarrassed. Finally, one woman said she thought they all knew as much as they needed to know from watching people do it in the movies.

glow
During one of the early wartime blackouts in London, Prime Minister Winston Churchill was told that the only thing that prevented a 100-percent perfect result was one little lightning bug who had completely ignored instructions. Churchill had the offender brought before him and demanded, "Why didn't you observe the blackout regulations?" "Well, it's this way, Sir Winston," said the blushing bug. "When ya gotta glow, ya gotta glow."

glue
Song parody (about do-it-yourself wallpaper):
"Wrapsody in Glue."

gneiss
A laminated rock, so called because it isn't ugly.

gnome
Resident of Alaska.

gnu

1. *There once was a gnu in a zoo*
   Who tired of the same daily view.
   To seek a new sight
   He stole out one night,
   But where he went gnobody gnu!
2. Once upon a time, there lived in a forest two families of amiable, hard-working gnus, who often enjoyed picnicking together. Each family boasted one young mischief-maker, however—though each mother was convinced her own little gnu was innocent.
   "You should punish that rascally brat of yours," shrilled one mother, finally. "A sound spanking might do him some good."
   "Spank my son, indeed!" huffed the other. "Why don't you go paddle your own gnu?"
3. "What's a gnu?"
   "Nothing much. What'sa gnu with you?"

goat

Of many a shepherd it's been said
Whenever he's lonely, he'll goat to bed.

goatee

A small goat.

gob

As the South Pacific maiden said resignedly when the sailor told her his leave was up, "Well, if you gob to go, you gob to go!"

gobble

"Someday," daydreamed a young sophomore, "I'm going to buy a place in the country with lots of chickens, ducks, and seven turkeys." "Why exactly seven turkeys?" her roommate wanted to know. "Well," she explained, "so that I can call it 'The House of the Seven Gobbles.'"

goblet

1. A young male turkey.
2. A small sailor.

God

1. A whole family, caught in a small boat during a sudden storm off the shores of Florida, was towed to safety in Fort Lauderdale by the ever-alert U.S. Coast Guard. "I always knew God would take care of us," said the composed five-year-old daughter of the boat-owner after the family got home. "I like to hear you say that," beamed the mother. "Always remember that God is in His heaven watching over us." "Oh, I wasn't talking about THAT God," the five-year-old interrupted. "I was talking about the COAST God."
2. Brigham Young awoke one night to hear a great voice saying to him "Go west, Young! Man, go west!" And Brigham, being full of wonder, replied, "If you God, I go. You God, I go."

go-getter
In some offices, the only go-getter is the guy they send out for coffee.

goo
The critic brushed off a particularly sappy romance by a best-selling lady novelist with *"Chacun à son goo."*

goon
A politician is sometimes a goon with the wind.

gopher
Banking term. (A loan officer's location is known as a borrowing-row dent.) A loan that's a poor risk is known as a "gopher broke."

Gordian knot
The way the ancients tied their neckties. Now, so do Gordian I.

gorge
To honor its famous native son, the actor, British Columbia has named the valley "Chief Dan Gorge."

gorgeous
The reason some women grow fat is because they start out being gorgeous.

gorilla
Short title for song popular in the pre-TV or active period in the U.S.: "Gorilla My Dreams."

gourd
There never is heard a discouraging gourd
When the deer and the antelope play.

goy
When comedienne Fanny Brice had her nose bobbed, she referred to her new self as, "A thing of beauty and a goy forever."

grab
A shoplifter is a shopper with the gift of grab.

grade
The new male teacher at the girls' school has been fired—just for trying to make the grade.

graft
1. A columnist is a paragrafter.
2. The construction of the dirigible R100 was a private venture. The R101 was built by government people and became a sort of graft zeppelin.

grain
In North Dakota there once was a farmer who lived on theft. Every year he would raid his neighbors' wheat bins, sell what he took and then go south to spend the winter living on his ill-gotten grains.

grand
A gambler in a Munich casino came home richer by two thousand marks one night. Climbing into bed, he slipped the money under his pillow and remarked to his wife, "In the morning I'm going to buy you a mink coat." Unfortunately, being excited over his success, he got up again a little later, returned to the casino and lost all he had won.
In the morning, his wife awoke him early and said, "Let's go and get that mink coat!" Her husband slid his hand under the pillow and sighed. "Go back to sleep," he mumbled. "I don't feel two grand."

granite
Rocks that have been around for a long time are often taken for granite.

grass
1. Today there's many a young bride who started out cooking with grass.
2. A grass widow is the wife of a vegetarian.

grate
The trouble with society today is that, in winter, people are forsaking the great outdoors for the grate indoors.

grave
Mercutio: *"Ask for me tomorrow and you shall find me a grave man."*

gravity
Man is gradually overcoming the problem of gravity, which is encouraging in view of the gravity of his problem.

great
A British comedian, in the course of promoting his approaching show, once published these lines:
Dear public, you and I of late
Have dealt so much in fun,
I'll crack you now a monstrous, great
Quadruplicated pun!
Like a grate full of coals I'll glow,
A great full house to see:
And if I am not grateful, too,
A great fool I must be.

greed
He was free of discrimination: He hated everyone, regardless of race, choler or greed.

grief
Perhaps it would be more truthful for today's newscasters to begin: "Here is a grief news report."

grill
Mixed grill: an ecumenical inquisition.

grime .
If you steal some money, the first thing to do is launder it: Grime doesn't pay.

grind
1. The censor always has a grind to ax.
2. It was for that reason that the stripper spent all her daylight hours for three months studying English literature. Then she entered a TV quiz contest and won $64,000 for knowing that Bacon wrote Shakespeare—regularly. Which proves that you can make more grinding than bumping.

grip
A desk clerk at the Beverly Hilton called the house detective. "There's something odd going on with the guy in 807, Mr. Edwards. Would you check?" When the detective returned to the lobby, the clerk asked, "Well, did you find any of our towels in his suitcase?" "No," said Edwards, "but I found a chambermaid in his grip."

gripe
A raisin is a dried gripe.

grippe
Two bouts of flu, one on top of the other, can ruin a golfer: He soon finds there's nothing worse than an overlapping grippe.

groan
Professional mourners are usually groan women.

groin
If you want to meet a handsome stranger, toss your groin in the fountain.

groom
It is of some consolation to the horse owner that a new groom sweeps clean.

gross
Gross ignorance is 144 times worse than ordinary ignorance.

ground
1. "Waiter, this coffee tastes like mud!"
   "Strange, sir, it was fresh-ground this morning!"
2. Aunt Jane went on a chopped-meat diet. On Monday she served Uncle Oscar hamburger, on Tuesday meat loaf, on Wednesday tartar steak, and on Thursday meatballs. On Friday he collared her in the kitchen and didn't mince words as he demanded, "How now? Ground cow?"

groundhog
Land baron.

group
Hate organizations are sour groups.

grouper
It does a West Indian fisherman's heart good to see a grouper fish.

grouse
You can always tell a girl is game if she doesn't quail or grouse.

grow
1. If you persist in punning, you will grow you mind.
2. Holland bulb growers' motto: "We grow with pride."

groin
"I think it's time for a navel engagement. May I kiss you on the groin?"

gruesome
"Father didn't shave for a week and gruesome whiskers."

grunt
"There's one poor thing about taking dictation from my boss," sighed the secretary. "You have to take a lot for grunted."

guess
"Company's coming," she guessed.

guild
The labor-union movement has been built on guild by association.

guise
Other women say she dresses like a tart, but she suits the guise.

guitar
Go-go music: If you guitar go, you guitar go.

gulch
Birds who follow ocean vessels.

gull
1. Lighthouse keepers are never lonely; there are always lots of gulls and buoys around.
2. So there's often a gull in the conversation.

gulp
Tequila: The gulp of Mexico.

guru
1. One of those Indian philosophers known as gurus hops around a great deal more than his fellow contemplators. That's why he's known as the Kan Guru.
2. In New York, there is a guru who lives in a tree house. So far as is known, he is the only tree guru in Brooklyn.

gust
Hurricane report: Gust story.

gut
1. "My nephew Mike has landed a job that takes a lot of guts. He puts strings on guitars."
2. "He doesn't like repairing rackets. I don't know why. Perhaps it's just a gut reaction."

3. "Well, in any case, he's onto a gut thing."

gym
A girl who always had trouble with names unsettled her parents when she returned from her first day at school and announced that all the boys and girls had been taken to see a film in the john.

gyp
An auction is a gyp off the old block.

*A small actor
is a **hamlet**.*

hhhhhh

H

A pupil who has trouble wrestling with the alphabet is known as a late H heaver.

habit

"Tell me, Father, is it all right for a young priest like me to go out with a nun?"

"Yes, my son—as long as you don't get into the habit!"

habitué

There's a chap in Atlantic City who makes a pretty penny being a habitué. He stands by a scale on the boardwalk, chanting to passers-by, "Habitué 165, habitué 174,..."

hack

Many a cab driver develops a hacking cough.

had

The successful starlet: a good time who's been had by all.

hail

1. Where all those damn Yankees are going to end up.
2. When Queen Elizabeth I made a state visit to the City of London, the Lord Mayor greeted her with, "Hail to the Queen!" Her Majesty stared at him. "How dare you hail," she demanded, "when I am reigning?"
3. The problem with show-going in a New York City shower:
   "It isn't raining rain, you know,
   "It's hailing taxicabs..."
4. The weatherman is often a hail fellow.

hair
1. "Johnny's So Long at the Hair."
2. The bald facts: Hair today, gone tomorrow.
3. One millionaire used to refer to his hippie son as "the hair apparent."

hake
Newfoundland joined Canada when its people could no longer stand its British leaders' cry, "Let them eat hake!"

hale
Sometimes an ill wind brings hale weather.

halibut
A true sportsman is one who goes fishing just for the halibut.

Hallelujah
Capital of Hawaii.

halo
St. Peter's greeting as you approach the Gates: "Well, halo there!"

halve
Two women were pulling and hauling at the same dress on a bargain counter. Finally, one looked at the other and warned, "What I halve I hold!"

ham
1. As the actor in the traveling roadshow admitted, "I ham what I ham!"
2. Which probably explains why the stage manager used to assemble the cast by calling "All hams on deck!"

hamlet
1. A small actor.
2. English breakfast of eggs cooked with ham.

hand
Aunt Nora has taken up palmistry to see what's in hand.

Handel
Printed on the wall over a toilet in a San Francisco restaurant is the misspelled request "Please Wiggel Handel." Below it some music-lover scrawled "If I do, will it wiggel Bach?"

handicap
"When you golf, do you have a handicap?"
"Yes, in case it turns cold."

handsome
"Whenever I come home on payday, my wife says, 'Glad to see you, handsome!' "
"Handsome?"
"Yes, handsome over!"

hang
1. "Don't worry," the prosecutor assured his new assistant before the latter's first murder trial. "You'll get a hang out of it!"

2. Or, as Benjamin Franklin, who had the hang of things observed, "We must all hang together, or, assuredly, we shall all hang separately."

3. After all, a Christmas stocking is just a childish hang-up.

hanker
An Indian chief asked his squaw one day, "What do you yearn for, my wife, to give you relief from that persistent sniffle?" Answered the squaw, "Tis but a linen cloth for which I hanker, chief."

Hans
Consulting with his German counterpart, the Dutch customs official agreed that one immigrant in particular should be restrained. As the Dutchman suggested, "Let's hold Hans across the border."

hansom
Her boyfriend was a cab driver. He was tall and good-looking. But the thing that she admired most was his hansom carriage.

hard
Lucky the husband who discovers that home is where the hard is.

hardship
The Pilgrim Fathers had many hardships. The first to arrive was the *Mayflower.*

hare
1. Operating a rabbit ranch is a hare-raising experience.

2. Elephant Stew
Cut up one elephant into bite-size pieces (approx. time—two months). Cover in brown sauce and cook on kerosene stove at 476° for two weeks. Yield: should serve 3,000 people. If you find it isn't enough, two rabbits may be added. The only problem is that some people might object to finding a hare in their stew.

harmony
Cooked grits.

harp
1. She kept harping—which at least showed pluck.
2. *"Harp!" the herald angels sing,*
   "Gloria, get a new G-string!"

harpy
Two girls who dyed really lived, until they tried green hair and became the harpies bizarre.

hart
Anthony: *Here wast thou bay'd, brave heart; Here didst thou fall; and here thy hunters stand. Signed in thy spoil and crimsoned in thy lethe. O world, thou wast the forest to this hart; And this, indeed, O world, the heart of thee. How like a deer, stricken by many princes, Dost thou lie here!*

hartebeest
The President and Vice-President of the United States were on a safari when a herd of animals thundered past. One of the animals came between them and, for a moment, the Vice-President was only a hartebeest away from becoming President.

Harvard
1. The academicians of Boston have a highly developed sense of belief in their own integrity. As they say, "It's Harvard against yours!"
2. (Hence the motto of Dartmouth: "We Try Harvard.")

hash
An American dish, served primarily at smokers. From this comes the saying, "More hash, less speed."

hatchet
During the French Revolution, Count de Beauvais plotted to overthrow the people's tribunal. Captured and sentenced to face the ax, he sought to save his life by sending a message that said he would reveal the others in his group of plotters. But somehow the messenger was delayed and the executioner lopped off the Count's head. A decree of clemency arrived only minutes later, but, of course, it was of no avail. If there is a moral to this, it is that you should never hatchet your count before he chickens.

hath
She hath a way
Anne Hathaway
                              Shakespeare (?)

haul
1. Municipal graft: city haul.
2. In Boston, there is a museum devoted wholly to the works of famous burglars. It is known as the Haul of Fame.

haunch
Our butcher was arrested yesterday by the morality squad and accused of playing his haunches.

haven
Ad heading: "Chocolate—the Sweetest Haven This Side of Music."

hay fever
An affectionate term of greeting for a fever.

head
1. In Scotland, a caretaker at a castle doubles as the local barber in the evenings. The sign on his cottage thriftily covers both occupations: "Duncan McInnis—Head Gardener."
2. A Navajo electrical engineer lost his big-city job and wound up installing lights in lavatories back home, thus becoming the first Indian to wire a head for a reservation.

headlong
A forceps baby becomes a headlong youth.

heap
It doesn't take a smart girl long to learn how to separate a heap from the goats.

heard
A hearing-aid company received a testimonial from a cowboy who said his work was a lot easier now that he could follow the thundering heard.

hearing
1. The Swedish movie star managed to get some vinegar in his ear one morning. Now he suffers from pickled hearing.
2. And in Newfoundland, where politics is seen as a fishy business, a politician is known as "a hearing choker."

hearse
1. The undertaker in Upper Upsalquitch has ordered a new vehicle—in light blue, this time. He thought it was time to try a hearse of a different color.
2. He purchased it in his wife's name so that if his creditors try to seize it he can say, "That's not mine, it's hearse."

heart
When the young American soldier knocked on the door of the town's only brothel, one of the girls peeked out of the window and reported, "There's an army man out there with a Purple Heart on!"
"Never mind about the color," ordered the madam impatiently. "Let him in!"

hear
A landlord is someone who would rather sleep than heat.

hedge
Lady Chatterley loved her gardener, even though he was a little bit too rough around the hedges.

heel
Sign in window of shoe repair shop beside a medical center: "Physician, heel thyself!"

heifer
It was a lazy summer day in the pasture and the four young bulls were having a bull session.
"I," said the first, "shall go to Rome and became a papal bull."
"I," said the second, "shall get a job in a brokerage office and become a Wall Street bull."
"I," said the third, "am determined to become a bull in a china shop."
"Okay," said the fourth bull cheerfully. "But listen to this bull-etin: Go out into the world if you want to. But I love it right here in this pasture and I intend to stay here for heifer and heifer and heifer!"

heir
1. Shortly after the Chinese invented the razor, a mandarin used one to slit the throats of his three offspring—giving us the first recorded case of a razor being used for heir removal.
2. The only son of a millionaire was run over by a steamroller one morning. The obituary notice referred to him as a compressed heir.

helm
1. Noah tried to teach the donkeys on the Ark to steer, but all they did was helm and haw.
2. He finally cried, "To helm with you!"

hem
Rosalind: *These burrs are in my heart.*
Celia: *Hem them away.*
Rosalind: *I would try, if I could cry 'hem' and have him.*

hemoglobin
Colloquial Spanish (circa 1520). Attributed to Mrs. Ferdinand Magellan when she was asked, "Is your husband home?"

hence
The roosters do the crowing, but the hence lay the eggs.

herd
1. Communism is doing it the herd way.
2. "There's a little henpecking in every good marriage," says Aunt Jane. "You always herd the one you love."
3. At the local fair, a group of cows about to be auctioned off broke loose and wandered in among the musicians from the local band. They gained so much attention that when they were finally brought back to the field for auctioning they brought twice the expected price. Which certainly seems to prove that a herd in the band is worth two in the bush.
4. Perhaps you have already herd that.

her
The State of New York is unfair, according to the National Undertakers Trust Society (NUTS). A new law there requires that every funeral parlor have washroom facilities for both sexes. The problem is that currently some parlors do not have a "His," though every one of them has a "Hers."

heresy
"Is that a crack in my soup bowl or a heresy?"

herr
My German barber likes to be addressed formally, so I always greet him as "Herr Dresser."

herring
Kipper: the original herring aid.

hew
There's a divinity that shapes our ends rough. The rest is up to hew.

hey
Folk dancing is making hey while the moon shines.

hex
When the witch doctor began to sing and dance, the missionary asked the chief, "What the hex he up to?"

hide
1. The small boy wandered into the shoe-repair store and asked "What do you use to fix the shoes?"
"Hide," said the proprietor.
"Hide? Why should I hide?" the boy demanded.
"Hide! Hide! You know, the cow's outside!" the proprietor tried to explain.
"Aw, who's afraid of an old cow?" muttered the boy, wandering off.
2. Three Indian squaws were admitted to the reservation's maternity ward at the same time. The obstetrician, Chief Whackum, assigned one to a buffalo hide, the second to an elk hide, and the third to a hippopotamus hide. The squaws on the elk and buffalo hides each produced a six-pound son. But the squaw on the hippopotamus hide mothered healthy six-pound twins. All of which proves, of course, that the sons of the squaw on the hippopotamus equal the sons of the squaws on the other two hides.

high
Life was simpler in the Old West: a high-strung person then was simply a horse-thief who had been caught.

highway
The class comedian picked up a zero when he was asked to use "highway cop" in a sentence and supplied, "Highway cop wid a headache every Sunday morning."

him
The police broke up the Greenwich Village wedding because there were too many hims in the service.

Himalaya
"Yesterday was Father's birthday so Mother made Himalaya cake."

hindsight
Musical term (from students who are living Hindemuth), refers to dance forms such as can-can.

hip
When doing the rumba you must keep a stiff upper hip.

hippie
1. Q. What weighs 2,500 pounds and wears flowers in its hair?
   A. A hippiepotamus.
2. "Hippie Birthday to You!"

hippopotamus
Henry Morgan's Shakespeare: "O, what a rogue and hippopotami!"

hirsute
Yesterday he was her suitor. Today he is hirsuter.

hiss
1. It's not hard to keep a trained snake happy. All he needs is a pot to hiss in.
2. The size or shape is not important so long as he knows it's hiss.

historian
"That's historian he's stuck with it."

hives
Mary had a swarm of bees,
And they, to save their lives,
Went everywhere that Mary went,
Since Mary had the hives.

hoarse
Centaurs were half hoarse because they lived in damp caves.

hogmanay
It is an ancient Scottish custom that on the last day of the year children should go from door to door demanding gifts of cake. It probably began in the 17th century. Later, however, they weren't allowed to hogmanay.

holidays
Male expression caused by excessive exposure to beauty on the beach.

hollow
She looked right through me and didn't even say hollow.

holly
The purpose of New Year's Eve is to give parents some relief from the Christmas holly daze.

holocaust
"If you want this area excavated quickly, Senor Antonelli, we could blow it out for you."
"How much does a holocaust?"

holy
When United States Senator Muskie was about to enter a Cairo mosque, one of his aides demurred about following the Islamic custom of removing shoes. He explained that he had a hole in one of his socks. Muskie shrugged it off. "After all," he pointed out, "we're in a holy place."

homily
Many a girl brought up on the Bible has become a homily woman.

hominy
Homely. (Southern U.S. term. Thus, liberals there are known as "hominy grits.")

honey
Ashton and Haydock Reporter: A thief went to work in the changing room

at Burtonwood Rugby Club. Honey was taken from the pockets of five players.

hood
The Godfather, the book (and movie) about organized crime, shows that for the Mafia crime is a relative thing. The story is a real hood-done-it.

hooligan
A pentagon with six sides.

hootenanny
A cross between an owl and a goat.

hop
English brewer's epitaph:
Here lies poor Burton.
He was both hale and stout.
Death laid him on his bitter bier,
Now in another world he hops about.

Hopi
A lady tourist at an Indian reservation noticed a swarm of kids outside one tepee. "How many children have you?" she asked the father of the brood. "Sixteen," he replied proudly. "My, my!" reacted the lady tourist. "Don't you have endless squabbles and arguments?" "Not at all," grunted the Indian. "We're just one big Hopi family."

horrid
The instinctive impulses of the prostitute are horrid.

hors de combat
Camp followers.

horse
1. A horse divided against itself cannot stand.
2. The firemen played their horses on the smouldering debris.
3. *The cry of the huntsmen, "Tally-ho!"*
   Sometimes leaves them too horse to go.

horticulture
When asked to define this word, American author Dorothy Parker proclaimed, "You can lead a horticulture but you can't make her think."

hose
1. At the Owens-Corning plant in the eastern U.S., a family of tiny frogs lived happily in some long Pyrex tubes stored behind the factory. Unfortunately, they were asphyxiated when the tubes were packaged. This proves that peepers who live in glass hoses shouldn't trust Owens.
2. When a successful gangster invested in a racing horse, he made its jockeys carry a length of rubber tubing instead of a whip. The result was that his horse always won by a hose.
3. Mabel got so excited as she read a sexy novel that she had to take off her

stockings and put them on again inside-out: She simply had to turn the hose on herself.

hot

A new way to give permanent waves is known as hot couture.

hour

As two young women strolled along Market Street in San Francisco late one evening, they noticed two sailors following them.
"Aren't those sailors out after hours?" one asked.
"I sure hope so!" observed the other.

house

Domestic wrangling: house opera.

howdah

As they say in Africa, "You can't ride an elephant if you don't know howdah."

hue

The U.S. National Bureau of Standards reports that there are ten million different colors. Hue can take your choice.

hull

The boy stood on the burning deck
Whence all but he had fled.
It was a hull of a spot to be in.

humility

Condition related to (religious) climate. Thus, one would say of prostrate Moslems, "It's not the heat, it's the humility."

humor

To err is humor.

humus

The pun is the lowest form of humus—earthy wit that everyone digs.

hunk

The making of a great stew can begin with a ragout bone and a hunk of hare.

hurt

1. When two hypochondriacs get together they always have a hurt-to-hurt talk.
2. The Marquis de Sade was a switch hurter.
3. Traffic slogan: Children should been seen and not hurt.

Hyde

Dr. Jekyll was annoyed by people who kept getting under his Hyde.

hyena

Tasmania's tiger's
Fierce to see,

Especially
Hyena tree.

hymn
The old maid encountered the Salvation Army band on the Chelsea street corner. After listening for a while, she dropped ten shillings on the tambourine that was being passed. "God bless you, ma'am," said the lass collecting. "Which hymn would you like?" The old maid didn't hesitate. "Oh, thank you!" she cried. "I'll take hymn with the big drum!"

hypnosis
The use of pot heightens the sense of smell, producing some hypnosis.

hypotenuse
The bathroom upstairs is occupied.

hysterical
As the horror movie approached its terrifying conclusion, a young lady began to fidget in her seat. The man sitting behind her leaned forward and whispered sympathetically, "Excuse me. Are you feeling hysterical?" "Oh, no!" she whispered back. "He's feeling mine!"

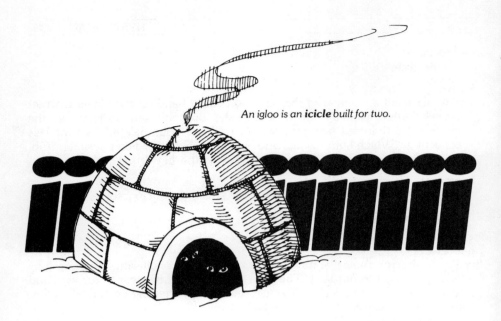

*An igloo is an **icicle** built for two.*

I

An egotist is a person who suffers from I strain.

ibid

Four spades; at least that's how ibidem for now.

ice

1. Pity the poor shepherd whose son never would obey! For instance, when his father told him explicitly not to lead the herd across their frozen pond, he was so anxious to get the chores over with that he grabbed the lead sheep roughly and tugged them across, thus succeeding in pulling the wool over his father's ice.

2. The Eskimo approach: "What's an ice girl like you doing in a place like this?"

3. *Hat stands,*
   Pub crawls,
   Sidewalks,
   Butterflies.
   Ice cream
   When I think of it!

ici

One of three types of U.S. resident of Japanese origin: Ici—those born in the U.S.; nisei—those born in Japan; and geesi—those who fly over for a visit and stay.

icicle

An igloo is an icicle built for two.

icing
"You come out of a cake at stag parties? What happens then?" "Icing for them."

icon
1. What pigs eat under oak trees.
2. When it comes to viewing religious artifacts, icon do without it.
3. "Excuse me. Is this the way to Lourdes?" "Yes. Icon down the road a piece."

idle
In his sunset years, the movie star became a movie idle.

idol
The young stonemason had just completed a monument to Baal. "Now what do I do?" he demanded of his boss. "Don't worry," the boss assured him. "The Devil makes work for idol hands."

igloo
Material used for keeping an ig from falling apart.

ignorant
"The old girl doesn't know anything; just ignorant."

iguana
"You want to see big lizard, lady? Iguana show you one."

ilk
The Holy Family is the ilk of human kindness.

ill
Giving suppositories is up ill work.

illegal
The difference between unlawful and illegal: The unlawful is outside the law. The illegal is outside the window.

illusion
1. The inept spiritualist sometimes makes unfortunate illusions.
2. The Russians have two kinds of planes; Snare and Illusion.

immerse
Conversion by Baptist standards requires that you go from bad to immerse.

imminent
Economist and writer Stephen Leacock was once introduced to an audience as "that well-known, imminent intellectual."

immolate
Two natives were about to be sacrificed to the gods for being tardy in returning to the tribe. One of them begged that the other be burned first. "After all," he argued, "immolate than I was!"

immortal
The priest and the nun crept into the crypt for immortal purposes.

impale
1. The thought of being fixed upon a sharp stake makes an impale.
2. A fence who also runs a bucket shop can end up impale.

impeccable
She wore so much lipstick that she was impeccable.

impolite
"He didn't even offer me a cigarette so why should I give the impolite?"

import
Opposite of outport.

impotent
1. When the queen's eunuch seized the throne it was a very impotent moment in history.
2. He became the first impotentate.

impregnable
"I'm afraid my poor wife can never have a child," sighed a frustrated husband. "Inconceivable!" commented a friend. "No, unbearable," said the husband. "Impregnable," amended the friend.

Inca
There was once a Peruvian prince who fished a maiden out of an enchanted lake and married her before the Inca was dry.

incest
1. To make an assertion or demand with emphasis and persistence. Also a term of concession as in "Well, if you incest!"
2. From a news item: There was something about that title, Old Incestors' Trading Corporation, that inspired confidence.

incinerator
A person who hints.

inclination
Said the Leaning Tower of Pisa to Big Ben: "If you've got the time, I've got the inclination!"

incongruous
Where U.S. laws are made.

incontinence
John Gunther, author of the enormously popular "Inside" books, once asked his publisher: "What am I going to do when I run out of continents?" The publisher promptly suggested, "Try incontinence."

inconvenience
Hotel washroom.

indigo

AN OFF-COLOR STORY

Miss Indigo Brown won a pot of gold on a vermilion-to-one chance which changed her life violetly pastel recognition. She joined the jet set, mingled with film scarlets and danced her umber with the cream of society. She finally met Sir Rhys Grey who, brushing aside her tintative resistance, said, "Let's get married, hue and dye." He taught her to lilac a politician and gave her her first khakis (for a Silver Cloud). Her flame spread. People called her a tartan worse. But one day she joined the congregation in the puce and realized how jaded she was. When the lesson was red, her cares blue away. She rose up, rust outside to the green and vowed to orange her life anew. Her buff had been called; it was all fawn nothing and she was black white where she'd begun. But would Sir Rhys let Indigo...?

infamy
"The only reason I can suggest as to why my former boyfriend is spreading such ugly rumors is that he has it infamy."

infatuate
"Perhaps your trichinosis was infatuate."

infernal
1. After the recital there was an infernal reception.
2. At it, the food played havoc with my infernal organs.

infidel
Needless to say, the Vatican is not inclined to believe infidel Castro.

influenza
He opened the window and influenza.

information
Appendicitis is caused by information in the appendix.

infra dig
If you have to shovel your own snow, you're infra dig.

ingest
He was so sure of his facts he said he'd eat his hat. Alas, many a true word is spoken ingest.

ingot
Motto of the Krupp steel barons: "Ingot We Trust."

inhale
He tried to make me smoke, but I said I'd see him inhale first.

inhibit
Blessed are the meek; for they shall inhibit the earth.

injudicious
How Hebrews use their spices.

inn
1. Brendan Behan achieved great fame as an inn fighter.
2. A motel is a love inn.

innuendo
1. American businessmen say of unsolicited orders that they "came in over

the transom." Rumors of possible orders come innuendo.
2. The Italian word for hemorrhoid medication.

inoculate
Artificial insemination: the inoculate conception.

insane
He lured her to the top of the Eiffel Tower and threw her in the river. As a result she was insane.

insect
There once was a despondent cockroach who committed insecticide.

insemination
Sex is more openly enjoyed inseminations than others.

insert
Many a bachelor feels the need to insert his masculinity.

inscrutable
The problem with falling in love with a mermaid is that she is inscrutable.

insight
The miserable medium finally gave up. "Tonight, I'm a failure. Everything seems to be coming insight out!"

insofar
Confronted by the slogan, "Modess—because," the advertising agency for Tampax struck back with, "Tampax—insofar."

insolvent
The other day a local dry cleaner fell into one of his vats and came out insolvent.

inspire
When you breathe, you inspire.
When you do not, you expire.

instrumental
The organist was instrumental in our marriage.

insufferable
Jane Ace: "Marge and I are insufferable friends."

insulate
"It's shocking to see you come insulate!"

insult
In case of illness, a doctor should aways be insulted.

intent
A camping honeymoon is apt to keep you two intent.

inter
There was a young man from Kilbryde
Who fell in an outhouse and died.

His heart-broken brother
Fell into another
And now they're interred side by side.

interdict
When former President Richard Nixon was involved in the Watergate scandal, it was observed that his opponents had managed to get interdict.

interfere
A busybody is a person with an interferiority complex.

interloper
A Texan whose home is on the range is suing for a divorce. He found his dear and an interloper playing.

intern
A young man in white passed a pretty girl in a hospital corridor. He cauterized and winked. She, intern, winked back.

internal
The ancient concept of the soul was based on the belief that hope springs internal.

interval
In music: The distance from one piano key to the next: an interval part of the composition.

intestate
It was ironic that after passing seven exams in Common Law he died intestate.

invade
Aggression is invading the issue.

inviolate
Poor old Vi!
It's been her fate
That no one's been
Inviolate.

invisible
An atheist is a man with no invisible means of support.

invoice
A Wall Street clerk recently had to be committed to a mental hospital: Every time he went to a tavern he kept hearing strange invoices.

Ionic
You Doric.
He Corinthian.
Ionic.

IRA
The pride of the Irish: "IRA rebel!"

Iran
"How did you catch that Persian plane?"
"Iran."

Iraq
In the Middle East there's trouble brewin':
Things are going from Iraq to ruin.

ire
The Church should have its mind on ire things....

irk
For the Devil makes irk for idle hands.

irregular
The inventor of laxatives was irregular fellow.

irritate
The desert could grow things if it got irritated.

isle
One thing about being a castaway; you're sure of a seat on the isle.

itch
Boy flea to girl flea: "How would you like to come up to my place and see my itchings?"

irrelevant
A scrap of dialogue from an old Marx Brothers movie illustrates how much the success of a pun can rely on fuzzy articulation:
"What has four legs and a trunk?"
"That's irrelevant!"
"That's-a right!"

Q. When is a door not a door? A. When it is a *jar*.

J

Chicago bars have their B-girls, so called because they always seem to be thirsty. In Paris restaurants you encounter the J-femmes.

jab

Boxing term, as in "Jab a good fight?"

jack

1. "Why do they call money jack?"
   "It lifts such a load off a fellow."
2. Famous American pornographer: Jack Meoff.

jackal

When jackass'd her to be his she
Gave jackal and jilted me.

jackass

1. See jackal.
2. Vulgar American expression, as in "Let's jackass and get out of here!"

jacket

1. His friend's suit was too big for Bill; jacket too much.
2. Besides, it had a funereal, hick jacket.

jade

Old Chinese prospectors never die; they simply jade away.

jag

When a cowboy heads out after a few days in town, often all he has to take with him are a jag, a bone and a hunk of hare.

jam
1. One strawberry to another: "If we hadn't been in the same bed last night, we wouldn't be in this jam now!"
2. Or, as the worker in the preserves factory said, "It's just one jam thing after another!"

Jamaica
The question his friends ask most often after a college boy's blind date.

jamboree
A woman who talks continuously in crowds.

jar
When is a door not a door? When it is a jar.

jargon
Sad report from moonshiner.

jasmine
Place where they dig modern music.

jay
An old man used to take home for supper any deceased birds that he found. Apparently, he had a jay dead appetite.

jeep
If you want a fancy vehicle, you musn't expect it to be jeep.

jelly
"Santa, why does your belly jiggle when you laugh?" "Ho-ho-ho! I guess because 'tis the season to be jelly. Ho-ho-ho!"

jejune
As you get older, it often seems jejune in January.

jenny
The cause of the Industrial Revolution was that the workers weren't having jenny fun.

jerk
As they ascended to the fiftieth floor, he smiled his sexiest smile at the pretty operator and murmured, "I'll bet all these stops and starts get you pretty worn out." "It isn't the stops and starts that get me," she snapped. "It's the jerks."

jest
The able court fool
Was a valuable tool
For easing the strain with a guest.
When things got up tight
He would say something bright
And the king would play it close to his jest.
2. (Writing these is simple: You jest put pun to paper.)

jet
 Bilingual graffito: Jet aim.

Jew
 So many comedians have been Jewish that this word has been worked over from almost every conceivable angle. Be that as it may, here's the story of the Baptist girl and the Jewish boy who fell in love in the hill country of Kentucky. When her father heard of their involvement, he said to her, "I want you to stay away from the pot licker!" "That's a terrible thing to call Hymie!" the girl protested. "Bah!" exclaimed her father. "What else can you call a Kentucky mountain Jew?"

jigsaw
 Oriental two-wheeled taxi.

jilt
 A Dutch lover became known as Don Quixote because he did all his jilting at windmills.

jinx
 He wasn't much of a golfer; he worked too hard on the jinx.

jitter
 During the last days of the British domination of India, the remaining English residents went through a great deal of gin and jitters.

jock
 Georgia athlete: a Cracker jock.

jocular
 Bennett Cerf was an incisive humorist; he always went for the jocular vein.

jog
 Container for liquids.

joke
 Good jokes never die; they only pass along. Example: The comedian's wife sued for divorce, claiming he tried to joke her to death.

Jose
 When young Jose, newly arrived in the U.S., made his first trip to Yankee Stadium, there were no tickets left for sale. Touched by his disappointment, a friendly ticket-seller found him a perch near the American flag. Later, Jose wrote home enthusiastically about his experience. "And the Americans, they are so friendly!" he concluded. "Before the game started, they all stood up and looked at me and sang 'Jose, can you see?'"

joust
 From The Ballad of the Fallen Knight: "It was joust one of those things."

jowl
 When the aspiring young boxer got too cheeky, the champion hit him a jowl blow.

Joyce, James
Famous Irish author ("Portrait of the Artist as a Jung Man," "You Lessees," etc.). When one of his later novels appeared, a reviewer commented: "Last night I chose to read a new book; it turned out to be an unfortunate Joyce."

Juan
At a golf club in New Mexico, a member returned unexpectedly to his suite to find his wife in the arms of the club's manager, Señor Juan. The outraged husband promptly pulled out a revolver and shot the intruder. The club's golf pro heard the shot and rushed into the room. Taking in the situation at a glance he clapped the husband on the back and enthused: "Bully for you, sir! At last someone around here has made a hole in Juan!"

Judaism
Religious belief in Judo, the philosophy of keeping people off-balance (a throwback).

judgment
The decision he handed down was so complex that no one knew what the judgment.

judicious
Ham is not one of the judicious.

judy
The American garment industry is dominated by judy-ism.

jug
One moonshiner finally invented a method for mass-producing his corn liquor—but he had a lot of trouble getting the jugs out.

juggernaut
Following the First World War, the Germans were so impoverished they didn't know whether they could afford another juggernaut.

juice
Population of Israel.

juicy
"When we went by that window, juicy what I saw?"

July
"On this august occasion, I may march."
"July!"

jumpy
The kangaroo finally gave in to the advice of his friends and went to see a psychiatrist. "What seems to be the trouble?" the mind-bender asked. "I don't know, doc," replied the kangaroo. "But lately, nothing I do seems to make me feel jumpy."

junction
If you come to an auction at a crossroads, you really should the junction.

jungle
 In Africa, Santa Claus arrives accompanies by jungle belles.

junior
 The month of June, wrote Ogden Nash, is the time when*"Ladies grow loony and gentlemen loonier;*
 This year's June is next year's Junior."

juniper
 1. A coniferous evergreen shrub. North American spelling of Guinevere, early English queen who married a beefeater from Gilbey Street by the House of Lords near The Tanquery (a local inn—see "tanked").
 2. "I took my girl friend out to see a tree farm today."
 "Was it fir?"
 "Only about ten miles."
 "I mean—cedar trees?"
 "Of course we cedar trees!"
 "Come on, tell me! Juniper?"
 "Once or twice—but I don't think she liked it!"

jut
 Some women have their breasts inflated with silicone so that they can join the jut set.

juvenile
 Spear used in track and field meets.

*"You shouldn't send a **knight** out on a dog like this!"*

K

For a long time, the U.S. Army has had a pack of trained dogs known as the K-9 Corps. The pack was originally used in the Second World War to herd European prisoners; they are German shepherds. These clever animals are all rated according to their cunning, with the best being known as K-G.

Kahluah

It was very embarrassing. Someone had stolen the detective's liqueurs—and he didn't have a Kahluah.

kalpa

A device for the measuring of cylindrical objects.

Kamasutra

Medical term: Sutra made of kama hair—preferred by gynecologists for areas exposed to humping. (There are eight kinds of kama, each of which provides eight types of sutra. Thus there is available sixty-four play.)

kamerad

German term for Kodak advertising.

kangaroo

There were two juice manufacturers in Australia, each of whom tried to keep one jump ahead of the other. Every time one of them would increase his package size, the other's kangaroo.

Kant, Immanuel

German philosopher, the father of Negativism, of whom it was once said, "If Immanuel Kant, the Aga Khan!"

kayak

You can't have your kayak and heat it.

keel
An ancient custom among pirates was to punish an offender by hauling him under the ship. The practice finally had to be abandoned because they were keeling too many people.

keen
1. Irish funeral song, or the singing thereof, e.g., "Do you keen John Peel?"
2. A wake is a keen party.

kerchief
Gesundheit!

Kew
1. Site in London of national botanical displays for which tourists line up.
2. Also scene of national billiard championships. Hence the term for protecting your shot: Kew Garden.

khaki
Parking a yellowish brown auto in the desert is fine—as long as when you come back you can find the khaki.

Khan
An American sailor on shore leave in Morocco was dazzled when a veiled beauty, doused with perfume and bedecked with diamonds, fell panting into his arms. A hundred yards behind her charged a howling six-foot savage, brandishing a naked sword. "Queek, queek," whispered the veiled lady, "which way to the Khan?"
"Lady," said the sailor solemnly, "I wish I knew. I've been trying to find it for an hour myself!"

kibbitz
Collective farm.

kick
The thrust of Oliver Cromwell and his supporters was to kicking out.

kid
As the girl goat said to the boy goat, "I don't mind going out with you. But please don't kid me!"

kidney
Anatomical: a young goat's elbow.

kilt
"The trouble with the bloody army," muttered the Scottish sergeant, "is that you're always getting kilt."

kin
Incest is having the kin you love to touch.

kindle
Jewish votive taper.

kindred
Fear of relatives.

kinetic
The appetite of relatives. Also the manner of dealing (etic = ethic) with in-laws.

kingdom
In the days of intermarriage among Europe's royal families, it was said that it was incest that made the kingdom.

kink
The permanent wave: kink for a day.

Kipling
Do you like Kipling?
I don't know; I've never kippled.

kipper
The male salmon would like his mate to stay around, but her urge to spawn is incurable: He just can't kipper.

kirsch
A profane beverage.

kit
A Customs inspector pointed to the cat a nurse was carrying and said, "You can't bring that into our country."
"Oh, but I have to!" protested the nurse. "That's my first aid kit."

kitchen
The chef is kitchen up.

kitchener
Person in charge of kitchen things. From famous British chef, originator of "Cook's Tours." During the First World War, the food shortage made famous the slogan, "Kitchener Needs Ewe!"

kith
1. Relative. Hence, "kithin' cousins."
2. Or, as A.F.G. Lewis has noted,
   Blood is thicker than water
   And kith is sweeter than wine.

kitty
If you have to drop out of the poker game, then more's the kitty.

knead
As they say in the massage parlors, "Everyone likes to feel a little kneaded."

knee
1. Joint between thigh and lower leg. Long an area of fascination for man, in fact, a very fascinating joint, once you get the hang of it. In early civilization, the knee was related to modesty. It is said that as a reminder that this was the area beyond which one should not go, the Pillars of Hercules had engraved upon them, "Knee Plus Ultra."
2. A priest tries to satisfy his kneed.

knell

Many a day ago, Gypsy Rose Lee was playing a sketch in a musical revue that called for the property man to ring a deep gong offstage at a certain point in the proceedings. One day the property man misplaced his gong. In desperation, he shook a little dinner bell he found on the shelf. The unexpected silvery tinkle caused Miss Lee to burst out laughing, and the punch line of the sketch was lost as a consequence. When she returned to the wings, she demanded that the property man be fired forthwith. The stage manager, who had been out having a beer while the act was in progress, asked the cause of her ire. Gypsy explained, "He ain't done right by our knell."

knickerbocker(s)

Loose breaches of etiquette. Hence "knickers"—people who borrow from (knick) strangers.

knight

1. Military follower, esp. one devoted to servicing a lady. Historically, probably best known was the Black Knight, famous for his criticism of a horse given to him by his lady (after she rejected him for catching a colt). "You shouldn't send a knight out on a dog like this!"
2. The Dark Ages were so called because they were run by knights.

knockwurst

"You certainly got the best of our deal!"
"Don't knockwurst!"

knot

1. A honeymoon starts with the morning after the knot before.
2. He wanted to enter the Sea Scouts but his efforts at rope tying came to knot.
3. *There was a young man named Gilotti*
   Who the love of a puppet oft sought. He
   Would dress it in lace
   And powder its face
   And then he'd do things that were knotty.

Knott

Epitaph in a Perthshire, England, churchyard:
Here lies John Knott:
His father was Knott before him,
He lived Knott, died Knott,
Yet underneath this stone doth lie
Knott christened, Knott begot
And here he lies and still is Knott.

know

1. The old English gentleman was working in his garden, assisted by his faithful Cockney servant. Two sailors who were passing by stopped to watch. "What kind of tree is that you are spraying?" one of them asked. "It's a pear tree," the gentleman replied stiffly.

The sailors winked at each other. "Looks more like a peach tree to me," the second sailor said. The servant was not accustomed to hearing his master contradicted. He shook his finger angrily at the sailors and cried, " 'E knows fruit, salts!"

2. The Russian's wife told him that it was snowing out, but he disagreed. "After all," he protested, "Rudolph the Red knows rain, dear!"

3. A gentleman who had been arguing until his patience was exhausted finally said to his opponent, "Sir, I do not wish you dead but I must admit I would be glad to see you know more!"

koala
Patients convalescing at Mercy Hospital in Melbourne are served a brew named for a local bear. It is a rather lumpy beverage. However, this is because the koala tea of Mercy is not strained.

Kodak
The Mohammedan equivalent of The Bible.

koodoo
Large white-striped, spinal-horned South African antelope. Topic of well-known African ballad: "Brother, Koodoo Spare a Dime."

kookaburro
The Australian laughing jackass. (Hence "kook.") Local pronunciation: "kickaburro"—from "kickaburro bird," a domesticated fowl trained by Australian farmers to ride outback on their burros and kick them along. Thus the kickaburro bird is the only one in Australia not to be down under.

Korea
Capital was her Seoul aim because she was a Korea girl.

kumquat
May and her mother lived in a bountiful California valley where they spent all their time preserving the luscious fruit. One day, deciding to try something new, they bought a load of kumquats and began the preparations for boiling and sugaring and all the rest. Finally, when the mother had everything all set, she called to her daughter to tell her that her part of the work could begin: "Kumquat, May, we're ready!"

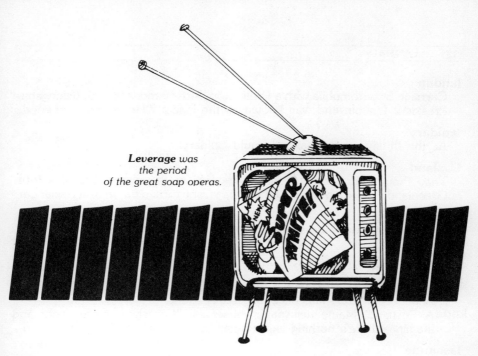

Leverage was
the period
of the great soap operas.

L

A famous writer once sent Christmas cards containing nothing but twenty-five letters of the alphabet. When some of his friends admitted that they had failed to understand his message, he pointed to the card and cried "Look! No L!"

label
French for "a good lay."

labrador
At the Westminster Dog Show in New York, a visitor from Canada asked, "Do you know the way to the labradors?"
"Yas'm," answered the attendant. "The gents' is in the basement; the ladies' down the hall on your right."

lacerate
Among famous women one should include the Marquis de Sade's girl friend, a lacerate highly.

lachrymose
"I've just written the saddest song that's ever been recorded," said Gordon Hotfoot proudly.
"What's it called?" asked Anne Scurry.
"Mighty Lachrymose," the famous singer replied.

lacquer
Your date won't go well with the Chinese classical dancer if you don't lacquer.

landau
Carriage or automobile with a folding top. Most famous in U.S. belonged to President Lincoln and was known as the landau "Hope and Glory."

lapidary
As the thirsty jeweler said, "I could lapidary!"

Lapland
They thought that the foreign-looking girl in the chorus line was from Greenland, but when she fell off the stage, she turned out to be a Laplander.

lapse
What we get when we sit down.

largesse
They said her face was her fortune, but what he liked most was her largesse.

lass
1. A beauty contest fast becomes a lass roundup.
2. A Portland, Maine newspaper observes: "For sheer tricks, fight and stamina, there's nothing like a small-mouth lass."

lassitude
Hybrid word: Scottish "lass" and French "*etude*"—the study of girls.

last
Of several meanings, best known is exemplified by the aria from *The Poor Shoemaker*, "Save the Last, Dance for Me."

lath
If choosing a carpenter to install laths, always pick a slow and careful man because he whose laths last, laths best.

Latin
They may be lousy lovers, but it's your fault for Latin them.

latitude
The best way to improve the world is to give people more latitude.

latrine
Properly, La Trine; The French Privy Council.

laudanum
The benumbing effects of excessive praise.

launch
Mental drifting, as in, "After ten weeks at sea, the captain was out to launch."

lava
The volcano song: "Lava Come Back to Me."

lay
1. September song: The lays dwindle down to a precious few.
2. An advocate of free love is known as a lay preacher.

lead
Early plumbing lead to many problems. One medieval poet wrote: "Somewhere in this common inn the lead sink's cuckoo."

leaf
When Eve tried to get out of the Garden without him, Adam called up to the Commanding Officer, "Eve is absent without leaf!"

leak
The control tower at a large airport warned a pilot that he had a hole in the bottom of his gas tank and told him to fly upside down to prevent all his fuel from spilling. "Hurry up!" the message warned. "Loop before your leak!"

lean
Mrs. Whitney Whitney Whitney III stalked into a butcher shop and glared down her narrow nose at the clerk. "I'll have two dozen chops," she said, "and see that you make them lean." "Yes, ma'am," said the clerk meekly. "To the left or the right?"

lease
A young lady from wealthy Lake Forest decided that she had had enough of her parents' soft life. She ran away to Europe to live on her own. Things didn't go too well and she finally ended up renting one of those little street-level rooms down by the docks in Amsterdam. There, at last, her American know-how came to her aid. She put a sign in the window that read: "Hello sailor! I'm Avis Herts. Love Me or Lease Me."

leash
"Why did the Doberman pinscher?"
"Because her leash had expired."

leave
Alimony is the high cost of leaving.

lecher
"You're really a dirty old man," said the chambermaid, weakening, "and I really shouldn't lecher."

led
The cowardly infantry officer was always reluctant to lead his men into battle, but when "Retreat" was sounded he experienced no difficulty in getting the led out.

Leda
Greek mythology has it that one day when Tyndarus was in the fields, Jupiter came up to him in the guise of a handsome swan and said, "Take me to your Leda."

ledge
A Hollywood stunt man who could perform any deed was called upon in one script to act as a kind of springboard. To help the white settlers escape the pursuing Indians, the script called for the daredevil to lie on a cliff's edge and

push out as far as he could so the settlers could use the extra distance provided to jump safely to the opposite cliff edge. The stunt man thought this particular deed so hazardous that he should be paid double time. But no matter how he tried, he could not convince the producer the stunt was worthy of extra pay. Morosely, as he went through with it and jutted from the cliff, he mourned to himself, "Here I am, a ledge-end on my own time."

ledger
1. Bookkeeping can end in disaster if you ledger self go.
2. Especially with a little ledger domain.

leech
In the early days of medicine, a doctor would never be caught with his leeches down.

leek
Peeling onions can give you a leeky eye.

legatee
French golfing expression, similar to British "l.b.w."

lei
Hawaiian—female of "beach boy."

lemming
Small Arctic rodent. In the absence of fresh fruit, the natives there drink lemming juice.

lemonade
Financial assistance with a bad car.

lentil
"Do you have any soup?"
"No, I'm sorry. It's lentil Easter."

leprechaun
Disease, common to Ireland, that makes your skin fall off.

lesbian
1. As Ruth said to Naomi, "Lesbian ardent pair."
2. "I guess I'd better admit it before you get any ideas," said the girl beside him at the bar. "I am a lesbian."
   "Oh? That's very interesting," the man on the make replied. "How are things in Beirut?"

lesion
The French Foreign Lesion fought against insufferable odds.

lessee
"Now lessee you skip the rent!"

lessor
The ambivalent businessman offered for hire a queer and a dyke and became, in technical terms, the lessor of two evils.

let
"I've never let a man I didn't like."

lettuce
"Shall we have a salad?"
"Yes, lettuce."

levee
The principal river in Israel has Levees on both sides.

lever
If a man asks a woman to help him with a crowbar, it's because he can't lever alone.

leverage
The period of the great soap operas.

lewd
The basic philosophy of the pornographer: The lewd giveth and the lewd taketh away.

liability
The measure of a politician.

libertine
An adolescent liberal.

libido
The French install them in their bathrooms.

lice
Discussing the Great Depression with his class, a teacher asked how many had heard of head lice. To his surprise most of the children raised their hands. He singled out one boy who got up and explained: "The head lice are on the front of the car."

lichen
He was so hungry he took a lichen for fungus.

lid
The dollar doesn't go as far as it used to, but if you're careful you can get by. To impress this message on his children, one American father took them to the spot on the Potomac River where, legend has it, George Washington threw a silver dollar across. The father took up a similar position and sent his hat spinning out over the water. It landed safely on the other side. "See?" said the father, wagging his finger. "A lid'll go a long way!"

lie
Here lies Bill, the son of Fred.
He lied alive; he now lies dead.

lien
In Shakespeare's "Much Ado About Loathing," it is said of Shylock, "Yon cashier hath a lien and a hungry look. Such mien is dangerous."

lieu

Sign in British hotel: Please Do Not Use the Bidet in Lieu.

lift

When young Papadopolis first came to call on his new girl friend, her mother took a look at him and whispered to her daughter, "Beware of Greeks wearing lifts!"

ligature

Pay attention. As in, "Ligature doing, nurse!"

lighter

There were three men in a boat with four cigarettes but no matches. What did they do? They threw out one cigarette and that made the boat a cigarette lighter.

lilac

In lilac time young lovers
In mutual admiration
Linger beside the lilac bush
And lilac all-tarnation.

limb

Mary had a little limb,
Its fleece as white as snow,
And everywhere that Mary went
Her limb was sure to show.

It followed that at school one day
She bent to get a rule
And made the boys all gasp and say,
"My, isn't Mary cruel!"

lime

Construction workers often find themselves with lime on their hands.

limelight

Commander Whitehead likes his gin and tonic but prefers the limelight.

linden

Asked why he was spraying the tree, the gardener replied, "I'm just washing my linden in public."

line

1. Up in the Rockies, where the only level spot is the railway, to get anywhere with a girl you have to lay it on the line.
2. Which is why poets should never drive trains; you never know when they're going to dash off their lines.
3. A girdle is a line tamer.

linen

As a guest said, it takes a heap of linen to make a house a home.

liner
"Where is the *Queen Elizabeth* now?"
"Oh, she's liner pier."

lingo
United Nations: An international lingo game.

lion
1. *To look like a lamb*
   March seems to be tryin',
   But you never can tell;
   It's probably lion.
2. A prominent broadcaster, on a big-game safari in Africa, was taken to a watering hole where the life of the jungle could be observed. As he looked down from his tree platform and described the scene into his tape recorder, he saw two gnus grazing peacefully. So preoccupied were they that they failed to observe the approach of a pride of lions led by two magnificent specimens, obviously the leaders. The lions charged, killed the gnus, and dragged them into the bushes where their feasting could not be seen. A little while later the two kings of the jungle emerged and the radioman recorded on his tape: "Well that's the end of the gnus and here, once again, are the head lions."
3. *If you want to try on*
   Rugs to rest,
   Fur is best;
   Especially to lion.

lip
You can always tell a dude in cow country because he shoots from the lip.

liquid
French for "chewing gum."

liquidate
Taking your girl friend out for a drink.

liquor
The young man fell back on candy and flowers when he found he couldn't liquor.

lisp
It wasn't that Mozart was jealous, it was just that he couldn't stand his friend's lisp.

litany
Sign in Montreal Catholic church: "Litany candles?"

literate
Mr. and Mrs. Bookworm often went hungry, but they always saw that their literate.

litigate
As a protest against his treatment at law school, the student litigate.

litmus
Drunken rodent.

litre
Tourist to waiter in Munich beer hall: "Take me to your litre."

litter
1. "Well, if she wants to have a big family, litter."
2. Riding on a dogcart leashed from Hertz, one terrier said to the other, "Heard from your beau lately?"
   "Yes, indeed," was the reply. "I had a litter from him Tuesday."
3. Pornographic novels: litterature.
4. To some, contraceptives are a litter pill.
5. But, as the sign on the trash can said, "Every litter bit helps!"

littoral
As A.F.G. Lewis has observed: "The phrase, 'George Bernard Shaw was born in Island,' is both a littoral mistake and a printer's Eire."

livelihood
Active gangster.

liver
1. Patent-medicine advertisement: "Life Not Worth Living? It May Be the Liver."
2. Name of novel about female surgeon: "Liver to Heaven."
3. A butcher in the Bronx got along well with every tenant in his building except a mysterious swami who occupied the attic. The butcher and the swami detested each other. One evening, however, the swami became very hungry. In desperation, he staggered downstairs to patronize his enemy's shop. "Give me a pound of liver," he commanded a clerk. The butcher beckoned the clerk to the rear of the store. "Here's our chance to put one over on that no-good!" he exulted. Pointing to his clerk's thumb, he warbled, "Weigh down upon the swami's liver!"

Liverpool
The British may not have a Blood Bank, but they do have a Liverpool.

lizard
Thomas Edison became known as "The Electrical Lizard."

llama
A South American version of the camel. It can be ridden by the tourist, but care should be taken not to a llama.

loaf
1. *It's some consolation*
   When a short vacation
   Is over and done,
   That half a loaf
   Is better than none.
2. You can't live by bread and loaf.
3. Shoe advertisement: "All the world loves a loafer."

loan
1. Out west, one finance company is known as "the Loan Arranger."
2. A hockshop is the loansomest place in town.
3. The novice banker paused in the midst of dictating his first letter to the pretty secretary assigned to him.
"Do you retire a loan?" he asked.
"Not if I can help it," she assured him.

lobster
Pitcher on a cricket team.

loch
Of all the lochs in Scotland, the most frequented is the Lock Upp, which is fed by the Tumbril (in Fairness).
Loch Upp is like a red, red nose
That's newly born and may,
Unless I can escape it soon,
Chase all my loch away.

locomotion
Usually a significant tapping of the forehead.

locomotive
When a citizen of Montreal was found lashed to the train tracks and somewhat the worse for the results, a reporter asked the police chief, "Do you think this was part of a foreign plot?" "No," said the chief. "I think there was a locomotive."

locust
1. A sotto voce imprecation.
2. The Japanese eat grasshoppers as a locust food.

lodger
"Mr. Perkins might be able to help you," she said as she took down a dusty lodger from the shelf.

logarithm
Catholic birth-control record.

Lohengrin
An opera about a happy cow.

loin
1. *A little loining is a dangerous thing,*
   But a good fall makes a bed spring.
2. The butcher, on having his attention drawn by the baker to a bunch of tarts, referred to them as a pride of loins.

Londonderry Air, The
A vulgar song about Londoners feeling a little behind.

lone
Don't worry about sharks who travel in pairs; watch out for the lone shark.

lonesome
The price of bachelorhood is the lonesome.

long
The man sat in the gallery,
His feet were in the orchestry.

—Longfellow.

longshoreman
"When it comes to making love," she said, "I would sooner have a short sailor then a longshoreman."

loom
Fruit of the Loom—American brand name. It is said that when the advertising agency suggested the name, the manufacturer wrote the head of the agency a congratulatory letter which began, "Blessed art thou, Harry, and blessed is thy 'Fruit of the Loom'."

loon
North American bird given to uttering a haunting cry when through feeding at night, i.e., when it's a full loon.

loot
While in Heaven the angels play on harps, here below we play with our loot.

lop
The foreman on a banana plantation is known as "the lop banana."

loquacious
She bumped into me and I told her to loquacious going.

lore
1. It's easy to strike gold in the U.S. Library of Congress because it is the country's lore body.
2. *The Exorcist* is a book (and movie) about sorcery in which it quickly becomes apparent that possession is nine points of the lore.

lorry
Popular British name for truck. Credited to Van Waggon, a big wheel at Carte Blanche and author of the song, "Whose Lorry Now?"

lot
A Florida real-estate man was so in love with his business that he made lots.

love
1. A term used in evaluating fruits—as in, *The Love of Three Oranges,* an opera about homosexual relationships in Northern Ireland.
2. A complaint sometimes referred to as "Wimbledon's disease." Symptoms include impulsive tendency to jump.
When the tennis ball soared high above,
Nellie rose to receive it like a dove,
But the strain of her reach
Caused her panties to breach
And her partner to cry out, "That's love!"

low
If you're in the mood for cows, you have low tastes.

lumbar
Lawyer: Did you say the plaintiff was shot in the woods, Doctor?
Doctor: I did not. I said he was shot in the lumbar region.

lunch
Newspaper item: "Police today lunched a roundup of gangsters."

lung
Pity the poor colon bacillus who got lost and had to take the lung way home!

lust
1. *"Tis better to have love and lust*
   Than never to have love at all."
2. Advertisement: "Going Overseas? Emigration, Business or Lust Pleasure? Immediate Passages Available."

lute
The prisoners' idea of having an orchestra failed because they all wanted the lute.

lye
Flattery is like soft soap; 90 percent lye.

lynch
"Should he be lynched or run out of town?"
"Oh, I don't know. A lynch is as good as a mile!"

lynx
He was a wild cat, but he looked like one of the missing lynx.

lyre
All music has a message—and many a lyre has told the truth.

*If you can afford a power lawnmower,
the **mower** power to you!*

M
A kindly doctor assures every patient, "This injection won't hurt a bit." Unfortunately, that's just an M.D. promise.

Machiavelli
I know a tailor who will Machiavelli good pair of pants for $30.

mackerel
Moby Dick, the great white whale, attacked the fishing boat and tried to mackerel over.

mad
1. "We had to shoot our dog this morning."
"That's too bad! Was he mad?"
"Well, he wasn't exactly pleased!"
2. A dictator is a self-madman.

made
*A team playing baseball in Dallas
Called the umpire a shit out of malice.
    While that worthy had fits
    The team made eight hits
And a girl in the bleachers named Alice.*

mafia
Literally, "my beloved." Perhaps the greatest contribution to English from the Italian. No other word so well sums up the ardor of the immigrant or so well expresses the source of strength behind so many extant politicians.

Other Italian contributions, such as "cosa nostra" ("doing our thing"), pale by comparison. Example of colloquial usage: "This coffin was just mafia."

magnet
1. Andrew Carnegie attracted a lot of criticism when he became a steel magnet.
2. To some, it is what you find in a bad apple.

mahogany
The southern farmer called the state troopers and reported that during the night someone had broken into his pigpen. "And now," he complained, "I haven't got mahogany more!"

maid
When Robin Hood cried "Carry on!"
Someone else Maid Marion.

mail
1. For spreading news, the female of the species is more deadly than the mail.
2. King Arthur: "How much will you take for this armor, Lance?" Sir Lancelot: "Ten cents an ounce, Art. After all, that's first-class mail!"

maim
Margaret Ann was excited at the prospect of going out with a new date, but then he insisted on using public transportation, a streetcar maimed desire.

make
Baron von Frankenstein was a lonely man until he learned how to make friends.

malady
A traveler in Africa fell ill and summoned a witch doctor, who examined him carefully, then presented him with a leather thong. "Bite off an inch of this thong every day," he prescribed. "Chew it carefully and at the end of a week you'll be as good as new." When he returned a week later, however, he found the traveler sicker than ever. The witch doctor demanded, "How come?" The traveler answered weakly, "The thong is ended, but the malady lingers on."

male
1. Old Greek proverb: A miss is as good as a male.
2. Artificial insemination has become a male-order business.

malice
At the peak of the Watergate scandal in Washington, journalist James Reston predicted that a book would eventually be written about it—called "Malice in Blunderland."

malicious
When fighting flares up in Belfast, the malicious called out.

mallet
Humorist Max Shulman has defined croquet as "pure hostility on the lawn," but adds: "I myself play with mallets toward none."

mammary
Old men in burlesque houses are just wandering down mammary lane.

manchineel
A member of the reptile family. Believed to be the snake in the Garden of Eden and thus, in the Bible, the first reptile mentioned.

mandate
A male escort.

mandolin
High official in ancient China.

mane
1. "Is that long hair really yours or are you traveling under an assumed mane?"
2. Cutting hair is a barber's mane line.

mania
An enterprising young psychiatrist has this slogan atop his letterhead:
"REMEMBER THE MANIA!"

mannequin
Modeling is a crazy business. It can turn you into a mannequin a moment.

maneuver
Cavalry motto: The best maneuver is horse maneuver.

manor
When the Hollywood starlet married an 80-year-old tycoon who could barely navigate, but who owned a dozen sumptuous homes in various corners of the world, she explained demurely, "I love him for his charming manors."

manse
When Richard Spong was undergraduate editor of the Dartmouth College newspaper, he sent a freshman cub to cover a wedding some miles outside Hanover. The bride—a Vassar graduate—informed the young reporter loftily, "You may say that when we return from our honeymoon, we will reside at the old manse." The story the freshman handed in to Spong read, "After their honeymoon, the young couple will dwell at the home of the bride's father."

mare
Chief officer of a city. From Latin "mare"—a see, as in See of Rome, etc.

marijuana
American-Mexican word, antonym for polygamy, as in, "Love them all, but marijuana."

marmot
A rodent of the squirrel family, of whom the marmot to be proud.

marrow
Making scrimshaw is often a marrowing experience.

marry
The call girl's wish: Marry Christmas.

Mars
Enthusiastic youth to friend, "That star over there is Mars." Unsympathetic friend, "Is it? Then the other one, I suppose, is pa's?"

master
A swinging family that really rates
Is Mr. and Mrs. and Master Bates.

mastodon
Dinosaur eggs taste best with French mastodon.

match
Her light-of-love turned out to be a bad match.

mate
"Are you the mate?" said a man to the Irish cook on a ship. "No," said he. "But I'm the man that boils the mate."

maternity
When the principal asked the new English teacher how long she planned to teach, she replied, "From here to maternity."

Maugham, Somerset
The college student left his Coca-Cola and his copy of *Of Human Bondage* on the restaurant table. When he returned, the book was missing. "Having trouble?" the waitress asked. "I sure am! I've found my pop but I've lost my Maugham!"

maximum
A huge British mother.

May
1. *And what is so rare as a May in June?*
   Then, if ever, come perfect lays;
   Then heaving, cries, the mirth are all in tune
   And overtly the bull dyke plays.
2. She's the May Queen I hope to be May King.

mayor
A female horse. Hence the axiom, "A strong mayor leads to stable government."

me
An egotist is a person who is always me-deep in conversation.

meager
An early winter makes a meager beaver.

meat
Widowed early in her marriage, she carried on working her husband's cattle ranch and for many years toiled at the arduous chores that go with raising beef for market. As the years wore on, her three sons took on more and more of the work until she was able to retire, watch the young men labor and the money roll in. One thing troubled her. In all those years, she had never been able to think of a good name for the ranch. One day a neighbor suggested she call it "Focus." "Why Focus?" the widow asked. "It should be obvious," she was told. "That's where the sons raise meat."

Mecca
Arab war-cry: "Prepare to meet your Mecca!"

medication
The guru refused to let his dentist freeze his jaw because he wanted to transcend dental medication.

medium
A fortune-teller gazed into his crystal ball and burst into laughter. His young lady client rose and smacked his face. "Why did you do that?" asked the astounded clairvoyant. "My mother," she said firmly, "always told me to strike a happy medium!"

meet
She (belligerently): "Why weren't you waiting at the station with the car to meet me as usual?"
He (meekly): "My dear, you'll never lose weight if you don't have a *few* meetless days."

melancholy
A dog that won't eat anything but cantaloupes.

mellow
"East Lynne" is a mellow drama.

menagerie
The equator is a menagerie lion running around the earth.

mend
The cross-eyed seamstress thought she had him all sewn up until she found that she couldn't mend straight.

menopause
The secret of being a happy woman over forty is not to worry about the menopause but the men who don't.

menstrual
Famous poem on the joys of coitus interruptus: The Lay of the Last Menstrual.

merci
An American boy on holiday in Paris met a cute little thing who struck his fancy. Just before flying back to Boston, he gave her a very generous present. Later, the Boston boy shook his head weakly as he staggered into the plane. "I'll say one thing for French girls; the quality of 'merci' is not strained!"

mere
The Lady of the Lake was a mere woman.

meretricious
Here's wishing you a meretricious and a Happy New Year.

Merideth
English epitaph:
Here lies one blown out of breath,
Who lived a merry life and died a Merideth.

mescaline
A sloppy Irish girl.

messrs.
When it comes time to eat, Frenchmen are the real messrs.

metaphor
Her hair cascaded over her apple-smooth shoulders when I metaphor the first time.

meter
1. Poetesses are known in America as meter maids.
2. *Each time she sat down to complete her*
   Ode to the famous love cheater,
      The things that he said
      To get her to bed
   Seemed to jump off the pages to meter.
3. Free verse: the triumph of mind over meter.

metronome
A city dwarf.

mho
"I'll be there in half a mho," said the electrician.

mews
The homeless poet scanned the property columns for a mews cottage.

miaow
"I'm learning to steal. A cat burglar is teaching miaow."

miasma
Infectious or noxious emanation: "In New York City, miasma's worse."

mien
A drama coach is a mien man.

millenium
Like a centennial, only it has more legs.

millstone
A dictionary of puns is a millstone on the road to learning.

minaret
The Shah: "Hurry, Scheherazade!"
The Shah's wife: "All right, dear. I'll be there in a minaret."

mine
1. As in "mine eyes," i.e., Kosher salad dressing.
2. I knew she was a gold-digger, so I made her mine.

miner
The handsome movie hero was told by his studio head, "It's time you had a different kind of role. In your next picture, you play a miner." The hero announced firmly, "Nothing doing! The last one I played with cost me $50,000!"

Ming
"You should see what that spendthrift Judy bought yesterday!" reported a neighbor. "She bought a Ming vase, if you please." "Maybe," suggested a poorer friend bitterly, "she wants it to go with her ming coat."

minimum
A tiny British mother.

miniature
You'd make a good art thief: One miniature there, the next miniature not.

mink
Never accept a fur coat unless it's in mink condition.

mint
1. Quote from an arrested forger: "I wasn't much of a salesman, but I mint well."
2. He then added proudly, "It's quite a sport, being an expert with the bad mintin' racket."
3. His wife bought a carpet in mint condition; it had chocolate on it.

mirage
Arab-Israeli relations are a mirage of convenience.

misconception
Women take fertility drugs because of a misconception.

miss
1. Pimps are often accused of miss management.
2. Miss Fortune has three friends; Miss Take, Miss Lead, and Miss Hap. Miss Fit says, "Call me Miss Ster."

mission
After he had entered the priesthood, the virile young man found the mission impossible.

missive
I really should write better letters. It's a near missive I do.

mislay
The members of the oldest profession are not really lost women; they are just mislaid.

Missouri
President Truman rarely overlooked an opportunity to bring a few cronies home to Independence for a spot of his wife Bess's superb cooking. As he put it, "Missouri loves company."

mist
"Well," said the grounded pilot bitterly, "if the fog lifts, it won't be mist!"

mistletoe
Athletes get athlete's foot and astronauts get mistletoe.

mizzen
When the storm had blown over, the captain of a small schooner emerged from his cabin, took a quick survey, and bawled to a new hand, "Ahoy, mate, where's the mizzenmast?" The new hand answered cheerfully, "Lord knows, Cap'n! How long has it been mizzen?"

moan
Suburban resident: "It's grand to wake up in the morning and hear the leaves whispering outside your window."
City man: "It's all right to hear the leaves whispering, but I never could stand hearing the moan of the grass."

moat
When the feudal lord complained that he wanted a moat around his castle, just like everyone else, his wife suggested that he build *two* moats. "After all," she said, "it's a good investment. You'll be getting the moats for your money!"

mobile
Truckers have mobile than most.

molasses
1. Additional girls.
2. "Do you-all want some molasses, son?"
   "But Mammy, I ain't had *no* 'lasses yet!"

molecule
The first thing to learn about a molecule is how to keep it from falling out of your eye when you sneeze.

momentum
What to give a person on the occasion of their leaving.

monastery
Place in ancient times where monsters were kept.

Monet
Seeking to make a good impression, the clod told the heiress he wanted to marry her for her Monet.

money
Sign outside an amusement park: "Children under 14 must be accompanied by money and daddy."

mongoose
1. Likely to produce a more violent reaction than a girl-goose.
2. A Scottish gander.

monk
When hard times came to the monastery, the abbot decided to set up a fish and chips shop at the entrance. Brother James was put in charge of frying the fish, and Brother Luke was put in charge of the potatoes. The local citizens soon learned to ask for one man or the other when they wanted just fish or just chips. One night a newcomer to the area went in. He wanted just fish and said to the man behind the counter, "I say, are you the fish friar?" "No," said Brother Luke, "I'm the chip monk."

monkey
A fool and his monkey are soon parted.

monogamy
He took a mistress just to break the monogamy.

monsoon
Two old maids bought a sailboat in the hope they'd find a monsoon.

moo
One day, Uncle Oscar's cow got loose in the shed and drank up a supply of ink he kept there. For days after, she mooed indigo.

moonshine
Down in Kentucky, a character who identified himself simply as Joshua was hauled up in court for making corn liquor in the woods. "Joshua?" mused the judge, with the hint of a smile. "Are you the Joshua who caused the sun to stand still?" "No, suh," declared the defendant emphatically. "I'se the Joshua that made the moonshine."

moor
1. Two thieves of Casablanca fleeced the town's richest citizen. As they made off with their loot, one observed to the other, "We must do this moor often."
2. Try the new Wuthering Heights cocktail—it's for people who always want just one moor.

moose
1. Someday, you moose take a trip to a wild animal farm.
2. A Scottish mouse.

morass
What censors think the girls in movies are showing today.

mores
From popular Latin-American song, "That's a Mores!"

moron
What censors think the girls in movies should have.

morose
A pessimist is a person who looks at the world through morose-colored glasses.

morsel
What foods these morsels be!

mortar
When the British troops discovered them, the German soldiers were mortarfied!

mosaic
A law governing tile makers.

mosque
Mohammedan motto: "A rolling stone gathers no mosque."

moth
1. Musicians' motto: "A Rolling Stone gathers no moths."
2. There moth be a better pun than that!

mother
A term of distinction used in southern U.S., usually applied to persons or things especially meriting recognition such as "Mother Courage," "Mother England," "Mother Ofay" and some mother things.

mount
The sex lecture has been termed the sermon on the mount.

mounting
A parrot flew into a taxidermist's shop by mistake. He noted that it was a stuffy place and watched what was going on with mounting apprehension.

mourn
"Dawn came too soon," she mourned.

mourner
Same as "nooner."
Only sooner.

mousse
An American in Paris was disappointed when he ordered a mousse and it was served without horns.

moving
In Inverness, a Mr. MacIntosh asked his new parlormaid, "Are ye

fond of movin' pictures, Jeanie?" "Aye," said she readily. "Guid, lass," he nodded, "then maybe ye'll enjoy helping me get half a dozen doon out o' the attic."

mower
If you can afford a power lawnmower, then mower power to you!

Mrs.
Cupid's aim is pretty good, but he still makes a lot of Mrs.

Ms.
Heading on a *Wall Street Journal* article about women wanting executive positions: "Msery Loves Company."

muddle
A beautiful gull that poses in pitchers.

muff
A millionaire cunnilinguist became known as the Midas Muffler.

mulch
Books about raising roses are too mulch of a mulchness.

mumbo jumbo
An elephant that can talk.

munch
1. If we chews we can go out to munch.
2. However, if the food isn't good, please don't munch on it.

muscle
A penis is a guided muscle.

mushroom
A love nest.

mussel
It is a commonly held fallacy that you should eat oysters for mussel tone.

Mussulman
Mohammedan weight lifter.

must
Clean off your mold if you must.

mustard
When all the troops were mustard, the enemy turned yellow.

mutilate
"I could get more sleep if the cat wouldn't mutilate every morning."

mutt
"That's a mongrel," she muttered.

mutton
Lamb stew is much ado about mutton.

Muzak
   "If Muzak be the food of love, no wonder I'm impotent."

muzzle
   "If you'll keep quiet, muzzle take you to the movies."

myna
   Stealing a myna bird is strictly a myna offense.

myth
   Female moth.

*Lord Nelson was a great **nasal** hero.*

N
1. In math, an indefinite quantity (N-y number).
2. In minstrel shows, a comedian (the N-man).
3. In cooking, a dropped salad (N-dive).
4. In marriage, a mother-in-law (N-sufferable).

nab
The reason New York City has so many Irishmen on the police force is that the Irish have the gift of the nab.

nacelle
Nose of an aircraft. Hence, nacelle drops: aircraft engine oil.

nag
Having paid to have a competing racehorse drugged, the handler was naturally concerned until he got a telephone call saying, "Don't worry, it's in the nag!"

nail
Motto of the RFD (Rural Fence Designers): The Nail Must Go Through.

naive
1. *Eve was nigh Adam;*
   Adam was naive.
2. Naive is near twilight.

name
There is little job opportunity in a zoo for a literary type unless you can persuade the management to hire a lion namer.

Nantucket
> There was an old man of Nantucket
> Who kept all his cash in a bucket;
> > But his daughter, named Nan,
> > Ran away with a man,
> And as for the bucket, Nantucket.
>
> > > > —*The Princeton Tiger*
> Pa followed the pair to Pawtucket
> (The man and the girl with the bucket),
> > And he said to the man,
> > "You are welcome to Nan,"
> But as for the bucket, Pawtucket.
>
> > > > —*The Chicago Tribune*
> Then the pair followed Pa to Manhasset,
> Where he still held the cash as an asset;
> > And Nan and the man
> > Stole the money and ran,
> And as for the bucket, Manhasset.
>
> > > > —*The New York Press*

nap
1. He bet his flannel shirt on a horse when he heard it was napped.
2. A sleeping-bag is a napsack.

nape
Medical text on neck ailments: "The Ached Nape."

narc
American colloquialism, as in, "A bust is an unexpected narc at the door."

nasal
Lord Nelson was a great nasal hero.

natty
Beau Brummell was a natty boy.

naturalize
The immigration official let her into the country because she had two naturalize.

nautical
When a TV quiz show is headed for the rocks, the crew sometimes takes to the rigging—which is very nautical of them.

naval
"You say he's a naval surgeon? My dear, they do specialize today, don't they?"

nave
There is no case on record of a church having excommunicated a nave.

navel
1. Ballroom dancing is sometimes termed a navel engagement.
2. The play *Spafford* was adapted from Peter De Vries' navel.

nay
The spring colt auctions are usually nay day celebrations.

neap
1. Tidal term: "As you grow, so shall ye neap."
2. Getting a boat launched at low tide is a neap trick.

neck
1. The skipper had taken his little daughter to bear him company. But she soon turned out to be the neck of the *Hesperus*.
2. "This will be over in necks to no time," said the executioner.

neckpiece
A flirt.

necromancy
Making love to the dead.

nectar
When the naiad brought the god his drink, he nectar.

nee
1. You can tell a well-bred horse by his nee.
2. Royalty is nee plus ultra.

need
The inventor of the doorbell was of great help to the knock need.

needle
1. To do a tapestry, you needle the wool you can get.
2. The doctor had to let his nurse go because she kept needling all his patients.

negligent
Male version of negligee.

neigh
1. When Man O'War ended his famous racing career and was put out to stud there wasn't a mare could say him neigh.
2. The chaplain of the Royal Household Cavalry is known as the Vicar of Neigh.

neither
Purgatory: The neither world.

Neitzsche
"You've made me feel so Jung, doctor! Now I'm not afraid to go out during Schopenhauers instead of staying in my little Nietzsche."

Nero
When learning the alphabet, it is important to remember that N is Nero.

nest
When out for poker with the boys, a man would do well not to play his cards too close to his nest.

net
In hockey, it's the net result that counts.

network
Many a broadcasting executive doesn't understand what makes the network.

new
When the Old Year has gone his way and the New Year has appeared, the proper salutation is, "I new year father."

newt
He was really a salamander but no one newt.

Nicholas
"But, Joe, I can't marry you. You're almost penniless." "That's nothing; the Czar of Russia was Nicholas."

Nick
Jolly old St. Nicholas is usually pretty tired after Christmas. But despite the whiskers, he's still not a beat Nick.

niece
Once upon a time there was a beautiful girl whose only living relative was her uncle, a famous sculptor. When her boyfriend went to him to ask for her hand in marriage he found the uncle at work on a statue. "What do you think of it?" asked the sculptor. "Well, sir," stammered the boy, "I like the head and arms, but the truth is, I love your niece!"

night
And God said, Let there be light: and there was night.

nighthawk
Smoker's cough.

nihilism
Egyptians pyramid their profits through nihilism.

ninny
Someone willing to look after children.

nipple
When it comes to drinking milk, a little nipple do.

nit
Destroying the egg of a louse is a nit loss.

nitrous
Type of chastity belt for evening wear.

nitwit
There once was a yarn about a girl named Pearl who was so darn woolly-headed, she didn't have anything to nitwit.

nix
Frustrations are nixed emotions.

no
1. The United Nations would be a great place if the Russians would just keep their noes out of it.
2. A Puritan is a man who noes what he likes.

noble
A farmer who only owns cows is a noble man.

nod
1. An auction is a place where you can get something for nodding.
2. Sleeping pills are nod addictive.

node
When conducting an experiment in tree grafting, it is important to keep nodes.

nomad
Why do gypsies never become insane? Because they lead nomad lives.

Nome
Be it ever so humble, there's no place like Nome.

nonce
A historian's mind is filled with nonce sense.

none
The height of insignificance; being none in a million.

nonentity
Egotism is a case of mistaken nonentity.

noodle
1. "Here, taste this. I've just invented noodle pickles!" "Hm. Tastes like *old* dill pickles to me!"
2. Walter Winchell article: "Things About a Restaurant I Never Noodle Now."

nook
Colloquially, a pimp can be defined as a nookie bookie, and a student of the act, as a nookworm.

noose
The king's jester punned incessantly until the king, in desperation, condemned the jester to be hanged. However, when the executioners had taken the jester to the gallows, the king, thinking that after all a good jester was not easy to find, relented and sent a messenger posthaste with a royal pardon. Arriving at the gallows as the jester stood with the rope already about his neck, the messenger read the king's decree: The jester would be pardoned, if he would promise never to make another pun. The jester could not resist temptation, however. He cackled out, "No noose is good news." And they hanged him.

Norse
Eric the Red was a Norse of a different color.

nose
1. A gossip is a person with a who nose.
2. Hebrews don't like pigs because some of them have tricky noses.

nostrum
An early book of cures was written by Nostrum Damus.

not
The trouble with being inhibited is that you're so tied up in nots.

notarize
If there was anything about her makeup you could authenticate, it was notarize.

nothing
Ophelia: *I think nothing, my lord.*
Hamlet: *That's a fair thought to lie between maids' legs.*
Ophelia: *What is, my lord?*
Hamlet: *Nothing.*

notion
Playboy magazine is a sort of literary love notion.

notwithstanding
Elvira went out on a date
All pressed and neat and sedate.
She came back in a mess
With stains on her dress
And explained as she paused on the landing,
"It's a lot of fun
"If it's done on the run,
"But it's easier to take notwithstanding."

nought
Love is all a bit noughty.

novelty
An army beverage made out of weekend leaves.

noxious
A bumpy airplane ride can make you feel noxious.

nth
The highest degree, awarded to students of nthologies.

nu
"What's nu?"—Start of a Greek letter.

nubile
A nubile maiden is better than one with old bile.

nuclear
Nuclear physics is better than the old, clouded kind.

nude
1. Novel by P.G. Wodehouse: *No Nudes Is Good Nudes.*
2. Or, as a later writer assured us: "It's a brave nude world."

nudge
The Christian's just desserts include nudge Sundays.

nugatory
Place where nugat is made.

nuisance
"I haven't had anything nuisance I got married."

numb
Before Sonja Henie became a world-famous skater, she practiced on outdoor rinks in Norway and was really a numb blonde.

number
A successful surgeon told a group of anaesthetists that he had a dowager coming up for an operation. "I need someone to administer the anaesthetic, even though she doesn't really need it. Who'd like to win a fat fee? Any number can play."

nun
1. Half a Mother Superior is better than nun.
2. Anyway, chasing girls in a convent is a nun sequitur.

nurse
The patient suffered a relapse as he was going from bed to nurse.

nurture
Breast feeding is living off mother nurture.

nut
1. Cashews are nut what they're cracked up to be.
2. *An octogenerian Jew*
   To his wife remained steadfastly true.
       This was not from compunction
       But due to dysfunction
   Of his spermatic glands—nuts to you.

nutmeg
"Do you like a novel to be spicy?"
"It does nutmeg much difference."

nyet
Communism can be measured by the *nyet* effect.

nymph
1. An imp with a hare lip.
2. Love is a disease of the nymph glands.

*Pity the defenseless skunk
whose spray pump is out of **odor**.*

O

Oscar Brown, a stout British don known to all as "O.B.," once had these lines addressed to him by a student:
*O.B., oh be obedient
To Nature's stern decrees
Or, though you be but one O.B.,
You may be too obese.*

oaf

When told that her new husband was a bigamist, the former old maid sighed resignedly and said, "Well, I suppose that half an oaf is better than none!"

oak

As the lumberjack said when he accidentally felled a tree on his pal, "By gar, it looks like this time the oak's on you!"

oar

1. A novelty act in the Ringling Brothers Circus involved a specialty by an authentic whirling dervish. One day when the circus was playing Madison Square Garden in New York, an enterprising young lady picked up the dervish and took him for a row on the lake in Central Park. Being a nervish dervish he couldn't sit still. Suddenly the boat tilted, and the frightened lady cried, "I'm afraid I've lost my oar, Derv."
2. Ordered to help row the lifeboat, the first-class passenger sniffed, "Do I have a choice?" "Certainly, sir," replied a sailor. "Either oar."

oboe

American tramp.

oblique
Salvador Dali painted oblique picture.

obscene
When Canada's Prime Minister, Pierre Trudeau, appeared to have mouthed an expletive in Parliament, it was said: "He prefers to be obscene and not heard!"

Occident
Perplexed Oriental father: "Our new son is very white!" His wife defensively: "Well, Occidents will happen!"

ocelot
In South America, there is a leopardlike cat that is doing very poorly, perhaps because it ocelot.

octopus
A person who can always see the brighter side.

oculist
A fish with legs.

odd
1. Many a private has avoided being sent into battle by pretending to be queer—which simply goes to prove that odd soldiers never die.
2. This is because a homosexual has the odds in his favor.
3. A Hialeah hen swallowed a tip sheet and began laying odds.

ode
1. *The poet is a pious person*
   Who frequently can turn his verse on
   To praise a lass or, in a pass,
   Uphold his code
   With what is ode.
2. When the poetic French perfume salesman fell in love with a chambermaid, he gave her an ode de toilette.

odor
Pity the defenseless skunk whose spray pump is out of odor.

offal
The Augean Stables presented Hercules with an offal problem.

offend
People who do not know shipboard terms sometimes assume that the poop deck is the offend.

offer
The pimp told his girl to get rid of her present client quickly because he had just found a better offer.

ohm
Unit of electrical resistance—known in British broadcasting as "the Ohm Service."

oil
1. "Shall I check under the hood?" asked the service station attendant, politely. "No thanks," said the car owner. "Oil be all right."
2. Working on a drilling rig means oily to bed and oily to rise.

olfactory
"Where is that awful smell coming from?" demanded the pollution inspector. "Is it from the new plant?" "No," sighed the company head. "It's the olfactory."

olive
If you order a martini with no olive or twist, you'll get the Dickens.

Omar
What Cleopatra really whispered to Mark Antony when he asked her if she was true to him was "Omar Khayyam!"

omelet
Charm worn around the neck—above the yolk of the dress.

Onan
"What's going on in there?" demanded Judah. "Oh," replied his daughter-in-law, Tamar, "he's at it again; Onan off."

onomatopoeia
The dog's reply when asked why he didn't need to go out.

ooze
Never contest the ownership of a swamp; it really doesn't matter ooze.

opal
I opal get a ring.

open
Keep open.

opportune
Any well-known operatic melody.

optimist
When Sam Goldwyn was at his height as a motion-picture producer (and charming everyone with his beautiful abuse of English), it is said that he rejected the script for a movie called *The Optimist* because he didn't think that a story about an eye doctor would sell.

orange
Orange juice going to have breakfast?

orderly
To qualify for work in a hospital, you must learn to carry a bedpan in an orderly fashion.

ore
The miner didn't know whether he had struck iron ore what.

orgy
Derived from title of American opera, Orgy and Buss.

oriel
Fish oriel; the staple diet of Newfoundland.

orifice
A gynecologist is a doctor who puts in a hard day at the orifice.

O'Rourke
Shortly after his book of oriental tales, "Lalla Rookh," had brought him European fame, Dublin's Thomas Moore was the dinner guest of Lady Holland, who told him candidly: "Mr. Moore, I have not read your Larry O'Rourke; I don't like Irish stories."

ortho
Medical term from Latin *ortho pro nobis*.

Oscar
"What is that?" asked the starlet, pointing to an item on the Academy Awards Dinner menu. "I don't know," admitted her escort, motioning for the waitress. "Veal Oscar."

otter
1. Expressing duty or rightness, as in, "Anthropomorphism otter be enjoyed."
2. Do unto otters as you would have them do unto you.

ought
Conscience is ought-to suggestion.

our
Committees count their time in minutes while wasting ours.

out
The new sheriff announced he was going to have it out on the main street at high noon, and the townsfolk fined him for indecent exposure.

outboard
Once upon a time, a man had a pet corn borer named Motor. One day his Motor was missing. The man rushed into the nearest cornfield and began stripping the cobs. Luckily, as he was stripping the seventh cob, outboard Motor.

outside
Sheffield Star: "And sometimes, bodice backs need to be of average size while the fronts must be made for outside bosoms."

outspoken
"I know I'm outspoken," she admitted. "I can't believe it," said her husband. "By whom?"

outtakes
Pornography to go.

outwit

A jealous young stockbroker asked his partner, "Who was that beautiful blonde I saw you outwit last night?"

oval

It has been suggested that our moon is not round, but ellipsoid. Let's face it squarely: That's oval! Especially since the moon has been round so long.

ovary

"Ovary nice, indeed!" exclaimed the egg.

overall

Mrs. Murphy's chowder needs an overall improvement. (See "overhaul" below.)

overbearing

The population explosion was caused by overbearing women.

overhaul

The Irish lady's elephant saddle needed repairing. They finally found the right man to throw the overhaul in Mrs. Murphy's howdah.

owl

Contrary to ancient belief, there is no fool like an owl fool.

ox

The farmer went to town to sell his cattle. Unfortunately he was lured into a crap game and returned home sans shirt and minus ox.

oxygen

1. The plural of ox.
2. In districts where police check the alcohol content of drivers' breaths, partygoers should always have a cup of Oxo before driving home. Then, if checked, they will be breathing Oxo-gin.

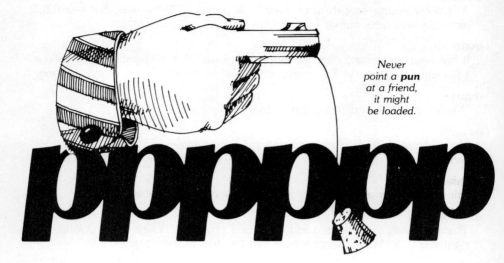

*Never point a **pun** at a friend, it might be loaded.*

P

His old wig and his new one are as alike as two P's.

pace
1. When Northern Dancer was in his prime as a racehorse, he encountered another racer one day who addressed him by name. Obviously puzzled, Northern Dancer confessed, "I can't remember your name, but your pace is familiar."
2. Male jogger to female jogger: "My pace or yours?"

pail
1. Don't be yellow. If you keep yourself in the pink, those Reds can't make you feel browned off, or blue, or even like kicking the bucket—i.e., a little pail.
2. *Jack fell down
And broke his crown,
While Jill turned pail
And ran.*

paint
Women paint what they used to be.

pair
1. After running a series of tests on the reaction of American males to various sizes of female busts, one of the psychologists sighed and asked, "How are you going to keep them down on the farm after they've seen Pair E?"
2. *Playboy* magazine has defined "falsies" as, "the enhancer to a maiden's pair."
3. The first marriage was fruitful; Eve liked her apple and Adam her pair.

pale
We assume that after their mishap, while up Jack got and home did trot, Jill was beyond the pale.

palomino
Italian for "friendly horse."

pan
1. All that some girls know about cooking is that a fresh egg should be slapped in the pan.
2. A critic is a man who pans for gold.

pane
When the glassblower inhaled, he got a pane in his stomach.

panhandle
All beauticians are panhandlers.

pant
A dog's tongue is the seat of his pants.

panther
"Look at the new animal trainer! His panther wet!"

papal
The voting structure of Rome is being revised so that the chief magistrate can become The Mayor of All the Papal.

par
There once was a kiddie named Carr
Caught a man on top of his mar,
*   As he watched him stick'er*
*   He said with a snicker,*
"You do it much faster than par."

paradox
You are dealing with a typical paradox when the specialist supports the original diagnosis.

parakeet
Ribald song title: "She Has the Biggest Parakeets in Town."

parallel
Tough break for the gymnast who fell off the parallel bars: He was parallelized.

parana
Let's get the orgy under way! Shall we undress Mabel first or parana?

paranoia
One mental-hospital patient to another, pointing to the two psychiatrists doing ward rounds: "Don't let that paranoia!"

paranoid
A couple in a car interrupted by a policeman.

paraphrase
Speeches would be more to the point if speakers would paraphrase here and there.

parasite
Resident of Paris.

pare
A boy begins to shave when he starts to think of paring off.

parfait
A gay golfer.

park
1. A wolf is a man whose park is worse than his bite.
2. Note on a mailed-in police ticket: "Parking is such sweet sorrow."

parlay
The average girl.

parr
He made his social entrée by ordering parr for the course.

parrot
1. The bird fancier's favorite song: "I Love Parrots in the Springtime."
2. The jungle commandment: "Honor thy parrots."

parse
Grammar books are parse for the course.

parsec
Golfer's disease, caused by frustration.

parsimony
Your father's estate.

parson
The Rev. Angus is so accustomed to getting discounts because of his profession that every time he places a long-distance call to another minister he says to the operator, "And remember, this is a parson-to-parson call."

parsonage
"At what age were you married?" asked she, inquisitively. But the other lady was equal to the emergency and quietly responded, "At the parsonage."

part
An official report on accidents in Canada reveals that twice as many men as women are killed each year. "This is unfortunate," it concludes, "because so many men are needed to open up the virgin parts of the country."

Parthenon
The Greeks may have invented the deep frieze—but they didn't think the idea worth Parthenon.

partisan
"You certainly got cheated on this loam, Comrade; the greater partisan."

partition
If you feel strongly about toilet graffiti, perhaps you should sign a partition.

pas de deux
Father of twins.

pass
Sign in an Acapulco hotel: "The Manager Has Personally Passed All the Water Served Here."

passable
Politics is the art of the passable.

passé
Father has spoken.

passion
Intrigued by his host's maid, the bachelor followed her about all evening. But each time that he went to make a pass he found that she was passion fruit.

past
She gave up the mail carrier for the grocery clerk because she was tired of waiting for the past man's ring.

pasta
An Italian restaurant can be judged by its pasta performance.

pastel
The figures he painted were distorted pastel recognition.

pasteurize
As the farmer said to his milkmaid, "Why won't you let me pasteurize?"

pasturage
A field of grass is like a person older than yourself.

patent
The rumor that an Irishman invented the microphone is purely a patent mike story.

patient
To be successful, a doctor must have a lot of patients.

patter
Sales resistance is the triumph of mind over patter.

paunch
The retired boxer refused a job as a masseur because he didn't like to pull paunches.

pauper
"You've got to help me, I'm a pauper."
"Congratulations! Boy or girl?"

paw
Radio announcers always have small hands; wee paws for station identification.

pawn
The Spartan mothers used to enjoin their sons: "Return with your shield—or pawn it."

pax vobiscum
What a waiter in Rome says when he spills peas in your lap.

pay
Notice to the person who has bills to pay: Please return it; Bill needs it.

pea
"No thanks, I've had all the vegetables I can eat," said Tom Swift peas-fully.

peace
1. As Cromwell cried, "Peace on you!"
2. This led to the development of Britain's fishing industry and the cod peace.

peach
"Just my luck!" sighed the sophomore, back from her blind date. "All he did was talk about how wonderful his mother is. Wouldn't you know? Of all the guys I could have gotten, I drew a son of a peach!"

peasant
This castle hath a peasant seat.

peak
Hydroelectric plants in high mountains produce off-peak electricity.

peal
Seeing three young ladies outside a burlesque house, the academic inquired of his friend, "Is that a tray of tarts?" "No," his friend replied, "I would call those belles a peal of strippers!"

peanut
Urologist.

pear
Unlikes attract in marriage; apples and oranges make fine pears.

peck
As the fat lady in the circus complained to her friend, "My appetite isn't what it used to be. Now I just peck my food; a peck of this and a peck of that." "I know," said her friend. "I thought that lately you've been looking a little pecked."

pedagogue
One who gets excited over feet.

pee
Writer-director Norman Corwin, permitting an actor to answer a call of

nature during a rehearsal: "I always want my actors to watch their pees and cues."

peek
Windows in the sides of swimming pools often provide a pike's peek.

peel
1. She was the apple of his eye until he started keeping it peeled.
2. "Do you think there's music in the stars?" "I don't know about that, but I know of the sun causing a belle to peel."
3. Sign outside a nudist camp: Come in Where the Peeling Is Mutual.

peephole
Slogan of the NAVY (National Association of Voyeur Yeomen): Power to the Peephole.

peer
A wistful woman in Wexford wrote to her favorite columnist: "For years I have loved a peer of the realm. I follow him wherever he goes, but he won't even give me the time of day. Should I continue to pursue him?" The columnist replied emphatically. "Obviously," he wrote, "you have missed the boat. Why go on hanging around the peer?"

Peking
A Chinese voyeur is known as a Peking Tom.

pelt
When we say, "It's raining cats and dogs," we mean it's pelting.

pen
When the warden was reproved for allowing prisoners to escape, he dismissed the incident as a slip of the pen.

penal
Penal colony: all-male nudist camp.

pencil
The prisoners would have been content to write home but the only pencil was on the window.

pendant
1. The proper form for Americans to use when importing medallions from Delhi is the declaration of Indian pendants.
2. A writer on the academic achievements of others is known as a pendant.

penial
Organ of society, as in "penial colony."

penitent
The erring priest wrote a letter of apology, but his bishop could not decipher his penitent.

peon
1. Britons never will be slaves, only Europe peons.

2. That's why they shouldn't peon each other.

peony
That flowery personality, Franklin P. Adams, once observed: "Take care of the peonies and the dahlias will take care of themselves."

period
A whole winter in the Antarctic was too long a sentence for him; it made the Admiral period.

permissive
The cost of mailing a letter is climbing so that it is immoral. Each year the Post Office gets more permissive.

Persian
One man's Mede is another man's Persian.

persistence
Failure is the path of least persistence.

pest
Unless teachers are better paid, they will begin to desert their pests.

peter
There was a young man from Glengozzle
Who found a remarkable fossil.
    He knew by the bend
    And the wart on the end
'Twas the peter of Paul the Apostle.

pheasant
O! What a rogue and pheasant slave am I!

phew
Last year the cheese-making priests of Quebec produced a million pounds of Oka. That's quite a phew!

philatelist
Person who lived in Biblical times.

philately
A twelve-year-old lad was a persistent and dedicated collector of postage stamps—until the kid next door bought an album, too, and began a collection of his own. "Jimmy buys every stamp I do," the twelve-year-old complained to his father. "He has taken all the fun out of it for me. I'm quitting." "Don't be a fool, my boy!" counseled the father. "Remember the old adage: Imitation is the sincerest form of philately."

Philip
Prince Philip of Great Britain bears a famous name. Who can forget the two worthy Scots mentioned in the old song, "Bonnie Dundee": "Come, Philip McCupp! Come, Philip McCann!"?

phlox
A British flower-lover has installed lights and cushions in his garden so he can watch his phlox by night while seated on the ground.

phonograph
A picture or likeness, so called because so many are phoney.

phrase
1. *Whenever I try to write a rhyme,*
   The same old words ensue.
   My teacher says to give it time;
   It's just a phrase
   I'm passing through.
2. Plagiarism: a phrase-lift.

Phyfe
As a rebuttal to the demands of American tourists, a British baker has perfected a new variety of doughnut. He calls it the "Phyfe." Soon, he hopes, every American visitor will be dunking Phyfes.

pianist
Vacationing in Ireland, an amorous American male trapped a leprechaun. In exchange for his freedom, the leprechaun agreed to grant one wish. Unfortunately, he was an old leprechaun and a little hard of hearing. The result was that the American spent the rest of his time in Ireland with a 12-inch pianist.

pica
Printer who never takes a customer to lunch.

pickerel
The briny old salt was in an awful pickerel.

picket
My mother was a labor organizer in a maternity ward. She always said, "Those scabs will go away if you don't picket them."

pickle
Irish whiskey is guaranteed to pickle your fancy.

pie
As evidence that engineers are not only ungrammatical but also do not belong in the kitchen, we submit their belief that pie are square.

piebald
What you can get from eating too many desserts.

piece
1. The artist was especially proud of his portrait of his mistress; she was his master piece.
2. The good ladies of Hadassah wanted to do something for peace, so they held a Fur Piece Fashion Show.
3. A conversation piece is a girl who likes to talk in bed.

piety
The reason they didn't serve pie at the Last Supper was because they had already had piety.

pigment
1. Two cans of paint got married. Not too long thereafter, the bride whispered happily to her groom, "Darling, I think I'm pigment."
2. Racial superiority is a pigment of one's imagination.
3. "Sow's things?" asked the boar—but no one knew what the pigment.

Pilate
The Crucifixion was really just a Pilate project.

pill
1. A pharmacy in the Bronx advertises itself as "The House of Pill Repute."
2. Where there's a Pill, there's a way.

pillage
It is the opinion of the doctor that the lawyer gets his living by plunder, while the lawyer thinks the doctor gets his by pillage.

pillow
The Israelites were led through the wilderness by a pillow afire.

pilot
When my Uncle Oscar announced that he had been promoted from orderly in the Air Force to pilot in the cavalry, a friend asked how he knew that he was a pilot. He said, "They've told me: 'Pilot here—pilot there'!"

pin
Some doctors practice acupuncture in order to pick up some pin money.

pinion
"What is the difference between a bird with one wing and a bird with two wings?"
"I give up."
"A difference of a pinion."

pinscher
It turned out that the Doberman was barking up the wrong tree when he tried to pinscher.

pint
The disposable bottle has brought the beverage industry to the pint of no return.

pistol
1. To stimulate an interest in grammar, the teacher asked for a sentence containing "cowboy," "Indian," "played" and "pistol." She was a bit discouraged when Johnny's sentence read, "The cowboy and the Indian drank beer and played poker until midnight, then they pistol two."
2. An all-night bar in Beverly Hills is called "Pistol Dawn."

pitcher
As the pancake said to the syrup, "You're so sweet you ought to be in pitchers."

pith
What kiddies do in the bafroom.

pitted
How did pitted prunes come into being? Well, it seems that the prune family, concerned that people were avoiding prunes because they resented having to remove and dispose of prune pits, decided they would henceforth be pitted—realizing that it's better to be pitted than scorned.

pity
The disillusioned new resident of Manhattan greeted his visiting parents on their arrival with, "Welcome to the pity of New York!"

pizza
One evening the dog lover brought home as food for his dog an Italian dish compounded of flour, cheese, and tomatoes. He thoughtfully tilted it against a door to make it more accessible for the dog. Then he summoned his wife and pointed out cheerfully, "There's no longer any need for you to plan that sightseeing trip to Italy next summer. Here, before your very eyes, is the leaning Pizza of Towser!"

plagiarism
Judge Jacob Brande: "All work and no plagiarism usually makes a mighty dull speech."

plaice
1. One worm to another, on meeting in a Dover sole, "What's a nice girl like you doing in a plaice like this?"
2. They subsequently become sole mates and he ended up singing "I've Grown Accustomed to Her Plaice."

plane
In Columbus, Ohio, a schoolboy's art assignment was to illustrate "America the Beautiful." The teacher recognized the flag, the map, the purple mountains—even the young artist's interpretation of "sea to shining sea." But she couldn't fathom the airplane in one corner that seemed to be covered with red and yellow balls. "Oh, that!" the seven-year-old student explained solemnly. "That is the fruited plane!"

planet
As the Martian explained on landing, "We're here by accident. We didn't planet this way."

plant
The promoters of the annual spring flower show had to postpone the opening because the exhibits couldn't be installed in time. The chairman admitted, "They caught us with our plants down."

plaster
The decorator was driven to the wall, and so he got plastered.

platitude
1. The all-encompassing speech usually suffers from longitude and platitude...
2. as the speaker rises to new platitudes of achievement.

platonic
A kind of tonic seldom associated with gin.

platoon
"I've just had a letter from my daughter. She's in love with a dozen soldiers. But she says not to worry—it's all platoonic."

pliers
Participants in a squeeze play.

plinth
Most thought the tuba player to be a low, square member of the bass, but she saw him as her plinth charming.

plot
1. Modern writers of detective stories find a sex element essential. They believe in having a chicken in every plot.
2. Lenin's tomb is a Communist plot.

pluck
1. Our butcher has fired his bird dresser because, although business was fowl, the young man didn't give a pluck.
2. Harpists are plucky fellows.

plug
The fire horse was the first spark plug.

plum
A carpenter had too much fruit in his lunch box and went plum loco.

Poe, Edgar Allan
The author of "The Fall of the House of Usher," etc. In his time, he was the Poe man's Shakespeare.

pointer
The duck-hunter's dog was very stupid. The hunter always had to pointer.

poison
In Brooklyn, the peephole's choice is an important poison.

pole
The first telephone pole was Alexander Graham Belinski.

police
Motto of the Mounties: "We Aim to Police."

polite
Every house should have a polite entrance.

polly
Q. What do they call hospitals for parrots?
A. Polly clinics.

polonaise
Sound of the ponies during a match.

polygon
A dead parrot.

polysyllables
"If you want your parrot to talk, you should begin by teaching it short words."
"That's strange. I supposed it would be quicker to use polysyllables."

ponder
Aircraft advertisement: "Off we go into the wilds you ponder."

Pontius
But don't blame the pilot; he was only semi-Pontius at the time.

pooch
An adventurous naturalist in Omaha has succeeded in crossing a bulldog with a hen. It now lays pooched eggs.

poodle
1. "It must be raining cats and dogs; I just stepped on a poodle."
2. If you are dogged by bad luck, it's like being up the creek without one.

pool
As they say in Texas, "There's no pool like an oil pool!"

pope
1. Sir Thomas Pope (of his daughter):
   She hardly is a fortnight old,
   And yet she is a Pope!
2. Contrary to rumor, the Vatican's income does not come from freezing holy water and selling it as popesicles.

poplar
Forestry is a poplar branch of science.

popsicle
A father hay slicer.

porcupine
"Pork is not a favorite dish of mine."
"So why is it that all through Lent,
It is for porcupine?"

pore
It is said that a human being has seven million pores through which perspiration and exhausted particles of the system escape. We are all pore creatures.

porn
> *We should mourn*
> *The astronomical*
> *And almost comical*
> *Growth of corn*
> *In motion pictures*
> *With strictures;*
> *When clothes are shorn*
> *A star is porn.*

porpoise
Two of the dolphins at the San Diego zoo were causing the staff embarrassment because of their continual public lovemaking. The curator finally hit on the idea of feeding them seagulls—their favorite dish—in such quantities that they would be too loggy for love. One day, as he went through the zoo on his way to the porpoise pool, he encountered an ancient lion, toothless and tranquil, lying across the aquarium gateway. The keeper stepped over the docile old beast. Immediately he was accosted by two detectives from the vice squad who curtly informed him he was under arrest. When the startled keeper asked why, he was told the charge would be the transportation of gulls across a staid lion for immoral porpoises.

port
1. Despite a violent downpour, the speaker managed to arrive at a banquet only an hour or so late. He was promptly served a beaker of extremely bad wine. Downing it with some distaste, he sighed and muttered, "Oh, well, any port in a storm."
2. A wine expert is a port authority.

portal
As the speaker observed, any portal do.

porte-cochère
Entrance to a Jewish restaurant.

portent
In the southern U.S., government-provided accommodation for indigents.

possum
Playing dead is easier possum folks than others.

pot
As the judge was in his chambers, he was incommoded by my request. I had to see him at his convenience. It's a potty system.

potash
Aesop wrote fables and sold his copyright for a mess of potash.

potpourri
Extreme Protestants are against combining the churches. They want no potpourri.

poultry
1. Mike Douglas, speculating on how failed theatrical ventures first became known as "turkeys," suggests that it may have been because so many of them are produced for a poultry sum.
2. "Are you interested in poultry?"
"A bit. I think Shakespeare was a good egg."

pragmatic
A type of hand gun made in Czechoslovakia.

prank
Examination papers: Pranks for the memory.

prawn
Louth Standard: "Why is it that tenants of Council property are treated like so many prawns on a chessboard?"

precedent
The only known cure for precedent is wintergreen.

predator
Old boyfriend.

premise
According to H. L. Mencken, two housewives arguing across back porches can never agree because they are arguing from different premises.

prepositions
The English professor got nowhere with his beautiful student by making stupid prepositions.

present
1. There's no gift like the present.
2. Le Beau: Three proper young men, of excellent growth and presence.
Rosalind: With bills on their necks, "Be it known unto all men by these presents."

president
When General Eisenhower became President, bridge became a favorite pastime at the White House. In one session, a daring Eisenhower finesse failed and he went down four tricks—doubled and vulnerable. "This," reflected the President, "is one of the few times anybody around here has set a president."

pressing
BLOUSE BUSINESS?
"Business is pressing," flared the tailor as he hemmed and hawed at being buttonholed. "I don't want to skirt the issue; we're taking a uniform trimming. We're yard up and a cuff is a cuff. I try to pleats my customers but I gusset won't work. You're no dummy, you can culotte what you twill. All I ask is bias strings so slack if I seam to tweed my customers right. Our business faces the thread of going vest.
"Cleaning and pressing? You can't take any stocking that. Shirt'll help. But

we're taking a clipping, and I'll hat to bolt the door and clothes down if we don't tie up more orders to suit.

"So far, it's just sew-sew; ascot my bank—all is knot loft but I pink we'll needle the credit we can collar."

pretense
That which comes before (pre) getting tense. Thus, a young lady viewing etchings might ask, "Has this all been a pretense?"

prey
Stalking game is a prey amble.

primate
Brigham Young's favorite wife.

prime
Some confusion exists in the U.S. over this word. "Pump priming" is well understood, especially in Washington, but the business use of the word is less clear. In broadcasting, for example, one hears of "prime time"—a period when a station or network seeks to prime its ratings (audience size) by offering something approaching real entertainment.

print
"Has your film come back from the drugstore, Mary?"
"No, but someday my prints will come!"

prior
Priests can't marry without prior approval.

prism
In the making of crystal, no levers are employed because iron bars do not a prism make.

private
Hamlet: *Then you live about her waist, or in the middle of her favours?*
Guildenstern: *Faith, her privates we.*

pro
1. Sex has its pros and cons. The pros get arrested—and the cons get married.
2. Three English professors, returning to campus, encountered a pushy group of young women who obviously were no better than they should be. Having managed to evade them gracefully, one professor—a Shakespearean scholar—chuckled, "What might one call such a congregation? A flourish of strumpets?" The second professor, whose specialty was Anthony Trollope, understandably preferred "a chapter of trollops." But the winner was the third and youngest professor's nomination, "an anthology of pros."

procreate
Psychologists are studying prostitutes to see what makes a procreate.

profit
In a socialist state, a profit is without honor.

promissory
> *In the world of crime*
> *There's many a time*
> *When a note has an ending gory,*
> *Especially if*
> *There's a bit of a tiff*
> *When the signer says of his promissory.*

prone
We are all prone to die.

propagate
There's no point in trying to breed a horse that hasn't the propagate.

prophet
In the Old Testament one finds the parable of the woman of ill fame who was arrested while trying to make a prophet. (It was in the period when the Pharaohs were learning to pyramid theirs.)

prophylactic
Article worn by Jews while praying.

proposition
When the semiliterate streetwalker unwittingly approached a detective, her proposition ended with a sentence.

prose
1. *A poet impresses the dons.*
   An athlete writes prose and cons.
2. Shakespeare's prose by any other name would smell as sweet.

prostate
Doctor: "I'm afraid I'm going to have to give you a prostate treatment."
Gay patient: "Oh, that's delicious! We'll be so much more comfortable that way!"

prostitute
1. They have arrested the woman lawyer who was moonlighting as a call girl. She has been charged with being a prostituting attorney.
2. The instructor of a Freshman English course ordered his students to write a paper about high society. One co-ed's paper began with a bang: "The Duchess of Dogwood was descending a staircase in the palace when she tripped, fell and lay prostitute on the floor." The instructor circled the incorrect word and penciled this comment in the margin: "Dear Miss James: You must learn to distinguish between a fallen woman and one who has merely temporarily lost her balance."
3. *"Do flautists lay aside their flutes*
   And listen when a prostitutes?"

protest
The assessment of a golfing expert.

prune
A plum that has seen better days. Example: Disharmony among the plum pickers is putting us all out of prune.

psalmody
If you sing badly, refrain and let psalmody else.

psychiatrist
A secret meeting between Psyche and Cupid.

pubic
1. Sex survey: a pubic-opinion poll.
2. As a rule, the penis can be gauged squarely as a pubic sentimetre.

puce
If you're browned off at religion, you shouldn't sit in the puce.

pudding
The trouble with cooks from Yorkshire is that they are always pudding you on.

pudendum
Privy parts, e.g., hole, seat, vents, roof, etc.

puerility
The state of being pure (as in virginity, although puerility does not necessarily ensure virginity).

Puget
A State of Washington school of sky pilots. Famous for its ability to produce pontificial tonality (The Puget Sound).

Pullman
The original sleeping car was so stuffy, it caused many Pullmanary complaints.

pullover
The embarrassed bride, afraid to admit to her new husband that she had been arrested for speeding, entered the fine in her checkbook as, "one pullover—$10.00."

pumpernickel
It may seem a bit awry, but while you are earning your bread, the fireman is earning his pumpernickel.

pun
1. A friend once asked Ben Jonson to make a pun. He replied, "Pun what subject?" His friend responded, "The king." "But," said Jonson, "the king is not a subject. He is king."
2. Never point a pun at a friend. It might be loaded.
3. Besides, you might kill a pun-pal.
4. And end up in the punitentiary.
5. However, on Good Friday, it Easter custom to throw hot, cross puns.

punch
1. The boxing commission is a punch board.
2. Many a battered boxer is permanently out to punch.

punctuation
"Do you understand the importance of punctuation?"
"Have you ever known me to be late?"

pundit
One who utters (French *dit*—says) puns. For years, our Indian friends were understandably Nehru-minded about this.

punishment
If no pun is intended, then no punishment.

punjab
A biting play on words; repartee of the highest order (French: *odeur*).

punkah
East Indian term of derision ("You punkah, sahib"). Hence, the British colloquialism "punk."

punny

THE PUNNY FARM

Down on the punny farm, we have many pets for you to meet (but not if you're a butcher). There is a cat named Astrophe, a camel named Lot, a bat named Acro, a boar named Doukho and a lynx named Miss Sing. Not far away, you will find a dingo named Ling, an English sheep named One-upman and a lion from Germany named Frau.

These animals and many more were named by the readers of *Maclean's Magazine*. Readers also named a grouse National Product and a raccoon Tour. They tagged a gorilla My Dreams and a deer Abby. There's a swan, they say, named Way Traffic and a shark named Noah. A locust, Housing, flirts with a mockingbird named Tequilla—or so we learned from a gander named Proper. From Great Britain there is a cod, called Save the Queen, and from Quebec a bee, Lingual. Not to mention Canada's pet doe, True, which arrived with a squid, Doo.

The accuracy of all this has been attested by an aphid named David.

pup
1. Q. What's a small dog suffering from chills?
   A. A pupsickle.
2. A prominent, well-to-do member of the clergy gave his teenage daughter a pedigreed pup for her birthday, warning her that the little dog had not yet been housebroken. Sure enough, an hour later, when the clergyman wandered into his daughter's room, he found her contemplating a small puddle in the center of the room. "My pup," she murmered sadly, "runneth over."

Purdue
Motto of Purdue University: *Tout Est Purdue.*

purl
Today, a handknit sweater is a purl of great price.

purpose
The difference between a tiger and a pussy is discernible in the purpose.

purr
1. Our cat has gone to fur and is pregnant, as purr usual.
2. Sam Levenson's cat was a rather pathetic animal several degrees below purr. It was always getting in the way. Sam's mother accidentally stepped on it one night, and its felines were hurt.
3. Marketing cat food successfully is a purr ad venture.

push
When he was a baby, his parents hired a maid just to push him in his baby carriage. He has been pushed for money ever since.

puss
Sarawak Tribune: "A warning should be given about Cat-Scratch Disease. The disease spreads, involving swelling and puss formation."

put
"There was a terrible murder in our rooming house today."
"Was there?"
"Yes; a paperhanger hung a border."
"It must have been a put-up job!"

putt
George Burns's favorite golf trick was sinking a ball from the top of a Great Dane. But he only did it when he felt like putting on the dog.

pyorrhea
1. Dr. Wylie stood looking down at the pretty young thing in his dental chair. "My dear," he said, "you've got acute pyorrhea." "Never mind that now, Doctor," snapped the young thing. "Just get on with your dentistry."
2. The seaport of Athens.

pyromaniac
The judge at the village fair's baking contest was pretty cool about the cakes but turned out to be a pyromaniac.

*The fireman's daughter
was a lusty **quench.***

Q

Every Q has its tail—and the bigger the Q, the sadder the tail.

quack

"What happens when geese fly upside down?"
"They quack up."

quack doctor

Veterinarian.

quadrangle

1. Argument in a private school or college.
2. So, "quadrant," a scholastic harangue.
3. And, "quadroon," the results.

quadrille

A dance for squares.

quadruplet

Newspaper item: "The young of the hoatzin, a curious fowl-like bird native to South America, are remarkable in having clawed fingers on their wings by means of which they are able to climb about tree like quadruplets."

quaff

It is in *Alice in Wonderland* that we encounter a queen with a Cockney taste for beer. She goes about ordering "Quaff with 'er head!"

quail

1. A kind of migratory bird allied to the partridge. Also known as the cowherd or flinch.
2. It is foolish to try to make game of a chicken by looking at it, under the impression that a steady gaze of the human eye will make it quail.

quaint
An anachronism is something which appears to be what it quaint.

quake
San Francisco warning to soufflé makers: You can't have your quake and eat it.

qualm
Momentary faint or sick feeling; the qualm before the storm.

quarrel
Marching song of the Irish Republican Army: "Roll Out the Quarrel."

quart
People who drink before they drive are putting the quart before the hearse.

quarterback
The difference between soccer and football is that when you lose on a football game, you get your quarterback.

quash
A game played by judges—in quash courts.

quasi
All actors are quasi. And some sailors are quasi in the head.

queasy
Asked how he survived crossing the Atlantic in an open boat, the adventurer replied, "Oh, it was queasy!"

queer
How queer to my heart
Are the scenes of my childhood
When fond recollection
Recalls them to view.

quench
The fireman's daughter was a lusty quench.

query
"I've laid on an exciting evening for us, Sam. Do you have a query?" "No, I'll bring a girl."

queue
It is said that the modern wearer of a "pony tail" hairdo takes her queue from the Chinese.

quibble
The fraternity of politicians is full of quibbling rivalry.

quiche
"Kiss me," she whispered. "I'm hungry," he replied. "Quiche me first."

quid
The Latin teacher noticed that one student was chewing gum in class and asked, "Quid est hoc?" "Sir," the student replied honestly, "hoc est quid!"

quiff
A midget had a date with a very tall girl. It was a quiff-hanger.

quill
When it comes to influencing people after you are dead, where there's a quill there's a way.

quintessence
An aphrodisiac which can have multiple results.

quip
The comedian is society's quipping boy.

quire
Twenty-four uniform sheets. Best known: The Ku Klux Klan Quire.

quirk
The followers of the Marquis de Sade were by no means all loyal. Several young ladies deserted him, complaining that it was all quirk and no pay.

quiver
Coaching one of her damsels for that first night with a member of royalty, the madame cautioned, "Remember, the lord loveth a cheerful quiver."

quondam
Things keep changing so quickly these days, it's just quondam thing after another.

quota
"She has made her share of puns, but I wouldn't want to quota."

*It is bad manners
to break your bread
or **roll** in your
soup.*

R
You can always tell if a lass is Scottish by the way she rolls her Rs.

rabbi
Pasteur found a cure for rabbis.

rabbit
1. Fast, speedy (as in Rabbit Transit).
2. Hare today and gone tomorrow.
3. A Welsh rabbit is a girl from Wales who works in a bunny club: She's Hefner self a time.
4. And can't kick the rabbit.

raccoon
Many cottages are going to raccoon ruin.

Rachmaninov
She thought her new boyfriend was creative but when he finally got down to it he wasn't a Rachmaninov to satisfy her.

radish
Health food can give you a radish complexion.

raffia
The fiber of an impoverished society.

raffle
After years of getting booed, the dancer finally had her feathers raffled.

rag
The pressure was on at the network. Production costs had to be cut. Finally,

one bright young producer broke under the strain to the point of writing as follows: "I believe I have found the ideal low-cost show for this network. It is a casual, simple show with a lot of general appeal. In addition, it can be heavily merchandised as a broadcasting 'first.' It consists of having two moths on camera. They just sit there informally and chew the rag."

ragout
A special concoction (stew), usually homemade and principally consisting of old rags. (Not to be confused with Mrs. Murphy's chowder—in which there was an overall difference.)

raid
There have been many forms of "raid" used. Setting aside raids of armed forces, where equals in rank attack each other (known technically as *parades*), we have seen short-winded collegians involved in *panty-raids* and suburban housewives stealing each other's cleaning women (*charades*) and the growing youth problem where the new morality leaves them *radiant*. But for the true meaning of the basic word, one must go back to early times, when "the three Rs" were in vogue (Raiding, 'Riting and 'Rithmetic). History records that raiding was so accepted that when word got out that Spain had hired someone to discover the United States, the Nordic countries countered by hiring an explorer who had subsequently become known as "Eric the Raid." (The word did not recur in this form until recent times when an injunction went out from a broadcasting network to "Raid Skelton.")

rail
A horizontal bar. There is one in New York known as "The Rail Thing."

railroad
Conveyances used by commuters, who spend their time on the road railing against the service.

raise
"I come to bury Caesar, not to raise him."

raisin
Because he was fond of good wine, former U.S. President Lyndon B. Johnson used to quote from the Bible, "Come now, and let us raisin together." (His opponents used to complete the quotation for him: "... saith The Lord.")

raison d'être
1. A term in poker, as in "I'll raison d'être."
2. Also used in bilingual dunning letters (sometimes spelled "Re: Son debt.")
3. What the U.S. owes the grape pickers.

rampant
It is the ewe that makes the rampant.

ramshackle
A chain used to tie up a he-goat.

range
"I saw a big rat in my cookstove, but when I went for my revolver, he ran out."
"Did you shoot him?"
"No. He was out of my range."

ranger
Container for rainwater.

rank
Touchstone: "*Nay, if I keep not my rank.*"
Rosalind: "*Thou losest thy old smell.*"

ransack
It isn't legal to ransack business on Sunday.

rapier
Some girls are rapier than others.

rapscallion
A man who hates onions.

rash
"You're in quarantine? So, what's your rash?"

rate
As the cooking-contest judge said, "It must have been something I rate."

raucous
Coarse, vulgar expletive.

raven
Some thought Edgar Allan Poe a raven maniac.

razor
One's first time encounter with a lady barber is apt to razor eyebrows!

read
1. The trouble with education today is that the little red schoolhouse is producing the little-read schoolboy.
2. Hilaire Belloc:
   "*When I am dead, I hope it may be said:*
   '*His sins were scarlet, but his books were read*'."

ream
"*To sleep, perchance to ream . . .*"

reap
1. A grain of wheat fell asleep in a field. When it awoke it was in a loaf of bread. "Good Heavens!" it cried, "I've been reaped!"
2. In Canada's prairie province, when someone goes against the grain, he is known as "Jack the Reaper."
3. Read it and reap.

rear
Adlai Stevenson once characterized Senator Barry Goldwater as "a man who thinks everything will be better in the rear future."

reason
Thomas à Becket was involved in literature, politics and religion—a man for all reasons.

rebate
To put another worm on the hook.

rebuff
To undress again.

recline
After the age of retirement, we are faced with the reclining years.

recluse
The hermit was arrested for speeding on the highway and charged with recluse driving.

rectangle
Result of a head-on collision.

rector
She was a nice girl but he rector.

rectum
Some say she rectum.

red
1. "What's black and white and red all over?"
   A. (Circa 1900) "A newspaper."
   B. (Circus Barnum & Bailey) "An embarrassed zebra."
2. Not being much of a parliamentarian, the tsar of all the Russias was soon in the red.
3. The staple diet of Russia is the reddish.

redneck
1. A hero (Southern U.S.). From General Lee Redneck, leader of the Confederate forces at Fagg's Ferry. It was of General Redneck that General Grant once said, "I don't know what he's got—but I think we're all getting a case of it." Redneck was finally cowed at Bull Run when his rear became exposed. Shot in the saddle, he left his mark upon the South.
2. Founder of the Ku Klux Klan and its first Kluk, Redneck's fierceness in battle was attributed to the fact that he didn't give a sheet.

redress
The strip show was slow in coming off, but fortunately there was no redress.

reef
At the Olympics, the winner gets a coral reef.

reefers
"Grass" reefers to marijuana.

reek
Pollution prediction: And the reek shall inherit the earth.

reel
1. A fishing trip is a reel treat.
2. She was only a fisherman's daughter, but when she saw my rod she reeled.

reflect
A philosopher is like a looking-glass; he reflects.

refugee
The man who blows the whistle at games.

refuse
In their apartment, the lights went out every time you plugged in an appliance. Disgusted, the young husband finally sighed, "Should we refuse to move or move to refuse?"

refute
The Vatican has been termed "the house of Pill refute."

regalia
As the jester said to his king, "Your Majesty, shall I regalia?"

rehearse
One thing about performing as an undertaker; you don't have time to rehearse.

reign
1. If household pets were to take over the world, they would be reigning cats and dogs.
2. The maharaja of a small province in India decreed that no wild animals could be killed by the populace. Soon the country was overrun by lions, tigers, panthers, elephants and wild boars. The people finally could stand it no longer and gave their maharaja an unceremonious heave-ho. As an Indian newspaper noted, it was the first instance on record where the reign was called on account of game.

reindeer
"Tell the buffalo for me—I think it's going to reindeer."

relay
The second time around.

relapse
The reformed alcoholic who falls from grace probably feels that he might as well relapse and enjoy it.

relief
In Autumn one sees
Many causes for grief

Because all the trees
Stand in need of relief.

remind
"I am a psychiatrist—may I remind you?"

remorse
Penitence is the remorse code.

renegade
Now that we have teenagers, we've been renegaded to the back seat.

repeat
Marry in haste, repeat at leisure.

repel
Advertisement: "No matter what your topcoat is made of, this miracle spray will make it really repellent."

repent
A reformatory is a repent house.

repetition
A tourist who had purchased an old painting in Rome took it to a reputable New York dealer to get his opinion of its worth. "Well," said the dealer tactfully, "I'd say it is either a Titian or a repetition."

requiem
A mass meeting of the dead where all cry, "They destroyed us. Now requiem!"

reservation
Bride-to-be: "Have you made any reservations for our honeymoon, darling?"
Bridegroom-to-be: "Certainly not—and I hope you haven't any either!"

reservoir
To protect the North American Indians, they were all put in reservoirs.

resolution
The earth makes a resolution every twenty-four hours.

resort
He met her first at a travel bureau
And they began to court.
She was looking for a vacation
And he was the last resort.

respect
She washed his car and then it rained and it was all respect.

rest
A proper Bostonian went to Las Vegas for a change and a rest. The hotel maids got the change and the croupiers got the rest.

retort
Asked to explain why he wasn't working, the chemist replied, "I have no retort."

retouch
Borrowing twice from the same photographer.

reverend
"The Mother Superior says that if I don't study harder, I'll be in this convent for reverend ever."

reward
1. *The Reverend Henry Ward Beecher*
   Called a hen a most elegant creature.
   The hen, pleased with that,
   Laid an egg in his hat.
   And thus did the hen reward Beecher.
2. "If he can't afford a private room anymore, we'll have to reward him."

rhapsody
An effervescent drink consumed during bull sessions.

rhesus
The king of Thrace
Fell in disgrace,
His kingdom all in pieces.
What took the place
Of his bloody mace
Was the people's faith in Rhesus.

rheumatic
Aging lover—an incurable rheumatic.

Rhodes, Sir Cecil
His generosity has enabled thousands of students to see the world through Rhodes Scholared glasses.

rhyme
They say you can't rhyme a word with "orange." Perhaps they're right. Anyway, what good is an orange rhymed?

rib
1. Eve was a rib off.
2. Three prominent Indians—the Swami of Sudan, the Gaekwar of Baroda and the Nizam of Hyderabad—were being entertained as state visitors. A crowd assembled and three hecklers each chose one of the visiting dignitaries to rib. It became so annoying that the representative of the host government called a security man and told him to shut up one of the hecklers so that the others might go away. "Which one of the ribbers do you want me to lean on?" inquired the guard. Came the reply: "Weigh down upon the Swami ribber."

ribald
1. Exposed ribs.
2. Incest is sibling ribaldry.

ricochet
Chinese jaunting car.

rid
When the garbage man cometh it's a rid litter day.

rider
Edgar Allan Poe was an oily American rider.

ridge
Venice we going to come to a ridge of size?

ridicule
Queen Victoria carried her handkerchief in her ridicule.

rifle
1. After the murder weapon had been found, the police began to search for the rifle owner.
2. Bootleggers sometimes add water to get the rifle.

rift
In the story of Tom Sawyer's trip down the Mississippi, there is quite a rift.

rigger
Lunenburg's finest undertakers, old Mort Morrison and his son Dave, are experts at rigging sailing ships on the side. However, the natives agree that although Dave is a mighty good undertaker, he's not the rigger Mort is.

right
Pop song (and Ma song, too—from the Me Song Delta): "I Could Have Danced All Right!"

rigid
The country girl who becomes a city madam has obviously gone from rags to rigids.

rile
Irishism: "It's a rile reason for fighting."

rinderpest
What you get if you let a reindeer hang around too long.

ringleader
The first one in the bathtub.

riot
Something made by two wrongs.

roam
A gypsy needs lots of roam. (Hence, "Romany.")

robin
A jailbird is often guilty of robin.

robot
Uncle Oscar didn't like to help with the housework, so he got a robot and every time there was work to do he would get out his robot and go fishing.

rock
His marriage is on the rocks—but things may improve when they get a bed.

rod
A fisherman off of Cape Cod
Said, "I'll bugger that tuna, by God!"
    But the high-minded fish
    Resented his wish
And nimbly swam off with his rod.

roe
Tralee in Ireland is famous for its cavier, marketed as "The roes of Tralee."

roil
Heading on news item re fishing rights: "Britain Roils the Waves."

roll
It is bad manners to break your bread or roll in your soup.

Roman
Many a savage has been converted by encountering a Roman Catholic.

Rome
Cassius: *"Now it is Rome indeed and room enough."*

Romeo
Speaking of Shakespeare, how much did Romeo when Juliet?

romp
Her face wasn't much, but she had a beautiful romp.

rook
When Polinokoff, the great Russian chess player, visited the United States, a fresh young reporter clapped him on the back at the airport and cried, "Welcome, Polly! Led any good rooks lately?"

roomer
In their youth, humorists Frank Sullivan and Corey Ford shared quarters in an inexpensive and rather run-down boardinghouse. Ford named the tiny apartment, "Cloister on the Half Shell." Sullivan referred to himself as "Ford's Ugly Roomer."

root
When planting bulbs along a road, the left side should be planted on Monday, Wednesday, and Friday. On Tuesday, Thursday, and Saturday you use the alternate roots.

rose
Every time he saw his senorita his mexicali rose.

rough
What the dog said when it sat on the sandpaper.

round
1. He's a fair boxer. His swing can make a round a bout.
2. Uncle Oscar has 200 cows. He thought he had 199 until he rounded them up.

rubber
"Contraceptives used to rubber the wrong way."

rubble
Evidence of chain-gang activity. Hence the work song "Nobody Knows the Rubble I've Seen."

rube
1. O.E. ending, now *rub* (a 16th-century change). e.g.: Hamlet—"*To sleep, perchance to dream. Aye, there's the rube!*" Cf. *Lady Chatterley's Lover.*
2. If Lord Chatterley had discovered her cutting up, it would have come as a rube shock.

rudiment
Before singer Rudy Vallee became famous, he had to improve his articulation—no one knew what rudiment.

rue
1. Being a streetwalker is rued business.
2. In his later years, Rudy Vallee persuaded Los Angeles to name a street "Rue de Vallee."

rug
1. Travelling by flying carpet is a rugged experience.
2. *Nelson Evening Mail:* "He is now being kept alive by an artificial respirator and massive doses of rugs."

rum
WHAT THE ALE?
Girlperson: Leave me beer I'll scream!
Boyperson: I'd like tequilla! I didn't ask gin.
Girlperson: Water you mean? Then wine you let me go? Orange juice sorry you hurt me?
Boyperson: Don't be soda pressed. Them martini bruises.
Girlperson: Oh, why Chianti leave me alone?
Boyperson: Look, vodka I do to make it all rye?
Girlperson: Well, we could give up this bourbon life. There's more rum to fight in the country!

rumba
Southern bistro.

ruminate
The Italians were short of milk because some ruminate the cow.

run
Rum runner: A cocktail made of equal parts rum and prune juice.

rune
The ancient tales of Germany were runed.

runt
1. Classified ad: "Small apartment for runt."
2. The difference between a pygmy tribe and a women's track team is that the pygmies are a cunning bunch of runts.

rupture
Modern dancing often seems sheer rupture.

ruse
A rose is a rose is a ruse.

rush
They abandoned the film about Moses after they saw the rushes.

rusk
The baker wanted to rebake his sliced bread but he was afraid to run the rusk.

russet
Consumed by Communism, e.g., the Hungary people were russet.

Russian
We like to sip Chinese tea slowly but samovar friends prefer Russian.

rust
1. Sign at a Detroit junkyard: "Rust in Peace."
2. Presumably, its owners rust after business.

Ruth
As Naomi admitted later, "Ruth is stranger than fiction."

rye
1. He tells jokes only when he's drunk. He has a rye sense of humor.
2. When the party's over he makes it all rye to the door.

*Flamenco dancing is a **Stamp Act**.*

SSSSSSS

S
> The India rubber man had a poor social life: every time he went to a party he made an S of himself.

sack
> As in, "Sack it to me!" (from the Japanese, for ordering wine).

sacrament
> Special gown worn by priests.

sad
> *Brave young Anne,*
> *King Henry's wife,*
> *Kept her head*
> *Most of her life.*
> *She spent her time*
> *A lot alone*
> *And never sad*
> *Upon the throne.*

safari
> "How are you enjoying your visit to Africa?"
> "Well, safari so good!"

sage
> A bored judge once whispered to another judge on the bench that one of the witnesses had a vegetable head. "How so?" "Well, look at him!" whispered back the first judge. "He has carroty hair, radish cheeks, a turnip nose, and a sage look!"

sailfish
Some men go fishing for anything they can catch. Others have sailfish motives.

sake
They went to a Japanese restaurant to get acquainted, but she said, "Let's hit the sake!" and they left early.

salaam
There was a Turk who was so polite that he always salaamed the door.

salivation
Pavlov's experiments with a dog became the salivation of psychology.

salmon
To go upstream to spawn, fish have to salmon their strength.

salt
1. Cooking up a romance with a sailor often starts with a pinch of salt.
2. If he's too aggressive it could become a salt and battery.

samovar
Russia has supplied samovar recipes.

sand
1. You can't starve to death on a beach because you can always eat the sand which is there.
2. "What do Christmas and a cat on the beach have in common?" "Sandy claws!"

sank
When King Louis XV's royal barge capsized in the Seine, Madame de Pompadour, the royal mistress, asked if her precious kittens had been rescued. Louis had to tell her, "Hélas! Un, deux, trois cats sank."

sap
There must be something feminine about a tree. It does a striptease in the fall, goes with bare limbs all winter, gets a new outfit in the spring, and lives off the sap all summer.

Sarah
1. *Schubert had a horse named Sarah.*
   He drove her to the big parade.
   And all the time the band was playing
   Schubert's Sarah neighed.
2. "Knock, knock!"
   "*Who's there?*"
   "Sarah."
   "*Sarah who?*"
   "Sarah doctor in the house?"

sari
A wealthy sheik was wont to while away his evenings appreciating the

gyrations of a native dancing belle. One night, however, a booking agent persuaded him to try Sari, a new importation from Paris. The potentate was displeased with the substitution and phoned the agent to announce curtly, "Sari wrong number."

sarong

A businessman in Malaysia had a wife who spent all her time worrying about clothes. One night he arrived home to find her in tears. In exasperation he demanded, "What sarong now?"

sauce

A famous Washington columnist, dining in the old quarter of Montreal, raved over the trout Marguery. He summoned the proprietor of the restaurant and said, "I'd like to have the recipe for this dish." The proprietor smiled and answered suavely, "I'm sorry, m'sieu, but we have here the same policy as you journalists. We never reveal our sauce."

sausage

When fire broke out in the wiener works you never sausage a mess!

saw

1. You shouldn't presume that stone can't be cut just because you never saw it.
2. A joke writer is a man who sharpens old saws.

sax

On occasion one encounters in show business an all-girl band. Unfortunately, many of them sound like the battle of the saxes.

scale

1. The convicted architect soon discovered that the prison walls were not built to scale.
2. The world's only musical fish? The rainbow trout—with its chromatic scales.
3. Sol Mizate's contribution to music shows great scale.

scandal

In China, before going into a house, you must get rid of your scandals.

scar

1. "Have I told you about my operation?"
   "Do you have a scar?"
   "Sorry, I don't smoke."
2. The American Civil War may well have left its scars and stripes forever.

scare

I know not where His islands lift
Their fronded palms in error;
I only know I cannot drift
Beyond his love and scare.

scarlet

In Hollywood, young ladies of the evening are sometimes referred to as film scarlets.

scent

1. A truck belonging to a wholesale perfume distributor was hijacked and thousands of dollars' worth of expensive toiletries and fragrances was stolen. The president of the company called the police a few days after the robbery and asked if the crooks had been apprehended. "Not yet," admitted the police chief. "But we know where the stuff's been scent."
2. A skunk may never grow rich but he makes a lot of scents.
3. In the animal world, he's the community scenter.

scheme

When he met her he thought she auto marry him, but she turned out to be a real scheme engine.

scherzo

A lady cellist lost her job because of making her scherzo short.

schnapps

A ginlike beverage that bites.

scraping

"Why were you hanging around so long at that steamroller accident?" "I was just scraping up an acquaintance."

scratch

It is easy for a dermatologist to build his practice; he just starts from scratch.

scrawl

Norton Mockridge's book on grafitti was called *The Scrawl of the Wild.*

scream

As an actor in horror movies, Boris Karloff was successful beyond his wildest screams.

screech

Filibustering is freedom of screech.

screen

"I like this hedge because it screen."

screw

1. Two Cockney ladies on a bus: "Going to see a ply by Shikespeare, are you? What's it called, luv?" "I'm not sure, but I think it's *The Timing of the Screw.*"
2. *There once was a girl named McGoffin*
   Who was diddled annoyingly often.
       She was rogered by scores
       Who'd been turned down by whores.
   And was finally screwed in her coffin.

scrimmage

Hopefully, the legitimate theatre will outlive the scrimmage.

script
"I can read you like a book," said Eve. "I'm not surprised," said Adam, who was completely script except for his flyleaf.

scrod
A woman hailed a taxi in Boston one day and asked the driver, "Would you take me down to the fish wharves? I'd like to get scrod." The driver looked at her. "You must be a tourist!" he commented. "Why do you say that?" the woman demanded. "Well," he explained, "no Bostonian would ever use that tense."

scrotum
On the west coast of North America, the Indians refer to an erection as a scrotum pole.

scrutable
The working surface in a massage parlor.

sculler
To be accepted at Oxford you must be both a gentleman and a sculler.

scurrilous
The music of the bagpipes.

sea
1. Pollution is getting so bad in Rome they are thinking of moving the Pope to the Irish Sea.
2. "Is this the first time you've been to sea?"
"Yes, when can I peak?"

seam
1. Hippies made poor tailors because they were always splitting the seam.
2. Being a garment worker is a seamy business.

season
1. It is generally recognized that there are four basic seasons: Salt, pepper, mustard and vinegar.
2. If you want to flavor food you must season one of these.

seat
The young usher had never seen a woman in a sari before. Offering the beautiful dark thing a program, he said, "Let me sew you to your sheet."

second
It isn't the minutes that pile up the pounds, it's the seconds.

secretive
Little is known about the salivary glands because they are so secretive.

section
What priests must do.

sediment
What he announced he had in mind.

see
1. Long bus tours sometimes make you see-sick.
2. At one time, the Catholic Church had to withdraw its maintenance of a diocese among the Seven Nations Indians. At last, however, the bishop returned. As he stepped from his canoe, the chief of the Indians greeted him with "Long time no see!"

seek
1. The Arabs have a famous detective. He is known as the Seek of Araby.
2. That's a seek joke.

seeking
Neptune is seeking.

Seine
One day, a man and his wife were seated at a sidewalk café in Paris. The wife ordered a martini, but her husband asked only for a glass of water. Then he signaled for a second round; as he put it to the startled waiter, "My wife will have another martini—and I'll have a little more of the Seine."

seize
Marc Antony got ahead because he was a girl-chaser. He kept yelling "Seize her!" Julius was so flattered he promoted him.

selamlik
Turkish kiss of greeting.

selenite
If an inhabitant of the moon ever came to Earth we'd probably keep him in a selenite.

self
My grandfather's cock
Was too large for himself
So it hung ninety years to the floor.

selfish
The net effect of running a trawler is too selfish.

sell
1. When con men become cons they are frequently sell mates.
2. Pregnancy begins with a single sell.

semaphore
Old news.

semen
Noah probably had no trouble sailing with all the semen aboard.

seminary
A place where they bury the dead.

senator
A creature half man and half horse.

señor
Mexican for "senior." In California, grape growers contribute palatial row houses for señor citizens.

sentence
"Give an example of period furniture." "The electric chair—because it ends a sentence."

sentiment
The floor of the ocean is covered with fine sentiments.

Seoul
1. While with the armed services in Korea, he fell in love with a native girl and they became Seoul mates.
2. Since money changed hands, you knew she was Seoul.
3. For a Seoul purpose.

sequel
A wolf is a man who treats all women as sequels.

serial
The Autocrat of the Breakfast Table was a breakfast serial.

serif
A printer tries to keep at least one jump ahead of him.

serrate
Wise sayings come and go
But old saws serrate low.

serum
The way some docs
Inject their flocks
Small wonder the patients fear 'em!
The cure produces burns and shocks;
They don't just prick, they serum.

servant
The little rich girl came back from her first trip to Sunday School and told her mother, "Oh, Mummy! They read us the nicest story! All about a Mr. Adam and a Miss Eve and what a nice time they were having under an apple tree until a servant came along and disturbed them."

setter
They couldn't afford a nurse for their children so they acquired a baby setter.

sew
A homemade dress often tends to look sew-sew.

sex
1. Latin for six. Still found in U.S. idiom: "Two's a party, three's a crowd, sex is good for you."
2. Or, as the hermaphrodite said, "I'll be with you in two sex."

sextant
   The captain was a bachelor whose only urge for women was satisfied by his sextant.

shack
   "See that big house over there? My friend just inherited it when his uncle died." "Well, it obviously came as quite a shack!"

shad
   In the spring, fishing can be a shad occasion.

shah
   Ruler. From Paddy Shah, early Irish king who signed all bills and treaties "per Shah." His early demise (he was not rugged) led to the exclamation "Aw, Shah!"

shake
   A hula is a shake in the grass.

shallow
   A budget forecast is a shallow device.

sham
   A hypochondriac has sham pain tastes.

shampoo
   An imposter bear.

shark
   There is a fishing boat down Key West way which has bumpers fore and aft. To the inquiring tourist, the captain explains that they are shark absorbers.

shasta
   Variety of daisy. Sometimes used as a nickname for a car because, "Shasta have gas, shasta have oil and shasta be insured."

shave
   When the wives of the members persisted in being careless in their use of the fairways, the Greens Committee at the golf course had a sign put up by the first tee:

DRIVE CAREFULLY!
THE WIFE YOU SHAVE MAY BE YOUR OWN!

shay
   "Whatsamatter?" demanded the drunk between the shafts. "I know the sign says no horses on this bridge but I'm the one that's doing the pulling!" "You're not being arrested for driving a horse," the policeman replied. "I'm giving you a ticket for shay-walking."

she
   A mermaid is a deep she fish.

shear
   The price of haircuts is becoming shear nonsense.

shed
As the critic wrote of the stripper, "Some things are better left unshed."

sheep
A New York investor saw an advertisement offering a stock market newsletter from Australia. Willing to try anything to change his luck, he subscribed. When the first issue arrived it contained just four words: "Buy sheep, sell deer."

sheik
1. There was an unscheduled free-for-all in a Baghdad harem one day. The Sultan barged in unexpectedly and his wives let out a terrified sheik.
2. Actually, Arab women really fear the wolf in sheik's clothing.
3. That's why they wear those sheik veils.

shelf
Shyness is thinking only of your shelf.

shellfish
As Molly Malone wheeled her wheelbarrow through streets broad and narrow it became apparent that she was a shellfish girl.

sherry
George Washington: "Father, I cannot tell a lie. I cut your sherry."

shin
Women with bad legs should stick to long skirts because they cover a multitude of shins.

ship
Many a girl has discovered too late that a sailor can be a wolf in ship's clothing.

shiver
"I lost my sister's slip, and she'll give me the cold shoulder if shiver finds out."

shoat
By the rude bridge that arched the flood,
Their flag to April's breeze unfurled,
Here once the embattled farmers stood
And fired the shoat heard round the world.

shock
Hollywood cocktail parties are devoted largely to shock talk.

shoe
When the slipper salesman had spent his last and was on his uppers, he cried, "Well, that's shoe business!"

shofar
1. In appreciation for his years of service, the synagogue gave its rabbi his own car and shofar.
2. Shofar, he hasn't blown it.

shoot
Despite everything the government can do to control inflation, rockets are still shooting up.

shore
She said he could kiss her on the groine—so he knew he was onto a shore thing.

short
1. A survey of juvenile delinquents in Glasgow reveals that more short boys have become involved in crime than tall boys. Apparently, many a boy turns to crime because he happens to be a little short. (A tall boy is above that short of thing.)
2. Bermuda shorts: natives of the island, usually under five feet in height.
3. They are much sought after as chefs, i.e., short order cooks.
4. Cruise ships approaching Bermuda announce their pending arrival by ship-to-short radio.
5. Napoleon: The short heard 'round the world.

Shostakovitch
Russian composer, best remembered for his ballad, "Shostakovitch Small by a Waterfall."

shotgun
An officer under the Mikado. The last one was fired in 1868.

shove
It pays to be pushy; all the world loves a shover.

show
1. At the court of Versailles, King Louis XV noticed during a reception that one of Madame de Pompadour's fourteen petticoats was sagging. "Pompy," he informed her gallantly, "your quelque shows."
2. One of the touring companies entertaining U.S. troops in Vietnam had its panel truck painted like the American flag—a flagrant example of show van ism.
3. Many a girl has gone to bed frightened by the late show.

shrimp
"Do you have any shrimps?"
"Just the busboy and the hatcheck girl."

shrivel
"Once you were my knight in shining armor. But that was before you reached the age of shrivelry."

sicken
"Aha!" cried Sherlock Holmes, "the plot sickens!"

sic transit
Motto of the Royal Ambulance Transport Society (RATS).

sigh
1. Early melodramas were known as sighed shows.
2. "There!" she said, standing on her tiptoes, "I am about your size." "On the contrary," said the disconsolate lover. "My sighs are about you."

simile
A widening of the mouth to explain pleasure.

simp
When King Edward VIII announced that he wished to marry a commoner, his mother counselled, "Don't be a simp, son!"

simpleton
Why a fool is like a twenty hundred weight.

sin
1. Extramarital relations can be curiously refreshing. One might call it sin and tonic.
2. *Daily Telegraph:* "The Manx Government plans to relax regulations on boardinghouses to make more beds available for tourist sin late August and September."

sincere
When the young advertising agency executive got promoted to New York, the first thing he did was go out and buy himself a sincere-sucker suit.

sing
The problem with the blues: It don't mean a sing if you ain't got that swing.

singe
When Monsignor Bishop was at his barber's one day he became aware of an unpleasant odor. "What is that I smell?" he demanded. "Oh," said his barber, "Forgive me, Father, for I have singed."

sinister
An unmarried woman.

sip
An elephant walked into a bar and ordered a martini. The place was empty except for himself and a lovely girl elephant at the other end of the bar. "Joe," he said to the bartender, "put another martini in front of me, then put another in front of each empty stool between me and the doll." "Sure," said Joe, "whatever you say." The elephant watched happily until the bartender was finished. Then he threw back his martini, shot to the next stool and drank that martini, shot to the next stool and gulped that one, shot to the next stool and..."Hey, elephant, what's going on?" Joe yelled. "Can't you see?" replied the elephant, "I'm going down to the she in sips!"

sit
As the condemned man approached the electric chair he muttered, "This is sit."

sitar
We wanted to hear a little Indian music but couldn't find a baby sitar.

skeleton
Sign outside a graveyard in Singapore: "Due to shortage of manpower, graves will be dug by our skeleton staff."

skeptic
An optimist is an anti-skeptic.

skid
Sign on a tire store: "We Skid You Not."

skipper
The captain took her for his mate but she turned out to be a skipper.

skoal
My nephew Mike was entertaining a new Norwegian friend at a neighborhood bar last week. The Norwegian lifted his drink and said, "Skoal!" "Of course it is," said Mike. "It's got ice in it."

skulduggery
The art of making haggis starts with skulduggery.

slake
The movie director said to his producer, "Those girls we hired for the brothel scene are hinting that they'd like us to go out with them. Would you like to buy some of them a drink?" The producer looked them over and shrugged. "Okay," he said. "When we're through shooting for the day, let's slake five."

slalom
A ski match can be a slalom occasion.

slay
1. The unsuccessful caveman was finally followed to work by his wife. As he stood indecisively among a herd of dinosaurs, his wife cried out in exasperation, "Don't just stand there, slay something!"
2. The pun *is* here to slay.

sleeve
The record store had two versions of Ravel's Bolero, but I don't like the sleeves.

sleigh
The Girl: "Let's go sleighing tonight!"
The Boy: "That could be fun—but I didn't realize you were so bloodthirsty!"

slight
When the masochist married, he admitted it was love at first slight.

slink
The attributes
Of bathing suits
For lasses of lithesome limb
Make me inquire

If this attire
Is worn to slink or swim.

slip
Cartoon caption: "No, no nurse! I said to slip off his spectacles and prick his boil!"

sloe
You can get plum wild if you drink your gin sloe.

sloth
To live in trees
High in the breeze
I'm somewhat loathe.
Perhaps that's why
Although I'm shy
I am not sloth.

slough
If you have a problem with a bunion, you should try *Slough off Despond.*

slug
Our housekeeper is so lazy she would sweep the dust under a slug.

smack
1. Corporal punishment smacks of sadism.
2. That is why the Marquis de Sade never invited anyone for dinner; his friends just dropped in for smacks.

smarmy
The unctious host
Did tend to boast.
Despite a yawn he'd talk to dawn
About his life in the army.
To anyone near
He'd quickly veer
With, "Let me tell you smarmy!"

smart
Social worker: "Tell me, Mrs. Smith, why do you whip your children so often?" "I do it to make them brighter. I never whipped one of them that he didn't acknowledge it made him smart."

smelt
Once the cooking problem was ironed out, the little fish smelt good.

smoke
As the big chimney said to the small chimney, "You're too little to smoke!"

smorgasbord
A disillusioned Swede inserted this ad in the local Swedish newspapers: "I am no longer responsible for my wife's debts. She has left my bed and smorgasbord."

smother
The affection of a big-busted woman is sometimes known as smother love.

snail
Old song: "There's a Long, Long Snail A-Winding."

snake
The Mayor of Upper Upsalquitch seized the animals of an itinerant circus so that his town could have a zoo. Unfortunately, he didn't get a fair snake.

snaky
Using long, thin logs supported by short ones crossed is a snaky way to build a fence.

snitch
Heading on a London *Times* story about a stool pigeon: A Snitch on Crime Saves Time.

snore
1. After serving at sea for a while, sailors are often given snore duty.
2. Marriage often seems a snore and a delusion.

snow
To breathe heavily while sleeping.

soar
1. Icarus was a soar loser.
2. Egotism is an I-soar.

socialist
A confirmed partygoer.

soda
People pour mixed drinks soda party will last.

sodden
Said the recently married husband as he graciously accepted another result of his wife's baking, "This is so sodden!"

Sodom
"Have you seen any of those pornographic films they're showing in town?"
"Not here. I Sodom in New York."

sodomy
1. Triad on tonic sofa. (Italian—from ballad, "O Sodomy-ia.")
2. Also found in U.S. bar lingo:
   "Water, you having?"
   "No, sodomy."

sofa
The amorous male: "How about coming over to my place for a whiskey and sofa?"
The cautious female: "Well, you could talk me into a gin and platonic."

soil
The Reverend Spooner, speaking to a group of farmers: "I have never before addressed so many tons of soil."

soirée
Love is never having to say you're soirée.

sold
A Canadian real estate firm boasts in its advertising that its name is a housesold word.

sole
The bishop had flat feet, rest his soles!

solfa
Vocal music has had its up and downs solfa.

son
An old Indian who had become a millionaire when oil was discovered on his reservation was very pleased when his two sons were finally accepted for membership in an expensive yacht club. For years, it seems, his one ambition had been to see his red sons in the sail set.

soot
When in the frosty midnight
He cruises through the air
What Santa needs for Christmas
Is fur-lined underwear.

But when sliding down the chimney
Toward the bright grate fire
Asbestos pants for Santa
Would be more sootable attire.

sop
A festival of Frankenstein movies
Is not an idea terrific.
They always put me to sleep;
A sort of sop horrific.

sophomore
After you get through your freshman year, you really sophomore.

sordid
Ice cream comes in sordid flavors.

sore
The old sheep clipper's back ached so much from yesterday's work that he couldn't make it back to the farm today. He had to send his young assistant, the sore shearer's apprentice.

SOS
Musical term: The same, only softer. Hence *Sostenuto.*

soul

1. Old puns are like old shoes; they are hard on the soul.
2. In the Vatican, the Pope is the soul proprietor.

soulful

Soulful music is a tonic.

soupçon

Some cooks add a dash
Of this and that to hash.
Others feel they've too far gone,
Just making sure the soupçon.

sour

Envy is sour heritage.

souvenir

The painted surface of a warring Indian.

soviet

Dinner was announced, soviet.

sow

A farmer who loved cows (because he had low tastes) also wanted to love his pigs, but goodness knows sow!

sox

Unisex footgear is known as heterosox.

spaniel

Drake fought doggedly against the Spaniel Armada.

spar

"What is the difference between a timid child and a shipwrecked sailor?" "One clings to his ma and the other to his spar."

spats

Back in the days when diplomats wore spats, their countries didn't have so many.

spay

If you want to do something about altering your cat, it may be consoling to know that the pain in spaying is mostly in the brain.

spear

An explorer in the interior of Africa encountered one tribe whose dexterity with spears astounded him. The chief's aim was particularly unerring. When the explorer produced a half dollar from his tunic, the chief speared it from a distance of fifty yards. He achieved the same result with a quarter. "Now," cried the delighted white man, "let's see if you can score another bull's-eye on this ten-cent piece." The chief demurred. "These tired old eyes of mine aren't what they used to be," he confessed. "Mind if I let my kid brother try it?" With that, he cupped his lips and bellowed, "Brother, can you spear a dime?"

specimen
Italian astronauts.

specious
Theologians have devoted much time to debating the Origin of the Specious.

spectacle
When two monocles get together and make spectacles of themselves, it creates glass distinction.

speculator
A speculator is a sort of endless stairway that keeps running up or down.

spell
1. When young Tommy was asked to spell weather, he took a deep breath and plunged in, "W-A-H-T-I-O-U-R." The teacher regarded him with amazement and said, "Tommy, that is certainly the worst spell of weather we've had around here for years."
2. And when the witch said "Abradacabra!" nothing happened, for she was an even worse speller.

spellbinder
Noah Webster.

spice
1. Plural of spouse—as in the newspaper columns headed "Add Spice to the Lovelorn."
2. A U.S. inventor has developed a way of spraying the odor of herbs on foods and thus creating the world's first aerospice industry.

spilling
At dinner one evening, little Willie upset the soup bowl. Then his older brother Max overturned a dishful of stewed tomatoes. Then sister Mae's slab of roast beef slid off the plate onto her newly laundered frock. Finally, Pop overturned a whole platter of ice cream covered with chocolate sauce. "Congratulations, Pop!" exclaimed his by now thoroughly exasperated wife. "You've won the spilling bee."

spittoon
Popular name for Cuspi D'Or's "Air for the Juice Harp."

spook
A medium is a big wheel with spooks.

spoor
1. As the rabbit said to the skunk, "My scent is spoor but mine own."
2. It was a rather spoorious claim.

sport
Every year, the leopard would win all the races at the Jungle Olympics, but he wasn't satisfied. He decided to try to make the broad jump. But no matter how hard he growled, she wouldn't budge. Which proves that a leopard can't change his sports.

spot
Which is why, when a tourist boasted on his return from Africa that while there he had spotted a leopard, one of his bored listeners said, "Oh, I had thought that they were born that way!"

spray
Confronted by danger, the mother skunk says to her children, "Let us spray."

spree
Headline over a story about a partridge smashing a picture window: "Partridge in a Rare Spree."

spring
"Speaking of bathing in famous springs," said an old tramp who had overheard a tourist, "I recall bathing in the spring of 1929. Of course, a lot of people took a bath that year!"

spy
The diplomat's song: "Can't Take My Spies Off of You."

squeeze play
Modern version of the French bedroom farce.

squid
"The trouble with you," said the psychiatrist to the octopus, "is that you're just a crazy mixed-up squid."

stable
Back in the horse-and-buggy days, they really had a stable economy.

stack
When the leader of the local Ku Klux Klan ordered pancakes, the black waiter put a giant firecracker under the platter and blew his stack.

stag
At the steel mill picnic, you should have seen the young bucks stag around! They finally all ended up on the stag heap.

stagnation
If all the women left the country, it would become a stagnation.

stair
Greta Garbo always took the elevator to avoid the stairs.

stalemate
A man who keeps telling the same old jokes in front of his wife.

stalk
1. If you're not getting enough celery, perhaps you should invest in a few good stalks.
2. Baby Ear of Corn: "Mama, where did I come from?"
   Mama Ear of Corn: "Hush, dear; the stalk brought you."

stall

When the innkeeper offered them accommodation in the stable, Mary whispered to Joseph, "Keep arguing. It's a stall!"

Stamp Act, The

Flamenco dancing.

staph

Colloquial abbreviation of "staphylococcus." The infection can spread so quickly that many firms have an executive in charge of staph relations.

stare

"There's surely one great advantage to short skirts."

"Yes?"

"They make it so much easier for the girls to get up stares."

stationary

They've designed a new automobile intended only for bucking traffic during rush hours on the highways. It's called a stationary wagon.

statutory

Statutory rape occurs when the deed is committed standing up.

steak

A young lawyer tried to call on Judge Mint one evening during the dinner hour. "I'm sorry," the Judge's maid told him firmly, "but His Honor is at steak."

steal

1. Pittsburgh is famous because the people there make iron and steal.
2. Which is worse than plagiarists who read Addison and steal.

steel

But, even so, we can all be steel friends.

steer

They went to the restaurant recommended for its roast beef, but it turned out to be a bum steer.

sterile

An oracle fell into an autoclave and came out a sterile medium.

stern

1. There is a popular music group in England composed entirely of rather plump young ladies. It is called The Rolling Sterns.
2. Steering a boat calls for stern discipline.

Stern, Isaac

Famous concert violinist of whom it was said, "He leaves no tone unSterned."

stew

"Good Heavens! Cannibals!"

"Now, now, let's not get in a stew!"

stick

"What is the secret of success?" asked the Sphinx.

"Push," said the Button.

"Never be led," said the Pencil.

"Take pains," said the Window.

"Always keep cool," said the Ice.

"Be up to date," said the Calendar.

"Never lose your head," said the Barrel.

"Make light of everything," said the Fire.

"Do a driving business," said the Hammer.

"Aspire to greater things," said the Nutmeg.

"Be sharp in all your dealings," said the Knife.

"Find a good thing and stick to it," said the Glue.

stiff

1. The loser in a beauty contest was being consoled by her hometown friend, "I'll bet the competition was stiff!" "No," said the fallen beauty bitterly. "But the judges were!"
2. To become a coroner, you have to take a stiff examination.

stile

For girls in the country, shorts are the best high stile fashion.

stink

After years of moving from one big mining job to another, the disgusted engineer finally exclaimed, "Great mines stink alike!"

stirrup

The cook wanted to serve horsemeat, but she couldn't stirrup any interest.

stitch

A funny accident can leave you in stitches.

stock

1. When the customer can't pay, the printer is stock.
2. "Here, boy," said the man to the city lad who was helping him drive a bunch of cattle, "hold this bull a minute, will you?" "No," answered the boy. "I don't mind bein' a director in this company, but I'm darned if I want to be a stockholder."
3. Or, as the women who sold rotten fruit for the pillory used to say, "Buy now while stocks last!"

stoic

Q. "How did Socrates get to Athens?"

A. "The stoic brought him."

stole

The gangster gave his girl friend a mink stole for Christmas. "Is it really a mink stole?" she gasped. "Well, honey, I can't guarantee that it's genuine mink, but it sure is stole!"

stone

It's a pity some people have to be stoned to get boulder.

stork
1. Pregnancy: The calm before the stork.
2. The reason the stork is associated with birth is that we all come into this world stork naked.
3. A birth announcement is a stork quotation.

stow
Once upon a time, the king of a jungle tribe was given a golden throne by his affectionate people. He was so proud of it—and so afraid of having it stolen—that every night before he went to bed he would hide the throne up on the rafters of his grass hut. Unfortunately, one night the rafter poles broke and the throne fell down and killed him. As the witch doctor later observed, "This certainly proves that people who live in grass houses shouldn't stow thrones."

straight
The first inhabitants of North America were Orientals who came across once they got their bearing straight.

strain
The truss-wearer's philosophy: Into every life a little strain must fall.

Strauss
Vienna—the city of Strauss and strain.

stray
Whatever you may think about Swedish movies, one thing seems certain; sex is here to stray.

stream
An old prospector, stranded in the Nevada wasteland and desperately in need of water, happened on a dry stream bed and then came upon another, only to find that one dry as well. "This," he lamented bitterly, "is what I call going from one ex-stream to another."

strike
The boxer's boast: "I've never met a man I couldn't strike."

strip
A visit to a lakeside beach
Can well be worth the trip;
Especially if you get a laugh
From seeing a comic strip.

stripper
He was afraid to go out with the burlesque queen because he didn't know how to stripper.

strumpet
Guitar player's girl friend.

stubble
Burma Shave roadside advertisement:

My job is keeping
Faces clean,
And nobody knows
The stubble I've seen.

stuck

The missionary was seized by cannibals, tied to a post and jabbed with daggers so that the savages could drink his blood. After a week he told the chief, "Look, I'm tired of being stuck for the drinks!"

stump

A good beaver is never stumped.

stupor

When Carrie Nation, the great suffragette, knocked out a man with her umbrella, a bystander was heard to mutter, "One thing about Carrie, she conks to stupor!"

sturgeon

The biggest operator in the freshwater theater is that old cut-up the sturgeon.

sty

For many a farmer, the price of pork has created a gold mine in the sty.

subpoena

Avant-Garde article title: "Subpeona Envy."

succor

After receiving a number of urgent requests for contributions "because of an emergency" from the badly-managed home for something or other, an exasperated donor wrote the chairman: "I'll have to ask you to remove my name from your succor list."

sucker

Being a headmistress is a job for suckers.

suite

1. When the great Arturo Toscanini first conducted an all-Bach concert, he pushed his orchestra so fiercely and relentlessly in rehearsal that they dubbed him "the Bach Suite Driver."
2. The only room the hotel manager could give them was part of a suite, the other room of which was occupied by a woman who had just been jilted. "If you want it," he told them, "you'll have to take the bitter with the suite."

sulphur

"I like those pretty matches. How much do they sulphur?"

summon

"I have to go to court tomorrow."
"Did you get a summons?"
"No, I think summons got me!"

sun
As Edgar Allan Poe observed, boyhood is a summer sun.

sunny
Comes before money. It's the foist day of the wick.

superficial
Inspector in a soup factory.

supertonic
High-toned product. A major key for people who are having treble with dandruff scales.

support
"Will you marry me?"
"No, I'm afraid not."
"Oh, come on, be a support."

surgeon
1. "My doctor looks nice in white, but I prefer the blue surgeon."
2. Caviar: The eggs of a surgeon.
3. An intern who is willing to keep studying can see himself surgeon ahead.

surplice
Some people regard the priesthood as a good investment because you can be sure of a surplice.

surrey
Song of the buggy thieves: "Whose Surrey Now?"

suture
"Why don't you stop going out with that doctor if he doesn't suture fancy?"

swallow
Fellatio is practiced every spring in Capistrano.

swan
Racing ballad: "Two Harts That Beat a Swan."

swat
Nothing makes one hotter
Than wielding a fly-swatter.
But yet it's all we've got
To teach those flies what's swat.

sway
A demagogue is a man who sways both ends against the middle.

swearing
"I didn't pay much for this suit, but swearing pretty well."

sweater
A divorcee once went to Jersey Island for a vacation because she had heard that there were a lot of rich widowers there. After two hot weeks she came home with a Jersey sweater.

Swede
If you decide to marry a Nordic widower with a large family, you've got to take the litter with the Swede.

swill
1. When pigs are eating they sure have a swill time.
2. Because where there's a swill, there's a whey!

swish
1. A gay daisy chain is a swish kabob.
2. The Queen of the Fairies can grant you your swish.

switch
1. Flagellation requires a switch hitter.
2. It's the switch that turns them on.

sycamore
I'm sycamore poplar trees.

sylph
Why is it that many a woman with a sylphlike figure insists on keeping it to her sylph?

synonym
The word you use when the children are listening.

syntax
What the girls at Madame Fifi's pay the cops.

Norwegians have
a **troll** sense of humor.

T

Even before they learn the alphabet, children discover what is not T.

tabaccer

Colloquial American: "I had a hot tip on a horse called Cigarette, but I didn't have enough tabaccer."

table d'hôte

The young actress discusses her sponsor: "He takes me to all the best restaurants. I just table d'hôte on him."

taboo

When the young missionary first arrived among the Polynesians, he tried politely to ignore their ancient, deep-seated beliefs. However, after living with them for a year he began taboo.

Taché, Sir Etienne

Early Canadian politician said by some to have been the "bag man" for his party; the first man to carry a Taché case.

tack

The aging member of the yacht club resigned, explaining, "I just can't tack it anymore!"

tactile

Although I am out of touch, I have a feeling it is better to glue than to tactile.

tail

"Could you walk a little faster?"
Said the Mountie to his frail.
"The Inspector's right behind us
And he's awfully fond of tail!"

taken
"Can you define matrimony?"
"Yes! You go to adore, you ring a belle, you give your name to a maid—and then you're taken in!"

talc
Acting on odors received, he scent a massage which became the talc of the town.

tale
1. The losing horse has a sad tale.
2. A commuting prostitute has a dickens of a time being the tale of two cities.

tall
It is better to have loved a short girl than never to have loved a tall.

Talmud
A student of Jewish law and legend sometimes has the feeling he is wading through some pretty Talmud.

tamale
One raw winter morning, a lady complained to humorist S.J. Perelman, "It's too cold here in New York!" "Go south of the border," advised Perelman. "It may be Chile there today, but it'll be hot tamale."

tan
Even though he got burned on a lot of deals, he ended up the richest tan in town.

tangle
The eternal triangle is usually right tangled.

tank
1. When Hitler "liberated" France, he surveyed the captured army equipment and muttered, "Is this all the tanks I get?"
2. Obviously, he wasn't very tankful.

tantrum
1. Two-seated bicycle.
2. *Dentists' anterooms*
   Give me tanterooms.

tap
A little prekindergarten girl in Louisiana explained to the playground supervisor that her mother, "tapped for a living." "Well, well, a tap dancer!" nodded the supervisor. "And where all does your mother tap?" Explained the youngster, "On her tapwratter."

tapir
She had sable hare, a small tapir waist
And lips you'd gopher miles to taste.

tar
When the resourceful captain lost a sailor overboard and saw him swallowed

by a whale, he took after the whale in a rowboat and, by the adept handling of an oar, managed to beat the tar out of him.

tarpon
You can always tell when a fishing trip has been a success; the boat comes back with tarpon.

tart
From a newspaper column on astrology: "An early tart helps as you begin to untangle yesterday's discrepancies. By evening you've earned a rest."

tartan
The Scottish call girl was called a tartan worse.

Tarzan
Short name for the American flag. Full name: Tarzan Stripes.

taste
An anthologist is a person who uses scissors and taste.

taut
Walking a tightrope must be taut.

tautological
Commendatory term, as in, "He tautological course free of redundancy and repetition."

taxis
The Americans were driven to the Boston Tea Party by British taxis.

tea
In England, you can get strip teas for one and sex a pot.

teak
It is said that at one point in his famous career, the Oriental detective Charlie Chan took up the hobby of collecting teakwood miniatures. He noticed after a while they were beginning to disappear one by one. Each morning one more would be gone. The only clue was muddy footprints on the floor. To Chan's trained eye they were clearly those of a small, barefoot boy.
On the night when he finally spotted the culprit, you can imagine his surprise when he found that, in reality, it was a black bear with a peculiarity; instead of claws it had feet like a little boy. As the bear snatched up a piece of the teakwood and lumbered off, the detective yelled, "Hey! Where you think you are going, boy-foot bear with teaks of Chan?"

teal
A kind of small freshwater duck so named because when it is feeding on the river bottom, only its teal shows.

team
As St. Jerome observed and every football coach knows, small minds can never handle great teams.

tear
1. *In Boston harbor*

Off the pier
The colonists shed
A final tear.
2. Most puns are not picked from the leaves of any author but bred amongst the weeds and tears of mine own brain.
3. *I would be strong, for there is much to suffer;*
I would be brave, for there is much to tear.

tease
The grass widow abhors the golf tease.

teat
"Our baby is learning to talk!"
"What was the first thing he said?"
"Well, the other morning he woke up and asked us, 'What's teat?'"

tee
Why does a golfer have a handicap?
It's fore putting tee in.

tee-hee
Chinese for waiter.

teens
Adolescent intercourse is a teensters' union.

telepathy
A means of contacting people, invented by William Morse.

Temperate Zone
A region where no one drinks very much.

tempo
The temperamental orchestra leader kept throwing tempo tantrums.

ten
1. Three young ladies were seated in a New York pub. One was called to the phone and was overheard to say "Fine! I'll see you there about eightish!" A few minutes later the second girl was called to the phone. "Nineish? That'll be great!" she said. Left alone, the third girl sighed and stood up. Turning to the men at the bar, she called, "Tennish, anyone?"
2. A cardsharp once had an extraordinary run of big hands and was smart enough to quit before his luck changed.
"Not another hand, gentlemen," he announced firmly as he cashed in his chips. "I intend to fold my tens and silently steal away."
3. The British lady of the night grew old and realized that she could no longer charge her former price. There was nothing for it but to change the tenner of her ways.

tennis
There once was a young lad who was counting on his Uncle Al to take him to the circus. On the big day, however, his mother told him that his Uncle Al had flown to Australia to see the Davis Cup tennis matches. "I didn't know

Uncle Al liked that game so much, Mom," mourned the lad. "Oh, but he does," she assured him. "Many's the time I've heard Alfred laud tennis, son!"

tequila
Charged with trying to push his girl friend out of a window, the Mexican protested, "We were just dancing. I wasn't trying tequila!"

termite
Termites are boring. They work with all termite.

tern
There's an odd type living in Sausalito who spends his entire day throwing rocks at sea gulls. He leaves no tern unstoned.

terrorize
"If that girl doesn't leave my husband alone, I'll terrorize out."

terse
The fit day of the wick.

Teutonic
Not enough gin.

Texas
The deadline for filing tax returns arrived. It was what Uncle Oscar used to call "The Night of the Big Snow." "Chico," said Groucho Marx sadly, "the time has come to discuss our taxes." "Datsa where my friend Ravelli lives," said Chico. "No, no," corrected Groucho. "Not Texas. Taxes. The dollars we have to pay the government." "Datsa what I said," insisted Chico. "Dallas, Texas."

Thai
A Siamese twin has a strong family Thai.

thaw
In feeding cowboys, all the modern cook has to know is how to be quick on the thaw.

theirs
A massage parlor often
Offers more than a scrub.
Yours is the risk
And theirs the rub.

thesis
Cryptic comment on a returned college essay: "Thesis awful!"

thick
Overeating will make you thick to your stomach.

thigh
1. One of America's financial experts believes that the market goes up along with a rise in ladies' skirts. Glamor stocks and miniskirts soared in 1967; the conglomerates and hemlines went down together in the spring of 1968.

Hot pants led the Dow Jones up in 1971. His moral: "Don't sell until you see the heights of their thighs."

2. In order to see them properly, you really need thigh-focals.

thing
Misspelling (U.S.) of English *think*. Exemplified in the poem:
A thing that I shall never see
Is a poem as lovely as a tree...

thirst
There is a bar in Tucson, Arizona, that has a sign reading, "Thirst come, thirst served."

Thomas, Ambroise
1. Composer of well-known opera *Filet Mignon*, from whence the aria, "Thomas These Days!"
2. (He catered Thomas appeal.)

thongs
What Thinatra things.

Thor
A Scandinavian god who, upon meeting the goddess Juno for the first time, announced, "I am Thor." To which she replied, "Well, come up and see me sometime—when you feel better."

thorax
Juno was a little disappointed with the thorax.

thrall
When Eric the Red returned home after discovering the New World, he brought back an Indian as a present for his mother. Later, she confided to a friend, "Eric has given me the thrall of a lifetime!"

three
A golfer who had the temerity to play on Christmas Day got into trouble. His first drive, on a short hole, went into the rough and hit a bird. He interpreted it as an omen and went home, for it was the first time he had seen a partridge on a par three.

throat
When the motion picture *Deep Throat* was first shown to the New York censors, one turned to the other at the conclusion and demanded, "What should we do with this filth?" The other grimaced and muttered, "Throat out!"

throne
Past tense of "throw." Example: When the African king tried to introduce contraceptives, he was throne for a loop.

through
Through puns we may someday understand why Alice through the looking-glass.

throw
1. The baseball pitcher had to play despite an injured arm. He was in the throws of agony.
2. Alice had a very bad temper for a little girl. That is why she threw the looking-glass.
3. Elbert Hubbard observed that a toreador is the power behind the thrown.

thrust
When New York's *Village Voice* ran a letter to the editor protesting the way a reader thought the paper was deifying sex, it appeared under the heading, "In God We Thrust."

thug
Any member of an Indian religious organization of assassins that was suppressed when the government made it illegal to play thug of war.

thumb
The Roman sports audiences used the thumb in voting on performances. Hence our phrase, "To thumb up the case."

thumbscrew
An awkward social gesture.

thyme
"Excuse me," said Basil to Rosemary sagely, "do you have the thyme?"

Tibet
First Chinese television show: "Tibet Your Life."

ticket
Closely planted bushes.

tide
In the boundless ocean, a father drop and a mother drop decided to teach their young offspring how to be a responsible part of the sea. After a month of intensive training, the father drop observed his son's performance with satisfaction and announced to the mother drop, "I believe we've taught Junior everything he has to know. I hereby declare him fit to be tide."

tie
Two boy silkworms were trying to score with a girl silkworm, but they ended up in a tie.

tier
For years, the residents of a mountain area in Italy farmed the slopes in carefully-constructed tiers. Then one day a prophet passed by and predicted that, for the first time in history, it was going to snow. Dismayed, the farmers wrote to Rome for advice on what to do. After some delay a tony young man appeared and said, "If you have tiers prepare to shed them now."

tight
Manufacturers of ballet costumes are always defending their tights.

tile
The owner of the new restaurant pointed to his floor with pride. "Those are genuine ceramics—imported from Austria," he boasted. When his guest did not look impressed, he protested, "Surely you've heard of the tiles from the Vienna woods?"

till
Organic gardeners till it like it is.

time
Coleridge lived during the time of The Ancient Mariner.

tin
It's said that the British army officer of the Kipling era began his career in childhood, playing with toy soldiers and the tin red line.

tine
She started going out with rakes and fell on hard tines.

tinkle
We really shouldn't do this to Shirley Temple Black, but it has been reported that when she first became a child movie star she was so nervous that she frequently had to go to the little girl's room. It is said that the film director would then yell, "Cut!" and wave her off the set, muttering to himself, "tinkle, tinkle, little star."

Tipperary
A song written during World War I as part of an abortive British campaign to teach generosity to the Scots. ("Rarie" is Scottish for "rare one.")

tire
1. One night, a car pulled up beside a convertible parked on a lonely road. The kindly car driver called, "Out of gas?" "Nope!" "Tire down?" "Nope! Didn't have to!"
2. Actually, the couple in the convertible were tireless.

titillate
A tardy meal for a breast-fed baby.

titmouse
Someone too timid to go to a burlesque.

titter
A titter ran through the audience—but he was soon arrested.

toboggan
The reason you attend an auction.

tocking
The little old clockmaker had a nightmare: He thought he heard the ticking tocking.

tog
1. In London's Saville Row there is a store that advertises "Mad Togs for

Englishmen."

2. Battledress: A tog of war.

toga

The sack of Rome.

told

1. Thomas Hood in "Faithless Sally Brown":
His death, which happened in his berth,
At forty-one befell;
They went and told the sexton
And the sexton tolled the bell.

2. Q. What did the puppy lisp when he sat down in the snow?
A. "My tail is told."

tome

1. Book on voyeurism: A peeping tome.
2. Do you feel a tome with a book?

tong

Trouble brewed in San Francisco's Chinatown recently, and Mayor E. Lee was earmarked for liquidation. The bullet, unfortunately, clipped an innocent bystander, Harry Lee. The following morning, Harry's widow received a note: "Please excuse. Mere slip of tong."

tongue

1. The battle of the sexes is really a tongue war.
2. The French art of self-defense is called Tongue Fu.
3. An advertising man has come up with the idea of putting slogans on the backs of postage stamps so that when you lick one, you'll go around for the rest of the day with the slogan on the tip of your tongue.

tonsure

When Samson was bald out, he became a bit tonsure of himself.

too

1. Ballet costumes are just too too.
2. Johann Sebastian was getting on in years when a neighbor's little girl asked him for a piggyback ride. "Carry me, Bach!" "Too old, Virginny!"

tool

Asked why he was still using a bent stick for hoeing, the happy hooker replied, "There's no tool like an old tool."

toot

1. A Los Angeles trumpet player has been sued for divorce. His wife claims he was toot-timing her with a tooty-fruity.
2. Old Hornblower was boasting about being an entirely self-educated man. Sneerwell, who heard him, said, "Ah, I understand! You were at a school where every man was his own tooter."

top

Shed a tear for the man who for one season played the French horn for a famous civic orchestra. In the middle of the opening symphony, his toupee fell into his instrument, and he spent the rest of the evening blowing his top.

Toronto
As sports promoter Jack Kent Cooke once remarked, "When you hit the ball you have Toronto first base."

torrid
There was a little girl
Who had a little curl
Right in the middle of her forehead.
When she was good
She was very, very good,
But when she was bad,
She was torrid.

tortuous
"I tortuous going to ask me out!"

toss
The trail horses at Jasper, Alberta, have minds of their own. But they are good sports: When one tourist insisted that his horse turn left and the horse wanted to turn right, the horse tossed him for it.

totter
Liquor is a form of totter sauce.

Toulouse-Lautrec
The famous French painter was once invited home by a *demi-mondaine* who asked, "What have you got, Toulouse?"

toupee
If anyone mentioned his bald spot there was hell toupee.

tour
1. "The twins are always together wherever they go; the tour inseparable."
2. Switzerland is very picturesque with its mountains touring among the clouds.
3. A couple of madams in Manhattan have opened their own travel agency. They call it The Tour House.

tourniquet
Tournament for croquet players.

track
Rather than be tied down, the railway worker's daughter made tracks for a better station in life.

tract
"Jehovah's Witnesses have tract me down!"

trail
A Mountie learns by trail and error.

tram

Running a street railway is just one tram thing after another.

tramp

1. When Marilyn Monroe was asked to appear onstage in the nude, she was advised against it by a friend, who told her, "It will tramp your style."
2. A poacher is a tramp in the woods.

transvestite

A special restrictive garment from the Transvaal. Used after puberty rites (*droits des publicains*) to keep young males from getting up tight.

Traubel, Helen

Famous opera singer. As Edward Johnson, when manager of the New York Opera Company, once remarked, "Nobody knows the Traubel I've seen!"

trauma

A psychiatrist is really a trauma critic.

tray

A homosexual waiter: tray gay.

tree

When former Israeli Premier Meir ordered the Suez Canal reopened to make the area easier to defend, the area was defoliated. In consequence, it became known as Golda Locks and the Bare Trees.

trek

Being routed along muddy roads is a dirty trek.

trend

The pressures of being in the fashion business drove the dress designer right around the trend.

trial

Unsure of how to handle the one girl arrested among a group of male offenders, the judge decided to trial the others first.

tried

1. "I see that you are drinking coffee, Judge. Have you ever tried gin and ginger ale?" "No, but I've tried several men who have."
2. Puberty is that time in every girl's life when she is fit to be tried.

trifle

Come, my love, and let me
Cover thee with confections—
Bananas, sponge cake, sherry—
And trifle with thy affections.

trigonometry

Being married to three people at the same time.

trillium

An aggressive florist can make a trillium.

trip
A travel folder is a trip-tease.

trite
Most of the best-selling paperbacks today come from the trite side of the racks.

troll
Norwegians have a troll sense of humor.

tropical
The Zulu is a tropical subject.

trot
The two diseases jockeys fear most are galloping consumption and the trots.

troubadour
In the third act of *Il Trovatore* we see the hero emerging through the troubadour.

trout
Without much urgin'
The sturgeon
With a swish
Puts other fish
Trout.

trowel
Although the construction of the new skyscraper was going well, one bricklayer suddenly lost interest in the entire project and threw in the trowel.

truss
After Madame LeGros told her friends what her *corsetier* had tried to do to her in the fitting room, he felt he couldn't truss her anymore.

try
A ne'er-do-well in Nantucket is so well known for his repeated failures that they call him "the Town Tryer."

tryst
Priest to altar boy: "Fear not, my son. In God we tryst."

tsar
If and when Russia again becomes a monarchy, the leader presumably will be a commie tsar.

tuber
The grasshopper is something of a singer, but the potato bug is a real musician. He plays on the tuber.

Tuck, Friar
He was once punished by being shut in an icehouse. This was widely deplored, since even then it was not considered sporting to ice the Tuck.

Tudor
The reason England has so many Tudor castles is that Henry VIII always liked to have an extra exit.

tuft
Worry causes falling hair: When the going gets tough, the tufts get going.

tug
1. In the Second World War the corvette was known as a tug of war.
2. That was stretching it a bit. The corvette had some design problems. It took the navy a while to get the tugs out.

tulip
A single rose
Can oft disclose
A love that's growing.
But if what's showing
Is a love to be won
Tulips are better than one.

tulle
A fine silk net used for veils and dresses. First created by French tulle and dye makers.

tumtum
Africans beat their tumtums because they can stomach the sound.

tune
Mozart was an opera-tunist.

turd
The elephant-keeper's complaint
Which he frequently cries in a scream,
Is that pachyderms show no restraint—
And that is the turd man theme.

turn
A maid at the Waldorf Astoria once got fired because she couldn't turn down a bed.

turnip
A speculative farm crop: "Let's plant it and see what'll turnip."

turtle
An elephant, finding a turtle at the edge of his favorite watering hole, stepped on it and crushed it into the mud. When asked by the king of the beasts why he had done so, he replied "Thirty years ago, when I was very small, that turtle bit my ankle. And, as you know, elephants have turtle recall."

tutti-frutti
A gay taxi driver.

twain
A train operated by a Norwegian-American engineer starts from Albany to

New York just as a train with a drunken engineer leaves New York for Albany. There's only one track, no switches or sidings, yet the trains do not collide. Why?

Because Norse is Norse and souse is souse and never the twains shall meet.

tweet

1. Uncle Oscar once reported that a neighboring farmer had a problem: Birds persisted in building nests in the mane of his favorite horse. A vet finally advised him to put yeast in the horse's mane, promising that then the birds would up and fly away. And they did, too. All of which proves, observed Uncle Oscar, that yeast is yeast and nest is nest and never the mane shall tweet.
2. Birds make tweet music.

twerp

An American adaptation and abbreviation of "terpischorian." A twerp (terp) is a man who gets caught short on the dance floor.

two

A bigamist is one who has loved not wisely but two well.

typhoon

A banker speaking sometimes sounds like a business typhoon.

tyrant

Conversation while dressing.

Tzigane

Hungarian gypsy washroom.

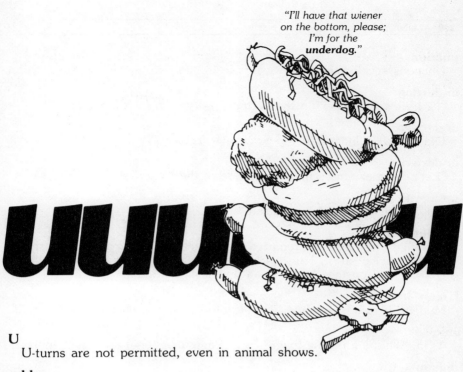

*"I'll have that wiener
on the bottom, please;
I'm for the
underdog."*

U
U-turns are not permitted, even in animal shows.

udder
When both contestants claimed to have won hands down, the milking contest ended in udder chaos.

ulcer
A county in Northern Ireland where a lot of Irishmen can't stomach one another.

umber
1. North American Indian word for rain. Most famous Indian rain dancer: Umber Ella.
2. The tourists pour applause when she does her umber.

umbilicus
Navel profanity, directed toward that part of early sailing ships where the humble (seamen) were billeted.

umbrage
Scottish place-name; the brage on the river Um (near Loch Jaw).

umpire
A judge or referee. Word originated in U.S. (New England area) as applied to one who judged baking at country fairs.

unanimous
"Why do you agree with me so completely all the time?" demanded Nan's husband. "That's why I think unanimous!"

unction
Unctions speak louder than words.

underdog
"I'll have that wiener on the bottom, please; I'm for the underdog."

underwear
Old song: "I Underwear My Sweetie Is Tonight?"

underwrite
"Let's keep expenses underwrite side of the ledger."

undulate
"I like watching dancers undulate show."

uninhibited
A United Press dispatch reported happily that a yachtsman feared lost in a violent Pacific storm has been found safe and cheerful. "He had been shipwrecked on the shores of an uninhibited island."

Union Jack
Mythical British hero who always flew to the rescue when courage flagged.

unique
As in, "This is a unique town." From Latin unus (one) and equus (horse).

unison
Offspring of unisex.

unsuited
An artist's model is a girl unsuited for her work.

up
Some days, it is better to stay in bed and avoid all the up evils.

upshot
John Wilkes Booth was guilty of the upshot.

upstairs
Kilted Highlanders are wary of the upstairs.

Uranus
Astronomer to offended female assistant:
"All I said was,'I can see Uranus quite clearly tonight'!"

urchin
Oliver Twist wasn't a bad boy, but someone was always urchin him on.

urination
Overheard in a UN washroom: "Urination of strange people."

urn
1. Potter's motto: "One good urn deserves another."
2. "What's a Grecian urn?"
   "Oh, about twenty drachmas a week after taxes."
3. "Of course, some have higher urning power," he added, evasively.

Uruguay

Groucho Marx in *Animal Crackers*: "You go Uruguay—and I'll go mine!"

utter

It's hard to survive on bread and utter nonsense.

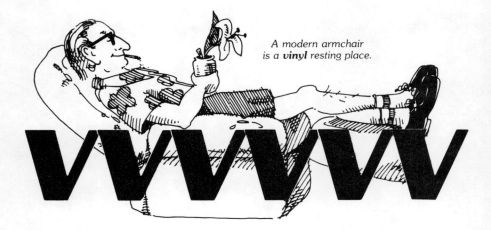

*A modern armchair is a **vinyl** resting place.*

V

And where do V go from here?

valet

After Howard Greene became famous as a designer of men's clothing, a pretentious gentleman wrote an article entitled, "How Greene Was My Valet."

vamp

The famed Lili Marlene of the Second World War was often seen in vamp light.

vampire

During a period when scandal rocked Great Britain as lord after lord was accused of consorting with ladies of ill fame, it was observed that, contrary to the North American practice, England tended to condemn the men, not the prostitutes. Apparently, the sin never sets on the British vampire.

van

1. A special truck designed for transporting hot foods is known as an "O" van.
2. But you never know van it will come.

Vandyke

A truck-driving lesbian.

vane

The cat on a hot tin roof is not a vane creature.

vanilla

Capital of the Philippines.

vanish
To make spots on floors disappear you should vanish them.

vapid
San Francisco has a vapid transit system.

vas
Would a male pill make a vas deferens?

vase
The very place
For flowers
Is a vase.
But if it has some flaws,
It may become
The vase that vase.

vassal
In feudal days, the laws were so stringent that a vassal couldn't have a leek.

vast
1. Texas is so proud of its size that it now has a military academy known as "Vast Point."
2. It is sponsored by the vasted interests.
3. Not to be confused with the school in the east, which is the vast of the Mohicans.
4. Or vast undertakings based on half-vast ideas.

Vat 69
The Pope's telephone number.

vault
After a stockbroker in San Francisco had illegally borrowed his customers' securities, he made the error of putting back too many and got a stiff sentence for being generous to a vault.

veal
As the eager bull explained to the reluctant cow, "You're only as young as you veal."

veil
Women's Lib: Tote that barge, lift that veil.

vein
A coal miner is a vein man.

vendetta
A lunch shared by vendor and vendee.

veneer
An ambitious Indian decorated his new wigwam with costly baubles, purchased via the mail-order catalogue. His neighbor, miffed because the new wigwam was getting too much attention, disparaged his effort and sneered, "Cheap Sioux veneer!"

Venice
Italian query, as in "Venice the next gondola?"

ventilate
It got stuffy around ten because the air conditioner only ventilate.

venture
"Sammy, you are now old enough to seek your fortune. It is time you venture way."

vermilion
This is what the pigment when he fell in the red paint and boasted, "I'm one in vermilion!"

verse
Just remember—no matter how bad these puns may be, it could be verse!

versify
The temptation is great
To quote or orate
From the words of the authors of prose.
Of course, I could do versify chose.

version
How Queen Elizabeth I was referred to in her period.

vertigo
An elderly lady hesitated at a busy intersection. A gentleman, noting her confusion, inquired, "Have you vertigo, Madam?." "Yes, I do," she replied. "Almost a mile."

vesper
In a church, it is an accepted custom never to talk above a vesper.

vest
1. A clothing salesman returned to New York from California feeling very happy because he had the vest all buttoned up.
2. Later, his employer got a call from a supplier. Two-piece suits were becoming popular and the supplier wanted to warn the employer that, in pushing three-piece suits, his salesman had made a vest mistake.

vestry
In churches, a device on which to hang vestments.

viability
1. Original spelling: vieability. Refers to competitive spirit in garment districts.
2. Used as term of flattery with respect to inquisitive Jewish children.

viaduct
Old vaudeville repartee: "You wanna viaduct?"
"Viaduct?" "It's cheaper than a goose!"

vicar
Candy is dandy but the vicar is quicker.

vicarious
"We can cross this rope bridge by ourselves. Vicarious?"

vice
1. A pornographer is one who offers a vice to the lovelorn.
2. Christ wanted to be a carpenter like his father, but he had no vices.
3. As the priest whispered to the young tart in the front pew, "What's a vice girl like you doing in a place like this?"
4. Offended by an item in that famous trade journal of show business, an actor commented, "*Variety* is the vice of life."

vice versa
Dirty Italian poetry.

vicious
"Best vicious for a Merry Christmas!"

view
"I chose this cliff to propose because I love view."

vigil
"I don't mind working at Homer nights but vigil keeps me awake."

vile
1. It was known as "The Fiddle Hotel" because it was such a vile inn.
2. Instruments in a school orchestra includes viles, strumpets, hornets, baboons and old boys.

villain
A wolf is a man who is ready, villain and able.

vim
She left the young man for the old because she'd had her fill of vim.

vinyl
Modern armchair: A vinyl resting place.

violate
In his youth he was very aggressive, but he hasn't been able to violate.

violet
That's why violet him.

V.I.P.
"You can tell I'm a man by the V.I.P."

viper
A snaky way of cleaning windshields.

virgin
As the clown said when a nun watching the circus parade from her balcony fell on him, "This is virgin on the ridiculous!"

virtuoso
Japanese virgin.

virus
Syphilis is the ultra virus.

visa
Passport endorsement permitting immigration (from: "visa friendly people").

viscount
Nobleman ranking below earl or count (from an estimate of his wealth: "He's so rich viscount?").

vise
"What's that you have there?"
"A clamp."
"Oh, so you're a vise guy!"

vituperation
Sir Winston Churchill recovered easily from illnesses because he had great powers of vituperation.

vivisection
The cry of Italian celibates.

vixen
A female fox
Met Goldilocks
En route to greet her bears.
Said Goldie sweetly,
"I'm completely
"Confused in my affairs.
"But come along;
"You may be strong
"Enough for vixen chairs."

vocal
Laryngitis is a sort of vocal anesthetic.

vocation
The priesthood is vocation without pay.

vodka
As the American cried when he saw his first Russian cocktail waitress, "Vodka girl!"

void
Chasm is a nasty void.

volley
War is volley.

volt
1. Place where people get buried.

2. The electric volt is named after Voltaire who was a shocking person.
3. He's currently in a cell in a state of shock waiting foraday for the circuit judge because he's charged with battery on the tube. Although he conducts himself well and offers no resistance, he refuses all food and asks, "Wire my insulate? I want to go ohm. Watt have I done? It wasn't my volt!"

vortex
The cost of conflict.

vowel
1. The growing use of profane speech is basically a vowel movement.
2. When it came to the language of love, his performance wasn't consonant with his promise; but he certainly knew how to vowel.

vulgar
1. The decimal system has its points, but fractions are often vulgar.
2. The most famous Russian is The Vulgar Boatman.

vying
The entrepreneur is a vying breed.

__West__ is what wabbits do
when they get tired of wunning awound.

W

Siamese twins occur most often among humans. For example, you seldom see a W.

wac

Member of The Coldcream Guards and the reason why so many soldiers, returning from leave, report that they are all wacked out.

wade

"Sure I'd like to swim! Can you wade a minute?"

wafer

Laxatives should be taken in wafer form. You just swallow one and wafer results.

waffle

"I see in the papers that a guy ate six dozen pancakes."
"Oh, how waffle!"

wail

1. Jonah had a wail of an experience.
2. "We have a United Kingdom family. My father is English, my mother is Irish. Our nurse is Scottish. And the baby wails."

waist

Everyone felt sorry for the Hunchback of Notre Dame because they hated to see his head go to waist.

wait

Senator from Alabama: "Think we should start a filibuster?"
Senator from Mississippi: "Yes, Ah do. It's time we threw our wait around."

waive
1. On his first visit to England, an ambitious American tried to crash a party at Buckingham Palace, but was tossed out on his derriere. Picking himself up gingerly, he observed, "Evidently Britannia will not waive the rules."
2. A pacifist is a flag-waiver.

wallaby
Australian cradlesong.

wallet
There is a clever artist in Peking who cultivates carp in his garden pool. When the carp attain full growth, he catches them, skins them and makes wallets out of the skins. He is, in fact, the only man in his country noted for carp to carp walleting.

Walpurgisnacht
From Germany comes the story of the fraulein whose hopes were Brocken by her Hartz desire. She was willing to find Saxony place and finally got Walpurgisnacht up.

wan
The director of the summer theater broke the news to the cast just before curtain time on opening night: The makeup kit had not arrived from the city. "But we are troopers," he reminded them. "The show must go wan!"

wand
The nice thing about being a fairy queen is that you can have anything you wand.

wane
1. After having been subjected to innumerable speeches of welcome, Prince Philip of England is alleged to have sighed, "It never wanes but it bores."
2. After many years, it finally became apparent that General Franco's reign in Spain was clearly on the wane.

wanton
1. The mini-skirt was tried and found wanton.
2. Many men believe that the heavier a girl is, the sexier she is. That is why they like wanton women.

ward
Half the fun of being an intern is the play on wards.

warm
Cargoes of rare birds were shipped to England from various European airports to stock a new zoo. Various instructions accompanied the valuable shipments. One set dealt with a tropical bird that had been shipped from the French air base at Orly near Paris. If the temperature wasn't high enough, the instructions said, the handlers were to use a small coat that had been sent along. The English air expressmen were totally confused by all the different instructions when the cargoes began arriving. "Does this coat go on the bird from Copenhagen?" one of them shouted. A mate who had read

the rules more closely shouted back, "No, it's the Orly bird that gets the warm."

wash

1. In stockbroker terminology, a "wash" (or "wash sale") is when someone is taken to the cleaners. Hence the injunction, "Wash it, Mac!"
2. When the ship sank, he grabbed a bar of soap and washed himself ashore.

Washington

Famous U.S. laundry known for its dexterity with dirty linen in bulk.

washout

The New Yorker was expecting a friend to arrive by train. Instead, he received a telegram: "Cannot come. Washout on line." He wired back promptly, "Don't worry. I'll lend you a shirt."

watch

Preoccupied with looking at the pretty girl farther down the bar, the newly-arrived young man said to the bartender, "I'll have a Scotch and watch her."

water

"Water, water everywhere—but not a drop to drink! Water we going to do?"

watt

Soon the power companies will be charging Heaven knows watt!

Watteau

A British expression.

wax

Forced to miss his golf game in order to clean floors, the husband waxed indignant.

weak

Doomsday is the last day of the weak.

weasel

At one time weasels were so prevalent in rural America that the trains had to make weasel stops.

weather

The meteorologist admitted, "We don't really know weather it will rain or shine."

wedlock

Socrates died from too much wedlock.

wee

If you've had your cough for seven days it's only a wee cold.

weed

1. Colloquialism, as in "Weed rather smoke than drink."
2. A gardening columnist got a letter crying for help from a suburbanite who despairingly signed himself "Constant Weeder."

week
Every dog has his day. And those with broken tails have their week ends.

weevil
Two boll weevils decided to give up farming and try their luck in the big city. One of them married the daughter of a rich termite and had a boll. The other failed at everything he tried and became known as the lesser of two weevils.

weigh
He crept up to the scales, stealthily dropped in a slug and silently stole a weigh.

weight
If you want an opportunity to be a jockey, you must weight for it.

weird
Horror-movie dialogue: "weird of mouth."

wench
The plumber insisted that the conductor stop the train and let him off. When asked why, he explained, "I'm on my honeymoon, and I've forgotten my wench!"

west
What wabbits do when they get tired of wunning awound.

wether
A castrated ram
Is not worth a dam.
He sighs a lot and never
Finds cows in heat
A special treat.
It's always gloomy wether.

whale
1. There is a whale who has retired from work at Marineland, Florida. But he still hangs around, cadging snacks from the tourists. In fact, he is becoming a real ne'er-do-whale.
2. Two Englishmen, alone in London for an evening, were discussing what to do. "Shall we go the flicks?" one suggested. "They're showing *Moby Dick*."
   "No, thanks!" exclaimed the other. "I detest sex films."
   "Oh, but this is about whales!"
   "Even worse," his friend said with a shudder. "I can't stand Welshmen!"

what
To be or not to be. What is the question?

whelp
The dog ran down the path, emitting whelps at every bound.

where
"Clothes are to where."

whether
Marvin is a meteorologist; he can look into a girl's eyes and tell whether.

whey
The Kurds have a whey of their own.

whine
1. Rise and whine.
2. The wealthy malcontent lives a life that is all whine, women and song.

whirl
Baton twirling is being taught in some areas as a school subject—but whirl it all lead?

whisker
The reason it is so hard to understand hippies is that you can't always hear a man who is talking below a whisker.

white
The minute Mr. Wong saw their new baby he started to protest, for it is well known in the Orient that two Wongs don't make a white.

whittle
Two tourists went to visit a wood-carver in the Black Forest. The American tourist was impressed with the man's volume of output and exclaimed, "Whittle man, you've had a busy day!" The German visitor was impressed with the fact that the American was impressed and cried, "Heil, whittler!"

who
The baby owl was just learning to talk. It kept saying "What? What?" until its wise old father explained, "Son, it's not 'What,' you know. It's 'Who' you know!"

whoa
The inexperienced rider returned his horse to the stables at The Greenbrier. (Actually, the horse returned him.) "This horse is very badly trained," he complained to the groom. "I'm sorry, sir," replied the groom. "We're very busy right now and I haven't time to listen to your tale of whoa."

whole
1. Confucius say, "Seven days on honeymoon make one whole week."
2. A New York fish store calls itself "Wholly Mackerel."

wholesale
The ambitious farmer was advised to go into the wholesale business, so he bought some well-drilling equipment.

whore
1. Song of the temporarily rejected husband: "The Menstrual Boy to the Whore Has Gone."
2. For those who like to wrestle, the madam can sometimes provide a whore de force.

3. "Well!" exclaimed the bank teller as he surveyed the bag of coins the small-town girl had brought for deposit. "Did you hoard all these by yourself?" "Oh, no, sir!" she replied. "My sister whored half of them."
4. Predicting the future of prostitution calls for a study of whorescopes.
5. A stag party sometimes turns into a whore show.

whorl
A police captain was shown two sets of fingerprints of a suspected robber. "These can't belong to the same man," he objected. "They're whorls apart."

why
Perhaps our foreword should have been entitled, "A Word to the Whys."

wick
The candlemakers are pulling for longer wick ends.

wicked
Advertisement: "FOR SALE, good mahogany bed table and wicked bath chair."

wicket
Although she used to fence with men, they loved her wicket gate.

widow
Advertisement: "Gardens dug, chimneys swept and widows washed."

wiener
American staple of diet named after Wien R. Schnitzel, famous Austrian chef who also gave his name to fast cooking (¾ time) as in the common cry of American youth: "Wiener we gonna eat?" and jocularly of cooking mistakes: "Wien R. blew it."

wife
1. Recipe for the ideal marriage: A short wife and a merry one.
2. A word to the wife is sufficient.

wiggle
Don't shake your head or the wiggle slip.

will
Going through the woods one day, a man came upon a boy with an apple on his head and a stopwatch in his hand. "What are you trying to do?" asked the man. Without moving, the boy answered out of the side of his mouth, "Time Will Tell."

wilt
A minister asked a nervous bridegroom, "Wilt thou take this woman as thy lawful wedded wife?" The groom stammered, "I wilt."

Wimbledon
English site of famous annual wimble matches, i.e., place where you can see the wimble done. (Wimble is a British jumping sport. Hence, "Jack be wimble. Jack be quick. Jack jump over the candlestick!")

wind
This word appears in several contexts:
1. In sports: "Who wind?"
2. At cocktail parties: "Wind we run out?"
3. In poetry (where license allows it to rhyme with "bind"):
   In Boston on a Saturday night
   Beans are a fare you often find
   And many a Bostonian has passed on
   After he has dined and wind.

winding
An eccentric bachelor passed away and left a nephew nothing but 365 clocks. The nephew now works full time winding up the estate.

window
The glazier took up gambling because he thought he knew how to window.

windrow
A married couple, educated but down on their luck, became itinerant farm workers and were hired by a woman rancher to harvest her hay crop. Since rainy weather was coming, she impressed upon her new hands the need for speed and long hours. She also urged them to be careful of the hay, for she wanted to exhibit the best of her crop at the Annual Fair. The pair worked long past sunset to cut the hay and place it in the neat lines necessary for proper drying. In the dark, somehow both cut themselves with their scythes. There was only one Band-Aid so the husband tore it in half and shared it with his helpmate. "You know," he said, as he covered his wife's wound, "this is romantic. Sort of share an aid in the night by a Fair lady's windrow."

wine
1. "Wine earth not stop drinking?"
2. "I will wine you will."
3. Champagne is the wine of least resistance.

wink
Flirting is just wishful winking.

wiper
Cleopatra instituted the practice of keeping a handkerchief tucked in her cleavage and thus became famous for taking a wiper to her bosom.

wire
As the tightrope walker asked himself, "Wire we here?"

wisp
Once upon a time, a domineering he-man married a mere wisp of a girl. He came back from his honeymoon a chastened groom, all too well aware of the will-o'-the-wisp.

witch
Back in the early days of New England, everybody went around wondering which was witch.

witless
Astronauts drift around in space because they are witless.

woe
If the Women's Lib movement's
Progress is slow,
Perhaps it's because
We instinctively know
If you take "men" from "women,"
You've nothing but woe.

wolf
The fat bachelor; all wolf and a yard wide.

womb
Twins usually get along well together because they start out as wombmates.

wombat
An Australian dildo.

wood
Sticks float.
They wood.

woodchuck
How much wood would the woodchuck chuck if the woodchuck could chuck wood?

wooden
I bought a wooden whistle
but it wooden whistle.
I bought a steel whistle
but it steel wooden whistle.
So I bought a tin whistle
and now I tin whistle!

word
1. A woman's word is never done.
2. When the Mormon message was brought forth from the wilderness, Brigham Young quickly realized that a Word in the hand...

worn
"Is anything worn under your kilt?"
"No, it's all in working order."

worship
It takes a good worship to defend the sees.

wound
Because of his wound
He swooned.
She left with a bound
And said, "See you wound!"

wow
Modern poetry makes "Sonnets from the Portuguese" seem pallid. Today's poet is more apt to start off, "Wow! Do I love thee!"

wrangle
Every time a new state is admitted into the American union and a new star added to the flag, someone refers to it as "the star-wrangled banner."

wrap
When the robbers held up the fur store, the leader ran off with the cash and left his accomplice to take the wrap.

wrath
We were wrathed this morning. Having ablutioned in the bathroom and repasted at the table, we agaped at how anyone could have so abased the English language. Two items had been newspapered and two nouns had been verbed: "Another western premiered on TV" and "Comedy show debuted." Really! We nearly corpsed but decided we'd wrather not.

wreck
1. Hollywood triangles usually end up as wreck tangles.
2. His unfortunate choice of mates left Jocasta and Oedipus wrecks.
3. "What's that quivering down there on the ocean's floor?"
   "Perhaps it's a nervous wreck!"

wrestler
Warning sign outside an apartheid-conscious South African sports arena: "The Wrestlers Are Native Tonight."

wretch
1. One of the most famous men in English history was King Wretched the Lyinghearted.
2. An American columnist once described an unhappy heiress as, "that poor little wretch girl."

wring
The London madam, disgusted with the way her girls left lingerie dripping in the bathroom, finally posted a sign on the mirror that read "Wring out, wild belles!"

writ
The Legal Eagle:
Antagonists find it hard
To flout him;
He always has
His writs about him.

write
1. Ladies' room graffiti: squatters' writes.
2. From a newspaper story: "In an Everton attack, Royle was injured and lay writing in the center of the field."

writhe
In addition to the different branches of arithmetic—ambition, distraction, uglification and derision—Lewis Carroll wrote that education consists of reeling and writhing.

wrung
He would have died of thirst if he hadn't wrung his hands.

wunderbar
A bar where you sit and daydream.

wurst
A Wisconsin farmer with poor relatives in East Germany heard that a food package they had requested had never arrived. To set their minds at ease, he cabled them, "Cheer up! The wurst is yet to come."

*When people talk to each other
in the Alps,
they **yokel**.*

XXYYZZ

X

    1. If you don't know how to vote, just X someone.

    2. A.F.G. Lewis asks:

*Is life really
Four nought
Or is it time
Two score
And XL?*

Xenophon

How Cyrus the Younger kept in touch with home office.

Y

The important thing is to vote, even if you don't know Y.

yacht *

*To reach the top in the navy
It helps to be swimming in gravy.
Forget what you're taught
And spend what yacht,
And you'll never start off as an A.B.*

yak

The farmer's wife in Tibet smelled something burning and rushed out to the barn moaning "Oh, my baking yak!"

*A variant:

*There was a young man from Biloxi
Whose approach to the draft board was foxy.
He showed up when yacht
But paddling a cot
And tried to tie up to the doc, see?*

yam
"I may be a lover of tropical tubers, but I yam what I yam."

yank
If you find yourself alone on a desert island, you've only yourself to yank.

Yankee
Name given to residents of northern United States by southerners prior to (and causing) the Civil War. Subsequently shortened to "Yank" or "Jerk." Origin believed to be name of Long Island laundry man, Yan Kee, famous for consistently turning out gray shirts.

yard
The trouble with gardening is that it's a yard life.

yarn
1. "I'll bet you can't knit me a sweater!" "I can make any yarn thing you please!"
2. Railroading expression: "Yarn the wrong track, you knit-wit!"
   Phrase was originally nautical: "Yarn the wrong tack, you knot-wit!"

yaw
"The helm with it!" muttered Captain Bligh. "The ship's all yaws."

yawl
"Captain, us southern boys sure hope yawl forgive us."

yawn
"I'll bet you a dollar I'll be asleep before you are!"
"Yawn!"

year
1975 was International Women's Year. Unfortunately, this recognition of women went in one year and out the next.

yearn
1. As an early ballad singer, Nelson Eddy had to yearn his own way.
2. A university is an institution of higher yearning.

yeast
Temperance slogan: "The sin rises in the yeast."

yegg
He was a good yegg, but a little cracked.

yell
Modern music has gone all to yell.

yellow
Dentistry originated in the Orient—and even today the patients yellow.

yelp
A silent dog is a friendly dog, as long as he isn't just yelpless.

yen
He had a yen for feminine company—but the geisha wanted two yen.

yeti
If you look Sherpa footprint may yeti merge from the snow.

yew
"I cedar hedge is growing."
"Yes, it's all up to yew."

yoicks
An exclamation. In America, usually heard as "Dem yoicks!"

yoke

A HORRIBLE EGG SAMPLE
"When a hen lays a square egg, the yoke is on her," proclaimed old Hog Dray, ever fateful. "Cheese, things aren't like whey rooster be! Now, it swan barn thing after an udder. Stalking turkey; a goose'll gobbler up—and that snow crop. Sow what, you shay? Shed up and down duck it; I ham the Lard of the Flies. Things are not good, Orwell. They won't lettuce have harvested rights. Weir all shook up, barley a bull to cope and nearly beet garden our salves.
"Wheat's going to turnip next, bray tell? It's yard to know, of horse. Butt plow the hill are waggon to carrion? Hay, I don't row, I'm oxen cow. Manure the expert. Ewe tell me, fodder!"

yokel
The way people talk to each other in the Alps.

yolk
Trying to preserve his savoir faire in a new restaurant, the guest looked down at the eggs the waiter had spilled in his lap and said brightly, "Well, I guess the yolk's on me!"

yonder
After the boring party, Mr. and Mrs. Matthews yonder way home.

yore
The historian's song: "My Time Is Yore Time."

you
1. Matilda had her nose altered, her face lifted and bought falsies for front and back. Her boyfriend sighed and asked, "What's you, Pussycat?"
2. It doesn't contribute to sobriety in New York City to see a mattress store called "Kleinsleep" or a clothing store named "Youtopia." The former presumably contributes youphoria. The latter might offer something yoursful.
3. Q. Why is the letter "T" like your nose?
   A. Because it goes before you.

your

Lush to bartender: "I'll have yours."
Other customer to lush: "What's yours?
Lush: "A double Scotch and water, thanks."

youth

1. There are times when the old folks wonder if the answer to all their problems might not be youthanasia.
2. After trying for years to disguise her age, Madame de Pompadour finally sighed "What's the youth?"

yule

There's no yule like an old Yule.

yum

"Well, Mama, now that the Day of Atonement fasting is over, what's to eat? Oh, yum! Kipper!"

Z

In other lands it's "zed" that's said.
The Yankees call it "zee."
But "zee" or "zed," you're still ahead
Till you come to the Zider Z.

Zanzibar

HOW THEY BABYLON!

Waitress: "Hawaii, Mister? You must be Hungary."
Gent: "Yes, Siam. And I can't Rumania long, either. Venice lunch ready?"
Waitress: "I'll Russia table. What are you Ghana Havre? Aix?"
Gent: "You want Tibet? I prefer Turkey. Can Jamaica cook step on the Gaza bit?"
Waitress: "Odessa laugh! Alaska, but listen for her Wales."
Gent: "I'm not Balkan. Just put a Cuba sugar in my Java."
Waitress: "Don't you be Sicily, big boy. Sweden it yourself. I'm only here to Serbia."
Gent: "Denmark my check and call the Bosphorus, Egypt me. There's an Eire. I hope he'll Kenya. I don't Bolivia know who I am!"
Waitress: "Canada noise! I don't Carribean. You sure Ararat!"
Gent: "Samoa your wisecracks? What's got India? D'you think this arguing Alps business? Why be so Chile? Be Nice!"
Waitress: "Don't Kiev me that Boulogne! Alamein do! Spain in the neck. Pay your Czech and don't Kuwait. Abyssinia!"
Gent: (To himself) "I'll come back with my France and Taiwan on Zanzibar is open."

zebra

Garment-industry invention to uplift young ladies in their cups. Hence, "Zebra won't stay up!"

Zend

Those ancient Iranian languages really Zend me.

zinc
1. The battery would not have been invented if someone hadn't stopped to zinc.
2. It's in the washroom.

zing
What Zider Zee zingers do.

zinnia
The florid American farewell: "I'll be zinnia!"

zipper
The girl who wears buttons cannot be rushed. There's no point in trying to zipper.

zombie
The trouble with revival through witchcraft is that zombie immune to it.

zoo
There was a young man from Long Sault
Who carried a toad in each shoe.
When they asked him to stop
He said with a hop
"I'm trying to get in Who's Zoo!"

Zoroaster
She refused to join any religious group until Zoroaster.

zounds
Noises.

Zucchetto
Ecclesiastic skullcap (R.C.) so called because when you become a priest zucchetto black one, when you're a bishop zucchetto purple, a cardinal zucchetto red and, if you make pope, zucchetto white. Word is the Italian diminutive of *zucca*, from the papal injunction "zucca tome, zucca tome." ("And the gourd was made flesh.")

zwieback
A crisp slice of well-bred conversation; a way of telling your host that you have both changed your minds and decided to spend the night.

appendixes

A friend once asked Ben Jonson
to make a pun.
He replied,
"Pun what subject?"
His friend responded,
"The king."
"But," said Jonson,
"the king is not a subject.
He is king."

Joseph Addison in
The Spectator
No. 61
Thursday, May 10, 1711

There is no kind of false wit which has been so recommended by the practice of all ages, as that which consists in a jingle of words, and is comprehended under the general name of Punning. It is indeed impossible to kill a weed, which the soil has a natural disposition to produce. The seeds of Punning are in the minds of all men; and though they may be subdued by reason, reflection, and good sense, they will be very apt to shoot up in the greatest genius that is not broken and cultivated by the rules of art. Imitation is natural to us, and when it does not raise the mind to poetry, painting, music, or other more noble arts, it often breaks out in Puns and Quibbles.

Aristotle, in the eleventh chapter of his book of rhetoric, describes two or three kinds of Puns, which he calls Paragrams, among the beauties of good writing, and produces instances of them out of some of the greatest authors in the Greek tongue. Cicero has sprinkled several of his works with Puns, and in his book where he lays down the rules of Oratory, quotes abundance of sayings as pieces of wit, which also upon examination prove arrant Puns. But the age in which the Pun chiefly flourished, was in the reign of King James the First. That learned monarch was himself a tolerable Punster, and made very few bishops or privy-counsellors that had not some time or other signalized themselves by a Clinch, or a Conundrum. It was therefore in this age that the Pun appeared with pomp and dignity. It had before been admitted into merry speeches and ludicrous compositions, but was now delivered with great gravity from the pulpit, or pronounced in the most solemn manner at the council-table. The greatest authors, in their most serious works, made frequent use of Puns. The sermons of Bishop Andrews, and the tragedies of Shakespeare, are full of them. The sinner was Punned into repentance by the former, as in the latter nothing is more usual than to see a hero weeping and quibbling for a dozen lines together.

I must add to these great authorities, which seem to have given a kind of sanction to this piece of false wit, that all the writers of rhetoric have treated of Punning with very great respect, and divided the several kinds of it into hard names, that are reckoned among the figures of speech, and recommended as ornaments in discourse. I remember a country schoolmaster of my acquaintance told me once, that he had been in company with a gentleman whom he looked upon to be the greatest Paragrammatist among the moderns. Upon enquiry, I found my learned friend had dined that day with Mr. Swan, the famous Punster; and desiring him to give me some account of Mr. Swan's conversation, he told me that he generally talked in the Paranomasia, that he sometimes gave into the Ploce, but that in his humble opinion he shined most in the Antanaclasis.

I must not here omit, that a famous university of this land was formerly very much infested with Puns; but whether or no this might not arise from the fens and marshes in which it was situated, and which are now drained, I must leave to the determination of more skillful naturalists.

After this short history of Punning, one would wonder how it should be so entirely banished out of the learned world as it is at present, especially since it has found a place in the writings of the most ancient polite authors. To account for this we must consider, that the first race of authors, who were the great heroes in writing, were destitute of all rules and arts of criticism; and for that reason, though they excel later writers in greatness of genius, they fall short of them in accuracy and correctness. The moderns cannot reach their beauties, but can avoid their imperfections. When the world was furnished with these authors of the first eminence, there grew up another set of writers, who gained themselves a reputation by the remarks which they made on the works of those who preceded them. It was one of the employments of these secondary authors, to distinguish the several kinds of wit by terms of art, and to consider them as more or less perfect, according as they were founded in truth. It is no wonder therefore, that even such authors as Socrates, Plato, and Cicero should have such little blemishes as are not to be met with in authors of a much inferior character, who have written since those several blemishes were discovered. I do not find that there was a proper separation made between Puns and true wit by any of the ancient authors, except Quintilian and Longinus. But when this distinction was once settled, it was very natural for all men of status to agree in it. As for the revival of this False Wit, it happened about the time of the revival of letters; but as soon as it was once detected, it immediately vanished and disappeared. At the same time there was no question, but as it has sunk in one age and rose in another, it will again recover itself in some distant period of time, as pedantry and ignorance shall prevail upon wit and sense. And to speak the truth, I do very much apprehend, by some of the last winter's productions, which had their set of admirers, that our posterity will in a few years degenerate into a race of Punsters: at least, a man may be very excusable for any apprehensions of this kind, that has seen Acrostics handed about the town with great secrecy and applause; to which I must also add a little epigram called the Witches Prayer, that fell into verse when it was read either backward or forward, excepting only that it cursed one way, and blessed the other. When one sees there are actually such pains-takers among our British wits, who can tell what it may end in? If we must lash one another, let it be with the manly strokes of wit and satire; for I am of the old philosopher's opinion, that if I must suffer from one or the other, I would rather it should be from the paw of a lion, than the hoof of an ass. I do not speak this out of any spirit of party. There is a most crying dullness on both sides. I have seen Tory Acrostics and Whig Anagrams, and do not quarrel with either of them, because they are Whigs or Tories, but because they are Anagrams and Acrostics.

But to return to punning. Having pursued the history of a Pun, from its original to its downfall, I shall here define it to be a conceit arising from the use of two words that agree in the sound, but differ in the sense. The only way therefore to try a piece of wit, is to translate it into a different language. If it bears the test, you may pronounce it true; but if it vanishes in the experiment you may conclude it to have been a Pun. In sort, one may say of a Pun, as the countryman described his nightingale, that it is *vox et praeterea nihil*, a sound, and nothing but a sound. On the contrary, one may represent true wit by the description which Aristenetus makes of a fine woman; when she is dressed she is beautiful, when she is undressed she is beautiful; or as Mercerus has translated it more emphatically, *Induitur, formosa est: exuitur, upsa forma est.**

---

*Dressed she is beautiful, undressed she is beauty's self.

THE PUNS OF SHAKESPEARE*
by Dr. F.A. Bather, F.R.S.

Nearly all the commentators on Shakespeare fell foul of the puns. Sir Sidney Lee, in his *Life of Shakespeare,* speaks of the depths of vapidity to which Shakespeare and contemporary punsters could sink. But it is more important to understand than to censure. The pun was a prevading element in Elizabethan literature and an important factor in the method of our early dramatists.

Why did the Elizabethans indulge in this verbal jesting? Some think it childish and that suggests the answer. Children, as they acquire the use of their mother tongue, delight to play with it. They make up jingles and seize on resemblances of sound. They revel in punning riddles and often some unfortunate name will dissolve a class in laughter. So too, as nations fashioned for themselves a language, they loved to prove their mastery of it in similar ways. Almost all literatures have passed through a stage in which the pun was an approved figure of speech. There are puns in the Pentateuch, in the great dramas of the Greeks, in Cicero and Virgil. In Japanese poetry, word-play and similar artifices are among the most admired ornaments.

The philosophy of the pun would lead us far. It is enough to observe the pleasure we take in the unexpected association of distinct ideas. A pun effects this by a similarity of sound. But it is clear that an association by unifying thought is deeper and truer than an association by the accident of language. Wit can be translated into another language, but if it resides merely in the words, it vanishes. The later Roman writers on style recognised this and verbal jesting disappeared from serious composition. But when Latin ceased to be the only language of literature, when the various languages of Europe came into their own, history repeated itself. The Elizabethans inherited a tongue in which the two strains of Norman-French and Anglo-Saxon had at last fused, and during the process had been enriched by contributions from sources so diverse as Scandinavia and ancient Rome. Englishmen discovered what a

*The original manuscript of this paper is in the New York City Public Library. It is based on the author's article in *Noctes Shakespeariance,* Winchester College, 1887.

wonderful instrument their language was and they delighted to play on it. Later critics again dwelt on how superficial was the humour of the pun and once more it disappeared from all productions that can claim to be called literary.

The development of the individual repeats in little the development of the race. Just as the pun, for the reasons above mentioned, fell into disuse among dramatists, so it may be expected to show a gradual decline in the works of him who, more than any other, is the representative of those dramatists. That this is largely the case has been recognised as a general principle by those who have studied Shakespeare's plays from a chronological standpoint. Thus, the late Professor [Edward] Dowden writes: "Shakespeare's early conceits, *puns*, frequent classical allusions, occasional overwrought rhetoric, all gradually disappear or subside; but these changes really belong to the growth of Shakespeare's taste and judgment." Still, no one before 1881 had attempted the scientific method of bringing this theory to the bar of fact. On the contrary, all would have said with Dowden: "These are things that cannot be precisely weighed and measured, although they can be clearly felt." Fleay, for instance, says of his metrical test that in it and in it *only* can quantitative results be obtained.

When I was still a boy in Winchester, it occurred to me that it should be possible to apply the statistical and scientific method to at least one of the points mentioned by Dowden. I therefore undertook the complete study of Shakespeare's verbal jests and quibbles. One might think that any person of intelligence should be able to see these things for himself without applying the ponderous method of statistics. Unfortunately, purely aesthetic criticism depends so greatly on the personality of the critic that its conclusions are often more entertaining than exact.

To Professor Dowden himself, for instance, no one will deny a large measure of aesthetic sense. And yet, hear what he says regarding the contrast of characters in *The Two Gentlemen of Verona*. "The *bright* and clever Sylvia is set over against the tender and ardent Julia; the clown Speed, notable as a *verbal wit* and *quibbler,* is set against the humorous Launce." After noting the words emphasised, you may perhaps be surprised to learn that, whereas Julia quibbles eleven times, Sylvia only quibbles once. The contrast may exist, but it does not lie in the quality of wit. As regards Speed and Launce, Dowden had more right on his side, for Speed makes twenty puns and Launce makes but nineteen. Another aesthetic critic, Mrs. Elizabeth Montagu, in her essay on the writings and genius of Shakespeare (1769) says: "As Falstaff, whom the author certainly intended to be perfectly witty, is less addicted to quibble and play on words than any of his comic characters, I think we may fairly conclude he was sensible it was but a false kind of wit, which he practised from the hard necessity of the times."

What are the facts? In *I King Henry IV* there are forty-seven puns; of those Falstaff makes twenty-one, Prince Hal ten, Hotspur eight. In *2 King Henry IV* there are fifty-two puns; Falstaff leads with twenty-seven, Prince Hal is again a bad second with six. In *The Merry Wives of Windsor* there are thirty-nine puns, of which eleven are credited to Falstaff, this being twice as many as are made by anyone else in the comedy. No character in the whole of Shakespeare's plays, or in those of any contemporary dramatist with which I am acquainted, exceeds Falstaff in quibbling. Were Sir John alive to read the above-quoted remark of Mrs. Montagu, he would surely once more ejaculate, "Lord, Lord, how this world is given to lying!"

In 1881, when I begun this study, the chronological order of Shakespeare's plays was not so accurately determined as it has been since. It was, however, generally agreed that Shakespeare's plays could be separated into four main periods which were thought to correspond with events and stages in the author's life. These were regarded as

(I) a period of apprenticeship,

(II) a period of manly vigour,

(III) a gloom period and then

(IV) a period of final calm.

According to that theory, a gradual decrease of puns was to be expected in successive periods. Taking the plays at that time allotted to the respective periods, the following were the proportions [percentages of puns] actually found:

I. 2.12; II. 1.36; III. .49; IV. .48.

Taking the chronology now generally accepted and dividing the plays into four corresponding periods, I find a rather different set of figures. The first period from 1591-1594, (that is to say from *Love's Labour's Lost* to *King John*) gives a percentage of 1.98. The second period from 1594-1600 (that is to say from *Midsummer Night's Dream* to *Twelfth Night*) gives 1.25. The third period from 1600 to 1609 (which includes the Roman plays and great tragedies) yields a percentage of .63; while the last period of romantic tragi-comedy, belonging to the years 1610 and 1611, gives .42. These latter numbers, if compared with the former, show apparently a more equable decrease in the number of puns. But if we divide the first period into two parts, the first containing *Love's Labour's Lost, Two Gentlemen of Verona, Comedy of Errors* and *Romeo and Juliet,* approximately the same plays as were contained in the first period of our former division, then this first half gives a percentage of 2.97, slightly higher than before; but the second half drops to 1.13, which is rather lower than the percentage of the next division. The reason for this will be seen directly. Meanwhile, it is interesting to observe that more accurate knowledge concerning the chronology of Shakespeare's plays, while by no means corroborating the old and somewhat fanciful division, based more largely upon purely aesthetic criticism, still does agree even better with our main hypothesis that there was a gradual decrease of punning as Shakespeare advanced in his art.

It may be as well to pause here to explain how these numbers are calculated. Each play was read with extreme care and every jest that depended on words alone, every double meaning and every quibble noted. On a first reading, many puns escaped notice, but these were usually detected afterwards by analogous undoubted puns in other plays either by Shakespeare or by contemporary authors. For example (Act II. Scene 2, line 271), Hamlet says to Rosenkrantz and Guildenstern, "Shall we to the court?" They reply, "We'll wait upon you." Hamlet: "No such matter. I will not sort you with the rest of my servants." Here I was at first doubtful, but on finding a similar passage in Ben Jonson I am now sure that a quibble was intended:

Silent Woman: I, 1, p.411 a:

La Foole: I am come to entreat you to wait upon two or three ladies to dinner to-day?

Clericourt: How, sir! Wait upon them? Did you ever see me carry dishes?

La Foole: No, sir. Dispense with me. I meant to bear them company.

The number of puns having being ascertained, the lines were counted in the Globe edition and the number of puns per 100 lines determined. This reduced all to a common standard. The necessity for this will be made clear by an example: there are forty puns in *Much Ado About Nothing,* thirty-seven in *Comedy of Errors;* but there are only 1,776 lines in the latter play, and 2,825 in the former, so that the percentages are—*Comedy of Errors,* 2.08; *Much Ado About Nothing,* 1.42.

When you make a diagram of the plays by the years in which they appeared and apply these percentages you end up with a gradually descending curve, the descent being more rapid at the beginning. This in the main corroborates our hypothesis. In the exuberance of youth, his brain thick with teeming fancies, his mind impressed by the euphuistic style of the day, Shakespeare simply revelled in his mastery of language and was no doubt eager to show that, whatever others could do, he at any rate could go one better. But, with *Romeo and Juliet* once behind him, he discarded the tendency to introduce puns on every possible and impossible occasion, and, for all that the critics may say, in subsequent plays puns are generally used either appropriately to the character speaking or with some other dramatic effect. This, however, does not prevent a continued decrease of punning, until the lowest point is reached in one of the latest plays, *Cymbeline.* This decrease is correlated with other well-known changes, a greater profundity of thought, a closer and more elliptical style and a more forcible, less regular metre.

So much for the general curve. When we turn to consider details, especially the apparent aberrances we find that they yield a ready explanation, perfectly consistent with the general hypothesis.

We first notice the sudden drop in *Richard III.* Here, we have to remember that between *Romeo and Juliet* and *Richard III,* there were produced the various parts of the revised version of *Henry VI.* Not only were they revisions of older plays, but it is clear that in the various revisions Shakespeare cooperated with another writer who is generally believed to have been

Christopher Marlowe. That poet, as we all know, gained his effect by the splendour and vigour of his words and rarely turned aside to trifle. The percentage of puns in *Henry VI* is therefore exceedingly small. Marlowe was killed in June, 1598, but *Richard III* was undoubtedly written under his influence. The same is the case with *Richard II*. It is therefore easy to understand why these plays should be relatively free from puns, but the Euripidean dialogue in *Richard III* and the general inaptness of the puns in *Richard II* are a set-off against their numerical weakness.

Just as Shakespeare's *Richard II* is obviously reminiscent of Marlowe's own *Edward II*, so Shakespeare's *Merchant of Venice* was suggested by and still bears traces of Marlowe's *Jew of Malta*. Nonetheless, Shakespeare was gradually throwing off the influence of Marlowe and this is seen in the puns no less than in the general treatment so that by the time *King John* is reached, we find the percentage of puns not very far below that of *Romeo and Juliet*.

But here again there is a sudden drop in *Midsummer Night's Dream*. For this there seem to be special reasons. The play is very different in character from any other play by Shakespeare. It is more in the style of a masque. It is a poem, and written in rhyme for the most part. It was probably composed, as Sir Sidney Lee suggests, to celebrate a marriage in high society. We may go even further and assume that it was actually performed for the first time before the contracting parties. Shakespeare, who knew so well how to accommodate himself to his surroundings, entertained his courtly audience with airy fancies and delicate poetry rather than with those jests wherewith he had occasionally condescended to tickle the ears of the groundlings.

In *The Taming of the Shrew,* the next play, the case is reversed. Here we have a roaring farce, or, if not entirely that, at least a comedy that has to be played with a strong farcical spirit. So much is this the case that, in order to give it the right setting, there is an Induction and the comedy is further removed from reality by being presented to us as a play within a play.

All's Well That Ends Well furnishes a rather more interesting problem— more interesting because it is rather more difficult. In this play, as Sir Sidney Lee points out: "early and late features of Shakespeare's work are perplexingly combined. The proportion of rhyme to blank verse is high, and the rhymed verse in which epistles are penned by two of the characters (in place of prose) is a clear sign of youthful artifice: . . . On the other hand, nearly half the play is in prose and the metrical irregularities of the blank verse and its elliptical tenour are characteristic of the author's ripest efforts." Although Sir Sidney Lee places this comedy in 1595, this is only on the somewhat doubtful evidence of [the critic] Francis Mere's allusion in 1598. Still, he points out that the play is not known in any edition earlier than the First Folio and the discrepancy of style suggests that the Folio text presents a late revision of an early draft.

In the three plays that followed it is interesting to observe how the puns gradually increased in quantity as Falstaff acquired prominence and how, with his disappearance, they fell again to a normal level in *Henry V*. The high number found in *The Merry Wives of Windsor* is of course due to the fact that this is nothing more than a farce, written, as the story goes, in the space of a fortnight. It seems to have been revised later. Nonetheless, certain passages seem to show that they may have been in part sketched out by the author at an earlier date (namely, the bitter allusions to Sir T. Lucy, his coat of arms and the deer stealing). The large number of Latin words is also a characteristic of early plays, perhaps while Shakespeare's schooling was still fresh upon him.

Nothing more calls for comment until we come to the three plays *Julius Caesar, Hamlet* and *Troilus and Cressida*. In *Julius Caesar* the percentage is low and in *Hamlet* it occupies about the position that it would have if the curve were regular, but in *Troilus and Cressida* it again rises slightly.

The fact is that there is a good deal of difficulty connected with the chronology of these plays. In a previous paper, I treated Julius Caesar as one of the doubtful plays, since at that time a view was prevalent that Shakespeare had written it in collaboration with some other writer, possibly Ben Jonson. No mention, however, is made of this view in Sir Sidney Lee's *Life of Shakespeare*. At the same time, as regards the chronology, Sir Sidney says, "internal evidence alone determines the date of composition."

The internal evidence on which he relies is the characterisation, the metrical features and the deliberate employment of prose. "All these traits," he says, "suggest a composition of the midmost point of the dramatist's career." It is, however, perfectly legitimate to add to the argument the evidence provided by the puns. This would certainly entitle us to place the play at a somewhat later date.

As regards *Troilus and Cressida* also, Sir Sidney says, the difficulties of determining the date are very great. All we know is that in February, 1603, the publisher, James Roberts, obtained a license "for the booke of Troilus and Cressida as it is acted by my Lord Chamberlain's men"; if the play was acted before this it must obviously have been written still earlier. And the regularity of the blank verse to which Sir Sidney alludes, as contrasted with the greater irregularity of *Julius Caesar* might even suggest that these two plays should change places in our scheme. If this were done, the descent of the curve would be almost normal. *Hamlet,* which is perhaps the play most characteristic of our author's genius, was written by him at the midmost point of his career and we find that the pun ratio also occupies about the mean position. It is, no doubt, a little high if *Hamlet* be considered as a tragedy and compared with the great tragedies of the succeeding period.

Hamlet, however, is a singularly composite play. It no doubt retains fragments of its predecessors by less experienced hands, and incorporates in its final form a large amount of topical and purely temporary matter, as for instance the controversial references to contemporary theatrical history.

Hereafter, the level of the puns drops and remains low all through the period of the late tragedies, only rising again in *The Tempest*. The rise is clearly due not to any emergence from a supposed period of gloom, but to the introduction of a strongly satiric and comic element brought from the outer world as a contrast to the mystical wonders of the remote island.

I would here draw your attention to a point which I have not previously seen noticed. It is the contrast between the rapidity of production in the early years of Shakespeare's career and the relative slowness in its latter half. In reality, the contrast was even greater than it appears because in the first half should also be included Shakespeare's contribution to the three parts of *Henry VI*, the publication of his poems and a good deal of dramatic hackwork, the tradition of which remains in the ascription to Shakespeare of such plays as *Titus Andronicus, Arden of Feversham* and *A Yorkshire Tragedy.* It is particularly noticeable how the period of world masterpieces was issued in by a year of comparative rest—and how during the first eight years of the XVII century these were produced at the rate of only one a year. It is clear that Shakespeare pondered more deeply over the subject matter, that he devoted more conscious attention to the style, and that, probably with no less conscious intention, he deliberately rejected the artifice of word play except when needed for a forcible dramatic effect.

I alluded to *Titus Andronicus,* and here perhaps I may be permitted to use it to illustrate the value of this method as a critical weapon. In his very interesting book *Did Shakespeare Write Titus Andronicus?* Mr. J.M. Robertson wrote: "As illustrating the inexactness of the earlier commentators. ...It may be noted that Stevens spoke of *Titus* as being non-Shakespearean in that it had neither double endings nor plays upon words. It has an abundance of both." Now an exact investigation reveals the fact that neither Stevens nor Mr. J.M. Robertson is correct. There are in *Titus Andronicus* just four puns. That is to say, .15 per hundred lines. The third part of *King Henry VI* has .14 puns per hundred lines and those two plays have thus absolutely fewer puns than any other play rightly or wrongly ascribed to Shakespeare. It is quite clear that these plays do not belong to Shakespeare's later period. Both external and internal evidence tell us that any connection that they may have had with him must have been in his early years when his pun ratio was relatively high. The proportion of puns in *Titus Andronicus* is therefore an additional strong argument against Shakespeare having had anything to do with it, unless in some slight re-arrangement of scenes.

Before passing from this topic, I would remind you once more that, even yet, the true chronological order of Shakespeare's plays is not settled by external evidence. Further, such chronological order as we have is the order not necessarily of writing but of production. Again, the text accessible to us is in many cases clearly understood not to be the same text as that which was first produced. In some cases one portion of a play may be of early and another of late date. We also have to remember that in some plays (*Henry VIII*, for instance) it is exceedingly difficult to decide how much is really by Shakespeare and how much may be due to some older writer or to some collaborator. It would be by taking separate portions of each play according to their true authorship and true chronological order that our curve of puns would give a true result. But even as it stands it is, I trust, clear that the method of enquiring into pun ratios has given us a new instrument of critical research—a method coming between the purely literary method of aesthetic appreciation and the purely scientific method of metrical test. It might therefore be possible to apply it to the elucidation of some of those doubtful points which I have just mentioned.

There are, however, other grounds upon which such a diagram might be criticised. "Mathematics", said [Thomas Henry] Huxley, "are like a mill; what comes out depends on what you put in." I am well aware that puns are of very different value and that for a true estimate they should be weighed as well as counted. To make such an estimate, a classification is necessary.

Now there are two main modes of classifying things, the first according to function, the second, according to structure. By the first method we consider whether the pun has a dramatic use or no. By the second we determine whether a pun is in itself good or bad.

It is a trite paradox that the worst puns are the best. Since the method according to function is more important in literary criticism, while the method according to structure is more important in grammatical criticism, both methods have their value in such an enquiry as the present.

I do not propose to explore here the classification of Shakespeare's puns according to structure or the method of punning. In one point, at any rate, the mode of introduction, we should observe a gradual advance in ease and in that art which conceals art. It is more interesting to pass at once to the classification of puns according to their function, that is to say, their dramatic purpose.

The first obvious division is into (a) puns with dramatic use; (b) puns without dramatic use.

This primary separation demands great care. There are so many ways in which a pun can be used with effect that one hesitates to stigmatise any as entirely purposeless. Turn, for example, to *King John,* II. i, 533, where the Dauphin Lewis is being betrothed to Blanch:-

K. Philip: It likes us well; young princes, close your hands.

Austria: And your lips too; for I am well assured that I did so when I
was first assured.

"Assured" had the meaning of "affianced", as we learn from *The Comedy of Errors:* ("Called me Dromio, sworn I was assured to her.")

Bishop Wordsworth is excited by this pun to a long note: "The intelligent reader, it is believed, would gladly part with such quibbles as this, which here and elsewhere disfigure the present play," etc. Walker, too, takes such exception to this pun that he would correct the "assured" to "affied". Yet the pun is not wholly out of place in the mouth of Austria. It is not the only bad pun he makes. He is the butt of The Bastard and he is certainly trying to be funny. The same pun occurs in *The Taming of the Shrew,* IV. iv, 91 and *Hamlet,* V. i, 125.

(A) Puns with dramatic use are futher divided according to (1) Character and (2) Incident.

(1) Puns of Character:

a. Light Comedy: Punsters are not rare, even in modern life; and in Shakespeare's day the fine gentlemen that could not turn his words inside out like a cheveril glove was esteemed but a poor fellow. Here come Biron and Rosaline, Benedick and Beatrice and Mercutio.

b. Low Comedy: But these must be made by genuine humorists, such as Launcelot, Launce and Speed. There is an idea that the Fool, as fully developed by Shakespeare, trusts less to puns than to real humour. Launce and Speed, who for this purpose must be reckoned as one fool, make between them nineteen puns, Launcelot ten, and Touchstone seven. Further, the puns made by Touchstone are far superior to those of Launce and Launcelot. Decrease in quantity and increase in quality was, however, to be expected on other grounds. Still, it is the case that the proportion relative to puns made by other characters diminishes in the ration of 10:8:7. The idea has, therefore, a small basis of fact.

c. Puns of a Diseased Brain: As a rule the character seizes on some prominent word or runs off at a tangent along a secondary line of thought thereby suggested. When Lear cries out on "Those pelican daughters," "Pillicock sat on Pillicock Hill" sings Edgar in the person of Mad Tom. So, too, Hamlet when he would seem mad mistakes Polonius. Frequently, however, these puns are most appropriate—"a happiness that often madness hits on, which reason and sanity could not so prosperously be delivered of." Such, for the most part, are the puns of the really mad Fool in *King Lear.*

d. Puns of a Weak Mind: a very interesting class, more apparent in the later plays.

(i) Showing poverty of true humour in the person that makes them. [Samuel Taylor] Coleridge points out that the wit of Antonio and Sebastian in *The Tempest* is of the lowest grade; the jokes never rise above puns nor the laughter above sarcasm. This is in true harmony with the characters of those dull villains. Antonio's wit is solely directed to render the good ridiculous and to make the descent to wickedness easy for Sebastian.

(ii) Showing deficiency of intellect or education. Such most notably are all those of Hostess Quickly, who continually mistakes words and many of Costard's in *Love's Labour's Lost.*

(2) Puns of Incident:

a. Art versus Nature: Puns and conceits are, like rhyme, often introduced in opposition to earnest sentences. They contrast the false with the true. In *Much Ado,* Benedick is a punster, Claudio rarely puns; but in V, i, where Benedick comes in earnest to challenge Claudio, it is the latter, alone, that jests and quibbles: "What a pretty thing man is when he goes in his doublet and hose and leaves off his wit."

b. The Pun Passionate: As converse of the above, the very fiercest feelings of our nature may provoke punning. This is the pun of scorn and anger and the pun, closely alllied, of contempt. To the psychologist it is perhaps the most interesting of all, for man is never so natural as when in a rage. Under this head fall many of Hotspur's puns, those of Gratiano in the Trial Scene and puns referring to Wolsey in *Henry VIII.*

1 Henry IV, Act I, Scene iii:-

Worcester:....Good Cousin, give me audience for a while.

Hotspur: I cry you mercy.

Worcester: Those same noble Scots

That are your prisoners—

Hotspur: I'll keep them all;

By God, he shall not have a Scot of them;

No, if a Scot would save his soul, he shall not;

I'll keep them, by this hand.

(Contrast Falstaff's, " 'S blood! 'twas time to counterfeit, or that hot termagant Scot had paid me scot and lot too.")

1 Henry IV, Act I, Scene iii:-

Hotspur: You say true:

Why, what a candy deal of courteousy

This fawning greyhound then did proffer me!

Look. 'when his infant fortune came to age'.

And 'gentle Harry Percy', and 'kind cousin';

O' the devil take such cozeners! God forgive me!

Good uncle, tell your tale; I have done.

Henry VIII, Act III, Scene i:-

Queen Katherine:...Is this your Christian counsel? Out upon ye!

Heaven is above all yet; there sits a judge that no king can corrupt.

Cam: Your rage mistakes us.

Queen Katherine: The more shame for ye: holy men I thought ye,

Upon my soul, two reverend cardinal virtues;

But cardinal sins and hollow hearts I fear ye.

c. The Pun Pathetic has often fallen under the lash of the commentators. When Posthumus in fetters confesses his debts to heaven and prays thus: "Great powers, If you will take this audit, take this life and cancel these cold bonds," Dr. [Samuel] Johnson exclaims "Another instance of our author's unfelicity in pathetic speeches!"

In Antony's conversation with the murderers of Caesar there are two lines which, on account of the pun in them, Coleridge has denounced as an interpolation and Hudson has stigmatised as "a foul blemish". Really, they furnish an excellent example of the Pun Pathetic. As Charles and Mary Cowden-Clarke say, "Antony, still in the mood of taking refuge in conceits and plays upon words from the sting of his suppressed indignation against Caesar's assassins, lets his fancy run riot in a figurative language that shall aggrandise his dear friend to the utmost":

...Here wast thou bay'd, brave hart;
Here didst thou fall; and here thy hunters stand,
Signed in thy spoil and crimson'd in thy lethe.
O world, thou wast the forest to this hart:
And this, indeed, O world, the heart of thee.
How like a deer, strucken by many princes,
Dost thou here lie!

The defence of this and similar word-play may be left to the poet himself, who recognised that punning is a natural safety-valve of feeling. "Misery," he says, "makes sport to mock itself," and "How oft when men are at the point of death have they been merry, which their keepers call a lightning before death!" Shakespeare has written few lines of greater pathos than the gay Mercutio's— "Ask for me to-morrow and you shall find me a grave man." *Romeo and Juliet* III, i.

The Pun Pathetic also serves by contrast to intensify the melancholy of the scene. This leads us on to

d. Puns of Contrast, pure and simple. To see the force with which a pun can be used let us turn to the terrible scene after the murder of Duncan, when Macbeth's nerve is giving way and Lady Macbeth works herself up to complete the bloody business.

Macbeth: I'll go no more;
I am afraid to think what I have done;
Look on't again I dare not.

Lady M.: Infirm of purpose!
Give me the daggers: the sleeping and the dead
Are but as pictures: 'tis the eye of childhood
That fears a painted devil. If he do bleed,
I'll gild the faces of the grooms withal;
For it must seem their guilt.

The sudden introduction of a jest amid the weird terrors of the scene startles us: it is a gleam of ghastly sunshine that suddenly strikes across a stormy landscape.

Already you will have gathered that the plays show a gradual increase in the dramatic handling of the pun. Among other features, we observe how wonderfully, in his mature plays, Shakespeare suits the method of punning to the character. In *As You Like It,* the puns of Touchstone are good but artificial, strongly contrasted with the perversely bad puns made by Jaques, the wrathful puns of Orlando, and the natural, merry puns of Rosalind. There are forty verbal jests in *Hamlet,* twenty-four being plain, evident puns; the vast majority are used with dramatic effect. The subjective tendency of Hamlet's own mind is marked by his making three-fourths of the total number—and many of these are used ironically with great force. The puns of the grave-digger are suited to his low-comedy character and to this level Hamlet approximates in the churchyard scene. The jests of Polonius are weak and ineffective, as of a man whose thoughts are superficial.

The pun, despised of the commentators, may seem but a small thing. Yet if any among you be incited to continue the study he will find it leads to many interesting fields of research. He will learn how the pronunciation of our English tongue has altered in the last three centuries, though the Cockney and several other dialects still retain some of the old sounds; he will become acquainted with many a curious custom and the slang terms derived from it. Many a passage that was before dark and perhaps meaningless will have for him meaning and beauty. He may even gain boldness to proceed to conjectural emendation of the text, for a pun in one place is often so closely simulated in another that the change of a letter would elucidate the sentence and make it, as the commentators say, "Much more in our author's manner." Finally, he will gain an increased reverence for the man who had such command over a newly-framed language that he could perpetrate in it the large number of ten hundred and sixty-two puns.

F.A. Bather
—Wimbledon, England, 1923.

Charles Lamb,
The Last Essays of Elia
Popular Fallacies - IX

THAT THE WORST PUNS
ARE THE BEST

If by worst be only meant the most far-fetched and startling, we agree to it. A pun is not bound by the laws which limit nicer wit. It is a pistol let off at the ear; not a feather to tickle the intellect. It is an antic which does not stand upon manners, but comes bounding into the presence, and does not show the less comic for being dragged in sometimes by the head and shoulders. What though it limp a little, or prove defective in one leg?—all the better. A pun may easily be too curious and artificial. Who has not at one time or other been at a party of professors (himself perhaps an old offender in that line), where, after ringing a round of the most ingenious conceits, every man contributing his shot, and some there the most expert shooters of the day; after making a poor *word* run the gauntlet till it is ready to drop; after hunting and winding it through all the possible ambages of similar sounds; after squeezing and hauling, and tugging at it, till the very milk of it will not yield a drop further— suddenly some obscure, unthought-of fellow in a corner, who was never 'prentice to the trade, whom the company for the very pity passed over, as we do by a known poor man when a money-subscription is going round, no one calling upon him for his quota—has all at once come out with something so whimsical, yet so pertinent; so brazen in its pretensions, yet so impossible to be denied; so exquisitely good, and so deplorably bad, at the same time—that it has proved a Robin Hood's shot; anything ulterior to that is despaired of; and the party breaks up, unanimously voting it to be the very worst (that is, best) pun of the evening. This species of wit is the better for not being perfect in all its parts. What it gains in completeness, it loses in naturalness. The more exactly it satisfies the critical, the less hold it has upon some other faculties. The puns which are most entertaining are those which will least bear an analysis. Of this kind is the following, recorded with a sort of stigma, in one of

Swift's Miscellanies.

An Oxford scholar, meeting a porter who was carrying a hare through the streets, accosts him with this extraordinary question: "Prithee friend, is that thy own hare, or a wig?"

There is no excusing this, and no resisting it. A man might blur ten sides of paper in attempting a defence of it against a critic who should be laughter-proof. The quibble in itself is not considerable. It is only a new turn given by a little false pronunciation, to a very common, though not very courteous inquiry. Put by one gentlemen to another at a dinner-party, it would have been vapid; to the mistress of the house it would have shown much less wit than rudeness. We must take in the totality of time, place, and person; the pert look of the inquiring scholar, the desponding looks of the puzzled porter: the one stopping at leisure, the other hurrying on with his burden; the innocent though rather abrupt tendency of the first member of the question, with the utter and inextricable irrelevancy of the second; the place—a public street, not favourable to frivolous investigations; the affrontive quality of the primitive inquiry (the common question) invidiously transferred to the derivative (the new turn given to it) in the implied satire; namely, that few of that tribe are expected to eat of the good things which they carry, they being in most countries considered rather as the temporary trustees than owners of such dainties—which the fellow was beginning to understand; but then the *wig* again comes in, and he can make nothing of it; all put together constitute a picture; Hogarth could have made it intelligible on canvas.

Yet nine out of ten critics will pronounce this a very bad pun, because of the defectiveness in the concluding member, which is its very beauty, and constitutes the surprise. The same person shall cry up for admirable the cold quibble from Virgil about the broken Cremona*; because it is made out in all its parts, and leaves nothing to the imagination. We venture to call it cold; because, of thousands who have admired it, it would be difficult to find one who has heartily chuckled at it. As appealing to the judgment merely (setting the risible faculty aside), we must pronounce it a monument of curious felicity. But as some stories are said to be too good to be true, it may with equal truth be asserted of this bi-verbal allusion, that it is too good to be natural. One cannot help suspecting that the incident was invented to fit the line. It would have been better had it been less perfect. Like some Virgilian hemistichs, it has suffered by filling up. The *nimium Vicina* was enough in conscience; the *Cremonoe* afterwards loads it. It is, in fact, a double pun; and we have always observed a superfoetation in this sort of wit is dangerous. When a man has said a good thing, it is seldom politic to follow it up. We do not care to be cheated a second time; or perhaps the mind of man (with reverence be it spoken) is not capacious enough to lodge two puns at a time. The impression, to be forcible, must be simultaneous and undivided.

*Swift

THE
UNSPEAKABLE
PUN*

English-speaking communities nowadays regard the pun as a very low form of humor—and they are particularly fearful of the obscene pun, which is a major variety of the form. The obscene pun is dangerous because it cleverly attacks the sacredness of taboo words, and it manages to do so with apparent innocence. A dirty story usually leads up to the punch-line by the use of taboo words, but a well-fashioned obscene pun never overtly uses taboo words. Rather, the pun allows two different words, which are pronounced in the same way, to be substituted for each other. Usually one of the two ambiguous words is taboo, but the teller of the pun claims innocence by leaving it up to the listener to connect the innocent and the taboo meanings.

A speaker who says "She was only a fisherman's daughter, but when she saw my rod she reeled," is really launching a sneak attack upon verbal taboos through the use of a pun. This well-known pun has endured probably because of the cleverness of its triple construction. On the level of a matter-of-fact utterance, the speaker could innocently claim that he had made a simple statement about a fisherman's daughter reeling in the line on a fishing rod. Even on the slang level, the speaker could also claim innocence of any obscene intent, because the statement could be interpreted as merely saying that the fisherman's daughter reeled with fright when she saw the *rod* (slang for "gun"). It is up to the listener, of course, to make the obscene interpretation: *rod* as "penis" and *reeled* as "sexually aroused." The nervous laughter that a pun such as this evokes is due to the listener's uncertainty about which of the meanings he should acknowledge. He could interpret the statement on a

*From WORD PLAY: WHAT HAPPENS WHEN PEOPLE TALK, by Peter Farb. Copyright © 1973 by Peter Farb. Reprinted by permission of Alfred A. Knopf, Inc.

matter-of-fact or a slang level, but then he would risk being regarded as dense or prudish. If he laughs, that means he has interpreted the pun on the obscene level—and thereby become an accomplice to challenging the taboos of his speech community.

The offering of a choice between two meanings, one innocent and the other taboo, is essential to the obscene pun. Because the taboo word is not expressed directly, the listener is therefore given the option either to accept the ambiguity or not to accept it (signified by his refusal to laugh nervously or by his uttering a deprecating groan). And the obscenity must be clever to be tolerated, as Freud pointed out in *Wit and Its Relation to the Unconscious:*

The technical means of which it (obscenity) mostly makes use is allusion, i.e. substitution through a trifle, something which is only remotely related, which the listener reconstructs in his imagination as a full-fledged and direct obscenity. The greater the disproportion between what is directly offered in the obscenity and what is necessarily aroused by it in the mind of the listener, the finer is the witticism and the higher it may venture in good society.

All obscene puns have the same underlying construction in that they consist of two elements. The first element sets the stage for the pun by offering seemingly harmless material, such as the title of a book, *The Tiger's Revenge.* But the second element either is obscene in itself or renders the first element obscene, as in the name of the author of *The Tiger's Revenge*—Claude Bawls ("clawed balls"). Any wit that the pun possesses must lie in the surprise presented by the ambiguity of the second element. The two-element structure is adaptable to a great variety of pun forms, such as the Punning Question: "Did you hear about the Arabs who were sitting under a tree eating their dates?" Or the Confucianism, which partakes of the traditional proverb with its pretensions of wisdom, thus adding an extra bite to the humor: "Confucius say, 'Seven days on honeymoon make one whole week.'" Or the eloquence of the Spooneristic Conundrum, which not only poses an unanswerable question but then cleverly replies to it by switching around sounds in the second element to avoid the actual use of an obscene word: "What's the difference between a pygmy village and a women's track team? The pygmy village is a cunning bunch of runts."